Instructor's Manual

TO ACCOMPANY

$\blacksquare$

EIGHTH EDITION

Statistical Techniques
in Business and Economics

Robert D. Mason
Douglas A. Lind
Both of University of Toledo

IRWIN

Homewood, IL 60430
Boston, MA 02116

Printed in the United States of America.

ISBN 0-256-12826-X

1 2 3 4 5 6 7 8 9 0 ML 9 8 7 6 5 4 3 2

PREFACE

This **Instructor's Manual** is one of several resources available to instructors adopting *Statistical Techniques in Business and Economics*, Eighth Edition. Included are suggested outlines for both quarter and semester courses. They are followed by solutions to all the exercises in each chapter. (In addition, the answers to the odd-numbered exercises are at the end of the text for student use. The answers to even-numbered exercises are in the margins of the Instructor's Edition.) Also included are the answers to the problems in the chapter review sections.

Finally, the **Study Guide** which accompanies the text has always been popular with students. There are easy to grade assignments at the end of each chapter which you might want to assign or use as extra credit. The answers to all of the assignments are at the end of this manual. If for some reason you have missed it, please review it for possible use in your course.

CONTENTS

NOTE TO INSTRUCTORS

The authors of the text and supplements, along with the reviewers, publisher, and typesetter, have made an extra effort to provide an error-free package. We hope we have succeeded.

Nevertheless, we would appreciate receiving any typographical or numerical errors you or your students find so that corrections can be made as quickly as possible in subsequent printings. Toward that end, we have included at the back of this manual several postage paid sheets. We hope you will jot down any corrections or comments, fold and staple the sheet, and drop it in the mail so that we can respond as quickly and effectively as possible.

Thank you for your support.

This manual is divided into three parts.

Part I
Part I includes several samples of syllabi for organizing your course.

Part II
Part II includes the answers and method of solution to all exercises in each chapter. In addition, the answers and method of solution to the odd-numbered exercises are at the end of the text.

Part III
Part III includes and answers and method of solution to all section review answers for chapters 1–4, 5–7, 8–10, 11 and 12, 13–15, and 16 and 17. In addition, the odd-numbered answers are at the end of the text.

Part IV
Part IV includes all the answers and method of solution to the chapter assignments in the **Study Guide** that accompanies the text.

PART I

SAMPLE SYLLABUS

Statistical Techniques for Business and Economics is designed to provide sound coverage of the basic techniques of statistics whether the text is used on the quarter or the semester system. The chapters beyond 15 are relatively independent, therefore instructors who choose not to cover various chapters or topics may do so without concern for loss of continuity.

In fact, some chapters such as 10 and 11 could be omitted and other chapters—say chapter 21 on quality control substituted.

Instructors are also urged to require that the computer be used. There are many software systems on the market which can be successfully employed. The authors have used MINITAB for many years and many examples from MINITAB are presented in the text. The Hall and Adelman package, available through Richard D. Irwin Co., is another possibility. SAS and SPSS are also available. Where should these computer problems be assigned? The multiple regression chapter and the ANOVA chapter are two possibilities. Others include after the descriptive material (chapter 4), during the nonparametric and chi-square chapters (chapters 16 and 17), or in the small sample methods (chapter 11).

A ONE-SEMESTER COURSE

The following outline is suggested for a one-semester course with three one hour meetings per week for 15 weeks. Four examinations are given during the semester.

Chapter	Topic	Meetings	
1	Introduction	1	
2	Summarizing Data	3	
3	Central Tendency	4	(omit geometric mean)
4	Dispersion	4	
	EXAM	1	
5	Probability	4	
6	Probability Distributions	3	(omit hypergeometric)
7	Normal Distribution	2	
	EXAM	1	
8	Sampling	4	
9	Large Sample Hypothesis	3	(omit Type II error)
10	Tests of Proportions	2	
11	Small Sample Hypothesis	3	
	EXAM	1	
13	Correlation	2	(omit rank correlation)
14	Regression	3	
16	Chi Square	3	
	EXAM	1	
	TOTAL	45	

The following outline is suggested for a one semester course with four one hour meetings per week for 15 weeks. Five examinations are given during the semester.

Chapter	Topic	Meetings	
1	Introduction	1	
2	Summarizing Data	3	
3	Central Tendency	4	
4	Dispersion	4	(omit geometric mean)
	EXAM	1	
5	Probability	4	
6	Probability Distributions	3	(omit hypergeometric)
7	Normal Distribution	2	
	EXAM	1	
8	Sampling	4	
9	Large Sample Hypothesis	3	(omit Type II error)
10	Tests of Proportions	2	
11	Small Sample Hypothesis	3	
12	ANOVA	3	(omit two-way)
	EXAM	1	
13	Correlation	3	
14	Regression	3	
16	Chi Square	3	
17	Nonparametric	3	(omit Kruskal-Wallis)
	EXAM	1	
18	Index Numbers	1	
19	Time Series	3	
20 or 21	Decision Making or Quality Control	3	
	EXAM	1	
	TOTAL	60	

A TWO-QUARTER

The following outline is suggested for a two quarter course with four one hour meetings per week for 20 weeks.

Chapter	Topic	Meetings	
1	Introduction	1	
2	Summarizing Data	3	
3	Central Tendency	4	(omit geometric mean)
4	Dispersion	4	
	EXAM	1	
5	Probability	4	
6	Probability Distributions	3	(omit hypergeometric)
7	Normal Distribution	2	
	EXAM	1	
8	Sampling	5	
9	Large Sample Hypothesis	5	
10	Tests of Proportions	2	
11	Small Sample Hypothesis	4	
	EXAM	1	
12	ANOVA	4	(omit two-way)
13	Correlation	3	
14	Regression	4	
	EXAM	1	
15	Multiple Regression	4	
16	Chi Square	3	
17	Nonparametric	5	
	EXAM	1	
18	Index Numbers	2	
19	Time Series	3	
20	Decision Making	3	
21	Quality Control	4	
	EXAM	1	
	TOTAL	80	

CORRECTIONS and/or COMMENTS I WOULD LIKE TO MAKE ON THE MASON/LIND *STATISTICAL TECH-NIQUES IN BUSINESS AND ECONOMICS*, EIGHTH EDITION TEXT OR SUPPLEMENTS.

Correction For:

___Text   ___Data Disk
___Instructor's Edition   ___Study Guide
___Instructor's Manual   ___Transparency Masters
___Test Bank

_____Name—Optional

_____
School

Additional copies of this form are included at the back of this manual for your convenience.

PART II

CHAPTER 1:   WHAT IS STATISTICS?

1. The collection of facts and figures is often referred to in everyday usage as statistics. Examples are: Greg Norman shot 68 to take the lead of the USF&G Classic in New Orleans; the yearly low of IBM common stock is 104¹/₂, and the high is 130⁷/₈.

   Here we define statistics as the science of collecting, organizing, analyzing, and interpreting numerical data in order to make more informed decisions. For example, to make a decision regarding a newly developed breakfast cereal, the Kellogg Company might have a sample of 270 persons selected at random try it and give their reactions. A sample of 10 pieces of steel wire randomly selected might be tested for tensile strength in order to make a decision about all the wire produced during the day.

2. The statistical techniques used to organize and summarize masses of numerical data are referred to as "descriptive statistics." The techniques applied to find out something about a population based on a sample are called "inferential statistics."

3. We could use these random sample results to infer something about all the executives. In this case, it would be estimated that about 30 percent of all executives have some degree of hypertension, found by (60/200) 100. This is just one illustration of the extensive use of sampling to infer something about a population.

4. A sampling plan needs to be generated. It might include taking a random sample of 10 jars of cherries every two hours, measuring the amount of liquid and weighing the contents of each jar. These results would be compared with the criteria established by the management. A report of the findings would be forwarded to management.

5. In order to suggest several sites to management, you would probably first collect data on the population in the metropolitan areas of Orlando, Birmingham, Atlanta, and other cities in the Southeast. Data on the availability and the prices of land, utilities, and so on need to be collected and analyzed. After a location has been decided on, an in-depth survey of, say 2,000 persons should be conducted to determine whether the park should be constructed to appeal to all ages, just children, or just adults.

6. a. Sample. Salary data is given for only five schools. There are many more in California including Stanford, UCLA, and so on.
   b. Yes. A professor's salary at California Maritime, for example, cannot be included at the same time with those at Azusa Pacific.
   c. About $50 thousand. If we arranged the salaries from low to high ($37.1, $45.6, $50.5, $59.7, $86.0) and selected a salary near the center, it would be near $50 thousand.

7. a. Sample. The 112 stocks are just a portion of the total number of stocks listed on the New York Stock Exchange.
   b. Nominal. The data resulted from counts and the order of the three movements is immaterial.
   c. Yes. A stock cannot increase, decrease, or stay the same at the same time.
   d. A statistic.

8. a. Sample. Only 800 out of the millions of voters were surveyed.
   b. Nominal. The data resulted from counts and the order of the potential candidates is immaterial.
   c. *USA Today* summed it up nicely by saying "No Democratic candidate is a threat."

9. American consumers' confidence in the economy in November 1991 (50.6) fell below the lowest level recorded during the 1982 recession. That low confidence (50.6) reflects growing uneasiness over job security by the American workers.

CHAPTER 2: SUMMARIZING DATA—FREQUENCY DISTRIBUTIONS AND GRAPHIC PRESENTATION

1. An array is an ordered list of the values from the smallest to the largest, or vice versa.

2. A frequency distribution is a grouping of data into categories showing the number of observations in each mutually exclusive category.

3. Mutually exclusive means that the classes are so formulated that a particular value can occur in only one class. As a result, there are no overlapping of classes.

4. Using the formula $2^k \geq n$, we suggest using 6 classes, starting with $40.00.

5. a. Using the formula $2^k \geq n$, we suggest 4 classes (although a minimum of 5 classes is usually preferred).
   b. Using formula 2–1, the suggested class interval would be 1.5, found by (31 − 25)/4. For ease of computations, 2.0 would be better.
   c. 24

   d.
	f
24–25	2
26–27	8
28–29	4
30–31	2
Total	16

   e. The largest concentration of scores is in the 26–27 class (8). Very few scores are over 30 or under 25.

6. a. Using $2^k \geq n$ would result in 5 classes.
   b. Using formula 2–1, the suggested class interval is 9.40, found by (98 − 51)/5. A class interval of 10 would be better.
   c. 50

   d.
	f
50–59	4
60–69	5
70–79	6
80–89	2
90–99	3
Total	20

   The fewest number of oil changes is about 50, the highest number about 99. The concentration of oil changes is between 60 and 79 per day.

7. a.
	f
0–2	9
3–5	21
6–8	13
9–11	4
12–14	4̶ 3
15–17	1
Total	51

   b. The largest group of shoppers (21) shop at Food Queen 3, 4 or 5 times during a two-week period. Some customers visit the store only 1 time during the two weeks, but others shop as many as 14 times.

   c.
Number of Shoppers	Percent of Total
0–2	17.65
3–5	41.18
6–8	25.49
9–11	7.84
12–14	7.84
Total	100.00

8. a. Using formula 2–1, the suggested class interval is 9.43.
   An interval of 10 is more convenient to work with. The distribution using 10 is:

	f
15–24	1
25–34	2
35–44	5
45–54	10
55–64	15
65–74	4
75–84	3
Total	40

   b. Data tends to cluster between 45 and 64.
   c. Based on the distribution, the youngest person taking the Caribbean cruise is 15 (actually 18 from the raw data). The oldest person was about 84. The largest concentration of ages is between 45 and 64.

   d.
Ages	Percent of Total
15–24	2.5
25–34	5.0
35–44	12.5
45–54	25.0
55–64	37.5
65–74	10.0
75–84	7.5
Total	100.0

9. The five values are 621, 623, 623, 627, and 629.

10. *a.* 81
    b. 5
    c. 97
    d. 30
    e. 11

11. | Stem | Leaves |
    |------|--------|
    | 0 | 5 |
    | 1 | 28 |
    | 2 | |
    | 3 | 0024789 |
    | 4 | 12366 |
    | 5 | 2 |

12. | Stem | Leaves |
    |------|--------|
    | 3 | 6 |
    | 4 | 7 |
    | 5 | 22499 |
    | 6 | 0113458 |
    | 7 | 035678 |
    | 8 | 0344447 |
    | 9 | 055 |

13. *a.* 50
    b. 1
    c. Using midpoints on the X-axis:

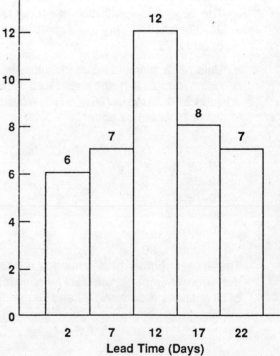

    d. x = 1, y = 5.

e.

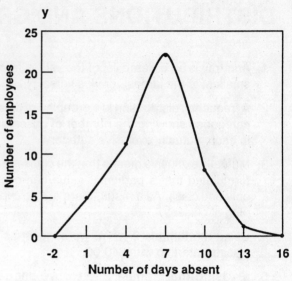

f. Out of the 50 employees about half (23) are absent 7 days. About 5 employees are only absent 1 day but 2 are absent about 13 days.

14. *a.* 40
    b. 2
    c. 2, 6, assuming we plan to draw a frequency polygon using the midpoints.
    d.

e.

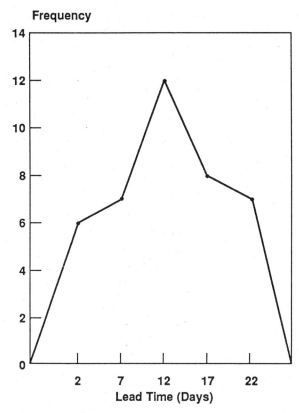

f. Based on the charts, the shortest lead time is 2 days, the longest 22 days. The concentration of lead times is 10–14 days.

15. *a.*

Time in minutes	Relative frequencies	
	Wilcox method	Lambert method
5–7	.060	.080
8–10	.213	.220
11–13	.530	.500
14–16	.143	.140
17–19	.054	.060
Total	1.000	1.000

b.

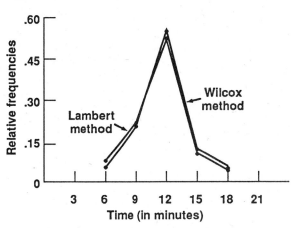

c. The distribution of times are almost identical.

16. *a.*

Amount of claim	Relative Frequencies	
	Five years and older	Less than 5 years old
$ 200–$ 499	0.1500	0.0215
$ 500–$ 799	0.6450	0.0530
$ 800–$1,099	0.1000	0.0920
$1,100–$1,399	0.0500	0.1200
$1,400–$1,699	0.0300	0.4515
$1,700–$1,999	0.0100	0.2245
$2,000–$2,299	0.0150	0.0375
Total	1.0000	1.0000

b.

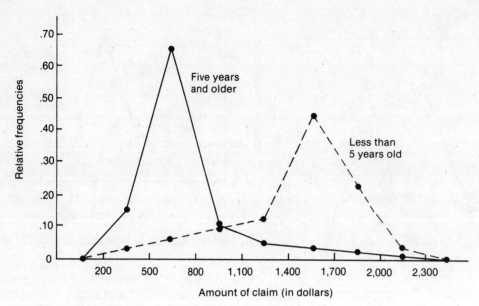

c. The claims for automobiles less than five years old are significantly greater than for those automobiles five years old and older. The typical claim for newer cars is about $1,550 and for older cars about $650.

17. *a.* 5, 17

b.

Days Absent	f	Cumulative frequency
0–2	5	5
3–5	12	17
6–8	23	40
9–11	8	48
12–14	2	50
Total	50	

c.

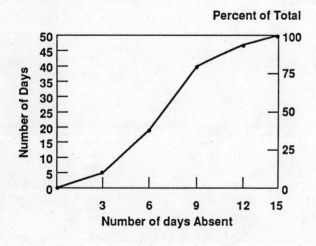

18. *a.* 13, 25.

b.

Lead Time	f	Cumulative frequency
0–4	6	6
5–9	7	13
10–14	12	25
15–19	8	33
20–24	7	40
Total	40	

c.

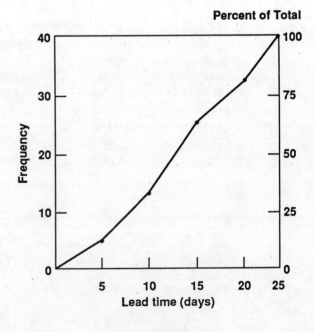

d. About 8.   *d.* 14.

19.

	cf
0–2	50
3–5	45
6–8	33
9–11	10
12–14	2
15–17	0

a. 33

b.

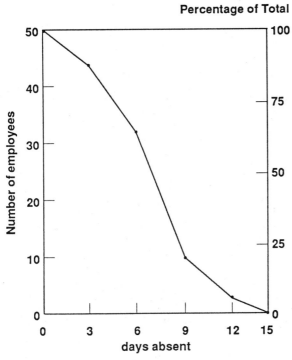

c. More than 45 employees were absent more than 3 days, 2 employees were absent 12 days or more, but no employees were absent more than 15 days.

20.

	cf
0–4	40
5–9	34
10–14	27
15–19	15
20–24	7

a. 15

b.

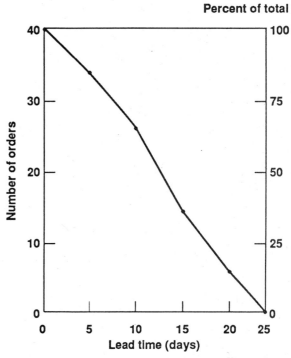

c. About 34 of the orders had a lead time of 5 days or more, 7 orders had a lead time of 20 days or more.

21.

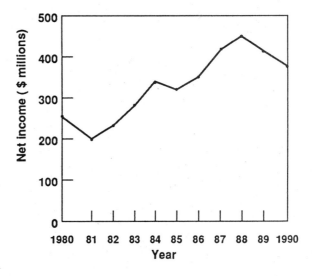

22.

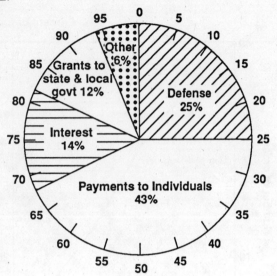

23.

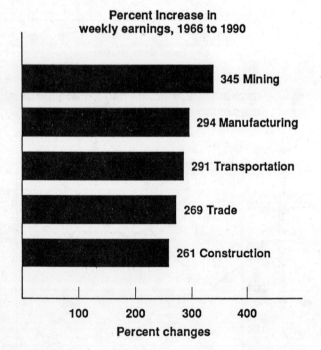

24.

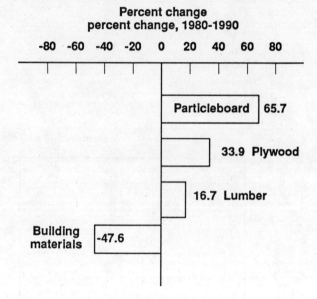

25. *a.* $36.60, found by ($265 − $82)/5.
   b. $40.
   c.

$ 80–$119	8
120– 159	19
160– 199	10
200– 239	6
240– 279	1
Total	44

   d. The purchases ranged from a low of about $80 to a high of about $279. The concentration is in the $120–$159 class.

26. Since there are only 20 observations $2^k \geq n$ suggests 5 classes (because $2^5 = 32$ which is greater than 20). Using 5 gives a class interval of 2.4, found by (34 − 22)/5. We use 2.0 as being more convenient.
   b. Using 21 as the lower limit of the first class:

Rate	Number
21–22	2
23–24	1
25–26	2
27–28	4
29–30	7
31–32	2
33–34	2
Total	20

c.

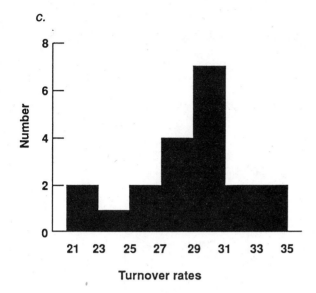

d.

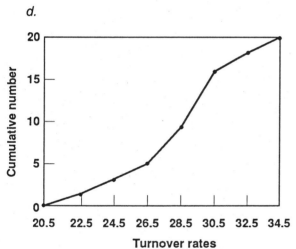

	Cumulative number Less-than
20.5	0
22.5	2
24.5	3
26.5	5
28.5	9
30.5	16
32.5	18
34.5	20

e. The concentration of turnover rates is between 27 and 30. The low is about 21, the high about 34. The rate of 18 patients per bed is quite low. It appears that the patients are being allowed to stay longer than in other hospitals.

27. *a.* Class interval is 21 or 22, found by (282/133)/7. We selected 22.

Stockholders (000)	Number of companies	Less than CF
130–151	6	6
152–173	8	14
174–195	5	19
196–217	4	23
218–239	4	27
240–261	2	29
262–283	3	32
Total	32	

b.

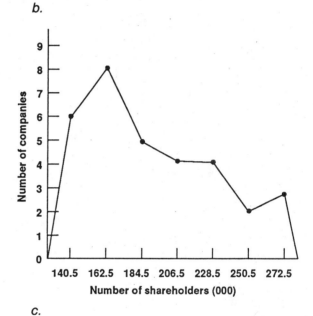

c.

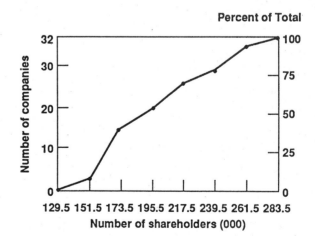

d. About 220 thousand, found by 3/4 of 32 = 24. The 24th company has about 220 thousand shareholders found by drawing a line to the curve from 24 and down to the X-axis.

e. The largest number of companies (8) have between 152 and 174 thousand shareholders. The smallest number is about 130 thousand, the largest number is about 284 thousand.

28. a.

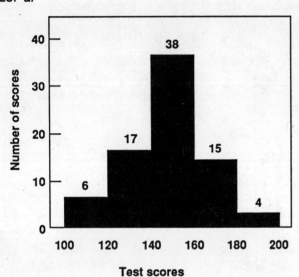

b.

c. The test scores tend to cluster between 140 and 160. A typical score is about 150, the low score is about 100, and the high score is about 200.

29. a.

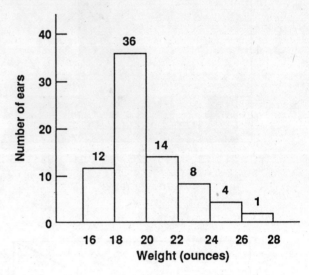

b.

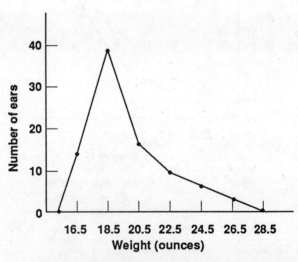

c. The weights range from a low of about 16 ounces to a high of about 28 ounces. The concentration of weights is in the 18 to 19 ounce class.

30. *a.* One possibility is:

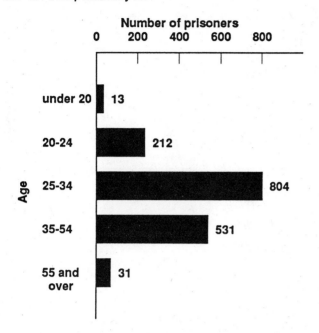

b. The largest group under sentence of death is the 25–34 age group, and very few are under 20 or are 55 or over.

31. Annual expenditure on a typical automobile.

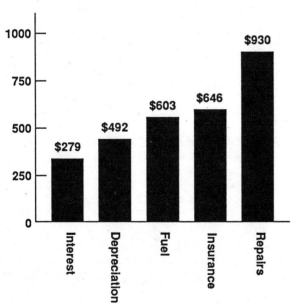

Another possibility is a pie chart.

32. *a.*

Balance	f	Cumulative frequency
$ 0–$ 99	9	9
100– 199	6	15
200– 299	6	21
300– 399	6	27
400– 499	5	32
500– 599	2	34
600– 699	1	35
700– 799	3	38
800– 899	1	39
900– 999	1	40
Total	40	

Probably a class interval of $200 would be better.

b.

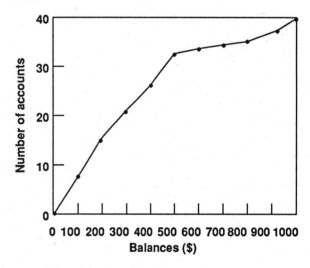

c. About 67% have less than a $400 balance. Therefore, about 33% would be considered "preferred."

d. Less than $50 would be a convenient cutoff point.

33. From MINITAB:
    MTB > stem c1;
    SUBC> increment 10.

    Stem-and-leaf of C1   N = 26
    Leaf Unit = 1.0

```
   2      6 | 57
 (12)     7 | 044555677779
  12      8 | 0355668
   5      9 | 1145
   1     10 | 3
```

34. *a.* Based on the MINITAB output below the fre-
    quency distribution would appear as:

	f	CF
65–69	2	2
70–74	3	5
75–79	9	14
80–84	2	16
85–89	5	21
90–94	3	24
95–99	1	25
100–104	1	26
Total	26	

    MTB > hist c1;
    SUBC> start 67;
    SUBC> increment 5.

    Histogram of C1   N = 26

Midpoint	Count	
67.00	2	**
72.00	3	***
77.00	9	*********
82.00	2	**
87.00	5	*****
92.00	3	***
97.00	1	*
102.00	1	*

    b. About 78 (the median). See Stem-and-leaf in
    the previous exercise. Answers between 75
    and 81 are possible (Mean = 80.96, median
    = 78.00).

c.

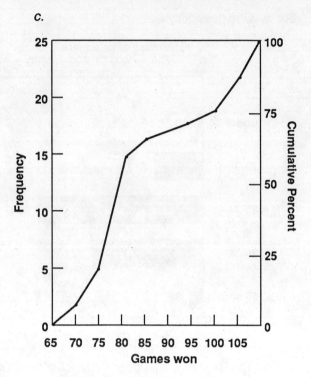

d. About 14 or 15.
e. About 75.

35.

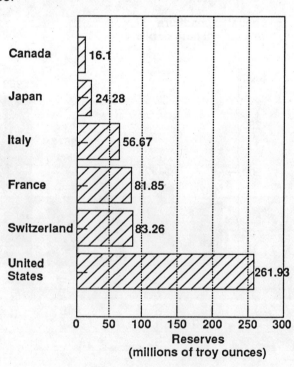

36.

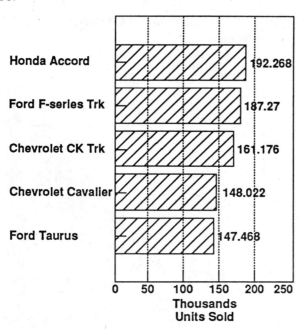

37. *a.* Using a class interval of $400,000, the salaries are: ($000)

	f
$0–$399	14
400–799	4
800–1199	3
1,200–1599	2
1,600 and over	4
Total	27

b. Fourteen out of the 27 players earn under $400,000. The others are scattered somewhat evenly from $400,000 upward with 4 earning $1,600,000 or more.

c. About 10 percent earn more than $2,000,000. This is approximate because we do not know the distribution of salaries above $1,600,000.

38.

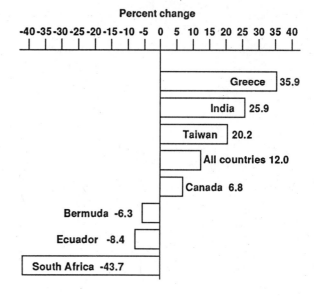

39. *a.*

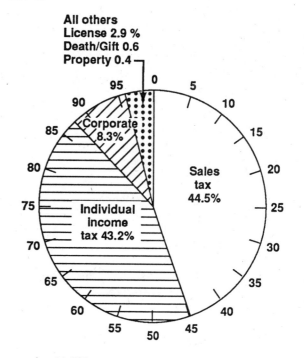

b. 44.5%.

40. *a.* Based on the MINITAB output below, the frequency distribution is:

	f
320–339	5
340–359	12
360–379	16
380–399	14
400–419	2
420–439	1

MTB > hist c1;
SUBC>   start 330;
SUBC>   increment 20.

Histogram of C1   N = 50

Midpoint	Count	
330.0	5	* * * * *
350.0	12	* * * * * * * * * * *
370.0	16	* * * * * * * * * * * * * * * *
390.0	14	* * * * * * * * * * * * * *
410.0	2	* *
430.0	1	*

b. MTB > stem c1;
SUBC>   increment 10.

Stem-and-leaf of C1   N = 50
Leaf Unit = 1.0

2	32	29
5	33	358
11	34	134789
17	35	124689
24	36	0125689
(9)	37	014456679
17	38	04569
12	39	002567899
3	40	0
2	41	0
1	42	
1	43	2

c. Practically all truck assembly during an eight-hour shift ranged between 340 and 400 trucks.

41.

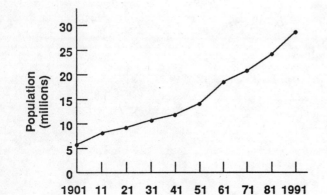

Another possibility is:

Population of Canada

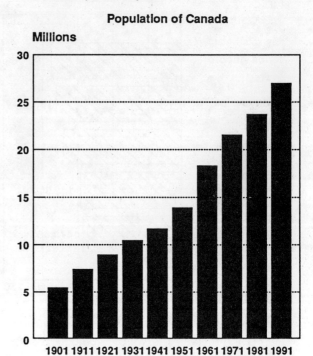

42.

Infant Mortality

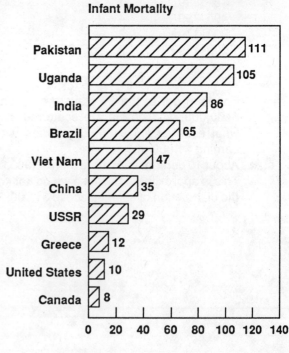

43.

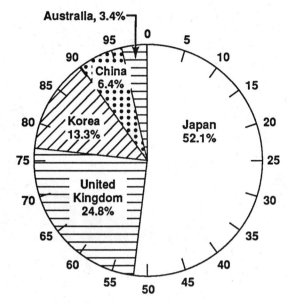

c.

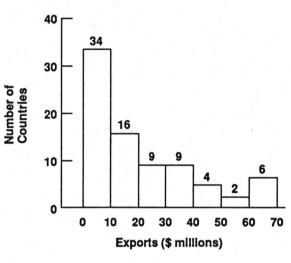

44. a.

	f	CF
$ 0–9	34	34
10–19	16	50
20–29	9	59
30–39	9	68
40–49	4	72
50–59	2	74
60–69	6	80
Total	80	

b. Using midpoints:

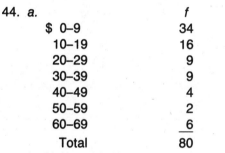

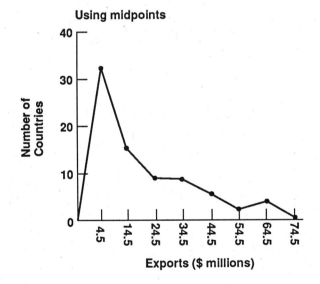

d.

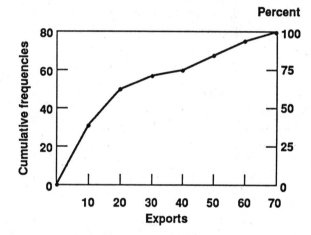

e. About $14 million (or $15 million).
f. About 50% of the exports are less than $15 million. The largest concentration is under $20 million. About 62% are in the 0 to $19 million range.

45.

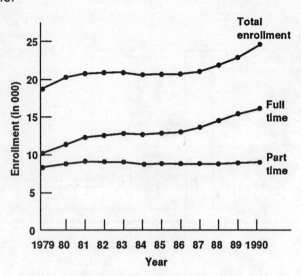

Total enrollment increased slightly due to in-creased full-time enrollment. Part-time enroll-ment remained about the same.

46. *a.*

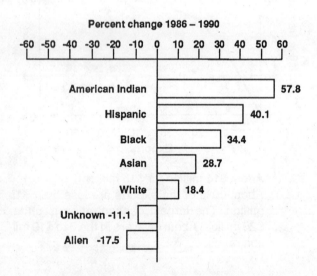

b. There has been a significant decrease in alien enrollment. Other ethnic groups increased percentagewise with the American Indian en-rollment having the largest increase.

47.

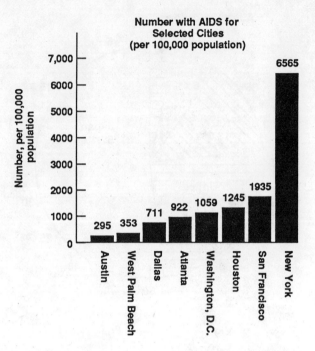

48.

Selling prices ($ thousands)	Number of homes	Cumulative frequencies
$ 90.5 up to $130.5	10	10
130.5 up to 170.5	34	44
170.5 up to 210.5	21	65
210.5 up to 250.5	9	74
250.5 up to 290.5	1	75
Total	75	

Another possibility is:

Selling Prices ($ thousand)	f	CF
$ 90.5 up to $110.5	3	3
110.5 up to 130.5	7	10
130.5 up to 150.5	16	26
150.5 up to 170.5	18	44
170.5 up to 190.5	12	56
190.5 up to 210.5	9	65
210.5 up to 230.5	5	70
230.5 up to 250.5	4	74
250.5 up to 270.5	1	75
Total	75	

b. About $160 thousand (Median = $160,000, mean = $166,000).

c.

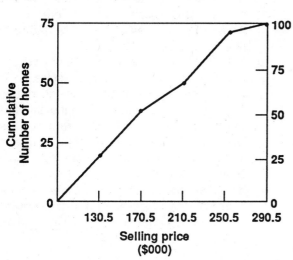

About $140,000.
About 98%.
d. Positively skewed.
e.

Positively skewed.

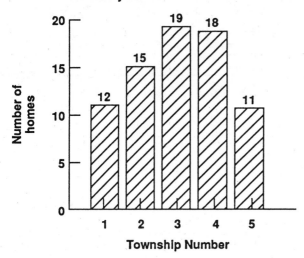

49. a.

Market Value ($ millions)	Number of companies	Cumulative frequency
$ 2,500 up to $12,500	159	159
12,500 up to 22,500	23	182
22,500 up to 32,500	9	191
32,500 up to 42,500	5	196
42,500 up to 52,500	0	196
52,500 up to 62,500	2	198
62,500 up to 72,500	1	199
72,500 up to 82,500	1	200
Total	200	

b. About $6 billion. Median = $6.1 billion, mean = $10.3 billion.

c.

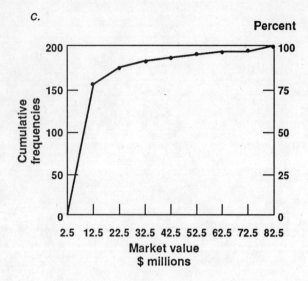

80% of the market value are less than $12,500 million.
About 13%. (Answers will vary.)
d. Distribution positively skewed with most of the market values less than $12,500 million.

50. *a.* Using $4 million as the class interval, the frequency distribution for total salaries of the 26 teams is:

Salary ($ million)	Number of teams	Cumulative number
$10.50–$14.49	1	1
14.50– 18.49	3	4
18.50– 22.49	6	10
22.50– 26.49	5	15
26.50– 30.49	5	20
30.50– 34.49	5	25
34.50– 38.49	1	26
Total	26	

b. About $24 million. (Median is $23.75 million.)
c.

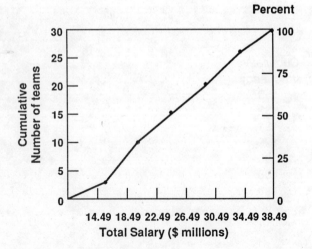

About 40% of the teams have less than a total salary of $23 million (or $24 million).
About 55% are paying less than $25 or $26 million in total salary.
d. The distribution of salaries is somewhat uniform in shape with 5 or 6 frequencies in most of the classes in the middle of the distribution. Yes, some of the teams are "out of line" with respect to total salaries. In this regard, 1 team salary is less than $14,490,000 and at the other extreme 1 team has a total salary in excess of $34,500,000.
e. Based on the following graph, it does not appear that there is any relationship between the fraction of games the team won and total salary.

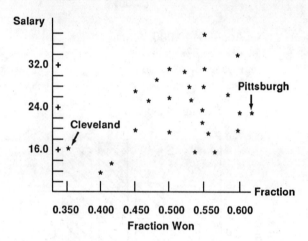

CHAPTER 3: DESCRIBING DATA— MEASURES OF CENTRAL TENDENCY

1. A sample mean is found by

$$\bar{X} = \frac{\text{Sum of all the values in a sample}}{\text{Number of values in the sample}}$$

Thus, it is a measurable characteristic of a sample.
A population mean is found by

$$\mu = \frac{\text{Sum of all the values in a particular population}}{\text{Number of values in a population}}$$

Thus, it is a measurable characteristic of the population of interest. Note that the steps for computing the sample mean and the population mean are the same. Only the symbols are different.

2. 1. If the data is interval or ratio level it has a mean.
   2. When computing the mean all the values in the sample (or population) are included.
   3. A given set of data only has one mean.
   4. The sum of the deviations of every value from the mean equals zero.

3. a. Mean = 7.0, found by 28/4.
   b. $(5 - 7) + (9 - 7) + (4 - 7) + (10 - 7) = 0$

4. a. 4.2 found by 21/5.
   b. $(1.3 - 4.2) + (7.0 - 4.2) + (3.6 - 4.2) + (4.1 - 4.2) + (5.0 - 4.2) = 0$

5. 14.58, found by 43.74/3.

6. $20.95, found by $125.68/6.

7. a. 15.4, found by 154/10.
   b. Population since it includes all the salespersons at Midtown Ford.

8. a. 23.9, found by 167/7.
   b. Population parameter since it includes all the calls during a seven-day period.

9. a. $54.55, found by $1,091/20.
   b. A sample—assuming that the power company serves more than 20 customers.

10. a. 10.73, found by 161/15.
    b. Sample of RN's.

11. $.775, found by ($10 + $37.50 + $30)/100.

12. $1.50 found by ($40 + $35)/50.

13. $11.50, found by ($400 + $500 + $1,400)/200 = $2,300/200.

14. $143.75, found by ($1,000 + $750 + $4,000)/40.

15. a. Nominal.
    b. Lecture, because it is the most frequently used method.
    c. No. Data must be at least ordinal scale.
    d. No. Data must be at least interval scale.

16. a. Nominal.
    b. Independent, because it was mentioned more often than any other political affiliation.
    c. No, because Republican, Democrat, and so on cannot be arranged from low to high. At least ordinal level is needed.
    d. No, because Republican, Democrat, and so on cannot be summed.

17. a. $96.70.
    b. No. It is the highest value.
    c. $91.40.
    d. $88.70, found by $620.90/7.
    e. Either mean or median.

18. *a.* 79.
  b. Yes. It is near the center of the values.
  c. 97.9 based on the following MINITAB.
  MTB > desc C1

	N	MEAN	MEDIAN	TRMEAN	STDEV	SEMEAN
C1	11	97.9	79.0	92.3	45.5	13.7

	MIN	MAX	Q1	Q3
C1	44.0	202.0	71.0	108.0

  d. 79.0
  e. Either the mode (79) or median (79). The arithmetic mean (97.9) is being pulled up by the 1985 number of dry wells (160).

19. Mean or median. Mode of 10 too low. Mean of 15.4 or median of 16.5 almost equal. From MINI-TAB:
  MTB > desc c1

	N	MEAN	MEDIAN	TRMEAN	STDEV	SEMEAN
C1	10	15.40	16.50	15.25	7.40	2.34

	MIN	MAX	Q1	Q3
C1	4.00	28.00	9.50	20.00

Distribution bimodal at 10 and 19.

20. *a.* When we need to average percents, indexes and relatives the geometric mean gives a more representative figure. Also, it is preferred when we need an average rate (percent) of increase from one period of time to another.
  b. Never larger. Geometric mean is always equal to or smaller than the arithmetic mean.

21. 11.18, found by using formula 3–6:

$8 \times 12 \times 14 \times 26 \times 5$	DISPLAY
Depress $\boxed{\text{2nd}}$ y^x	174720
Depress reciprocal of 5 (.20) =	11.180688

22. 5.41, found by using formula 3–6.

$2 \times 8 \times 6 \times 4 \times 10 \times 6 \times 8 \times 4$	DISPLAY
Depress $\boxed{\text{2nd}}$ y^x	
Depress reciprocal of 8 (.125) =	5.4131998

23. 62.5%, found by using formula 3–7:

$926.429 \div 30.948$	
Depress $\boxed{\text{2nd}}$ y^x	29.93502
Depress .1428571 =	1.6251099
Depress – 1 =	.625

24. 12.7%, found by using formula 3–7:

$54.87 \div 9.19$	DISPLAY
Depress $\boxed{\text{2nd}}$ y^x	5.9706202
Depress .066667 =	1.126509
Depress – 1 =	.126509

25. Since the exact values in a frequency distribution are not known the computed mean can only be an estimate.

26. 12.17, found by using formula 3–8:

$$\bar{X} = \frac{\Sigma fX}{n} = \frac{365}{30} = 12.17$$

In the following MINITAB, set C1 are the class midpoints, C2 the frequencies. The symbol * represents multiply.

27. 46.79, found by using formula 3–8:
  $\Sigma fX/n = 3,275/70 = 46.79$.

28. $59.67, found by using formula 3–8:
  $3,580/60 = $59.667.

29. 44.3 years of age, found by 2,215/50.

30. Median = 12.0, found by

$$9.50 + \frac{15 - 9}{12} \,(5)$$

Mode = 12.0 midpoint of the class containing the greatest numbers of frequencies.

31. Median = 47.12, found by

$$39.5 + \frac{35 - 19}{21} \,(10)$$

Mode = 44.5.

32. *a.* Median = 26.8 years, found by

$$26.5 + \frac{25 - 23}{20}\,(3)$$

    b. Mode = 28.0 which is the midpoint of the 27 – 29 class.

33. *a.* 17.90 miles per gallon, found by

$$15.5 + \frac{15 - 7}{10}\,(3)$$

    b. Mode = 17. It is the midpoint of the 16 – 18 class.

34. *a.* 1,200 tons (same as mean). Half of values above the median, half below it.
    b. 1,200 tons (same as the mean and medium) values on either side of the mean is equal 100.

35. *a.* Median = 10.8. B. Half of the price-earnings are above 10.8, the other half below 10.8.
    b. Mode = 10.2. A. More price-earning ratios are 10.2 than any other value.
    c. Mean = 11.1. C 11.1.

36. *a.* 12.6 inches, found by [2(12.9) + 12]/3.
    b.

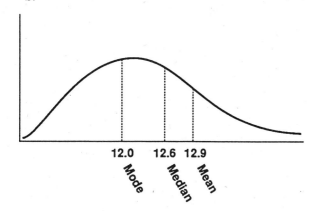

37. *a.* 81.0, found by [3(78.0) – 72]/2.
    b.

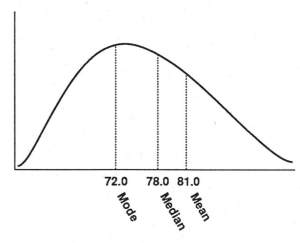

38. *a.* Mean = 5, found by (6 + 4 + 3 + 7 + 5)/5. Median is 5, found by rearranging the values and selecting the middle value.
    b. Population because all clients were included.
    c. $\Sigma (X - \bar{X})$ = (6 – 5) + (4 – 5) + (3 – 5) + (7 – 5) + (5 – 5) = 0.

39. *a.* Mean = 21.71, median 22.00
    b. (23 – 21.71) + (19 – 21.71) + . . . + (22 – 21.71) = 0

40. Mean = 34.06. Median = 37.5 (See MINITAB).
    MTB > describe c1

	N	MEAN	MEDIAN	TRMEAN	STDEV	SEMEAN
C1	16	34.06	37.50	34.86	12.84	3.21

	MIN	MAX	Q1	Q3		
C1	5.00	52.00	30.00	42.75		

41. Mean = 70.53, found by 2,116/30.
42. Mean = 80.96, found by 2,105/26.
    Median = 78.0, found by $(77 + 79)/2$.

43. Mean = \$672,963, found by \$18,170,000/27.
    Median = \$345,000 which is the middle value.
    There are a few very high salaries pulling the
    mean upward. Therefore, the median is a more
    representative salary.

44. 370.08, found by 18,504/50.

45. 15.6%, found by:
    165470 ÷ 44871

			DISPLAY
Depress	2nd	y^x	3.6876825
Depress .1111111 =			1.1560393
Depress −1 =			.1560393

46. 0.940 percent.

47. 61.68 percent.

48. 83.215 percent.

49. Arithmetic mean = 60.14%
    Geometric mean = 55.209%

50. 15.44%.

51. 227.4667 pounds, found by
    $[7(240) + 4(212) + 3(190) + 1(314)]/15$.

52. a. \$97, found by:
    $$\frac{100(\$70) + 60(\$100) + 40(\$160)}{100 + 60 + 40} = \frac{\$19,400}{200}$$
    b. \$112, found by:
    $$\frac{160(\$100) + 40(\$160)}{160 + 40} = \frac{\$22,400}{200}$$

53. a. No. The 3,333 pounds assumes that there are
    an equal number of containers weighing
    1,000, 3,000, and 6,000 pounds respectively.
    This is not the case.
    b. 2,500 pounds found by [(60 × 1,000) + (40 ×
    3,000) + (20 × 6,000)]/120. Each of the three
    size containers is weighted by the number of
    containers.

54. a. 164.19697 grams, found by 10,837/66.
    b. 161.5 grams, found by
    $$159.5 + \frac{\frac{66}{2} - 30}{15} (10)$$

55. 19.74 years, found by:
    $$19.5 + \frac{\frac{515.6}{2} - 249.8}{168.6} (5)$$
    Half of the unmarried mothers are under 19.74
    years old and the other half over 19.74 years old.

56. a. \$35,706.02, found by:
    $$\$29,999.50 + \frac{\frac{100}{2} - 39.5}{18.4} (\$10,000)$$
    Half of household incomes are above
    \$35,706.02, the other half below it.
    b. \$24,999.50. It is the midpoint of the
    \$20,000–\$29,999 class. It appears most fre-
    quently.

57. a. \$30,082.49, found by:
    $$\$29,999.50 + \frac{\frac{100}{2} - 49.8}{24.1} (\$10,000)$$
    Half of the incomes are below \$30,082.49, the
    other half above it.
    b. \$24,999.50. Midpoint of \$20,000–\$29,999
    class. Appears most frequently.

58. a. 2, because that number appears most fre-
    quently. More families have two income earn-
    ers than any other number.
    b. Median. Mean cannot be computed because
    of open end (4 or more).

59. *a.* 45.84 years, found by

$$44.5 \ + \ \frac{\dfrac{1829}{2} - 854}{450} \ (10)$$

Half of the divorced males are younger than 45.84 years, the other half older than 45.84 years.

b. 43.29 years, found by:

$$34.5 \ + \ \frac{\dfrac{2827}{2} - 837}{656} \ (10)$$

Half of the divorced females are younger than 43.29 years, the other half older than 43.29 years.

c. Males 49.5. Females: distribution bimodal (two modes), 39.5 and 49.5.

60. *a.* Mode.   *e.* Positively skewed.
    b. Arithmetic mean.   *f.* Arithmetic mean.
    c. Geometric mean.   *g.* Median.
    d. Symmetrical.   *h.* Mode.

61. *a.* $3,330, found by [3($3,220) – $3,000]/2.
    b. Mean. It is being pulled up by extreme values.
    c. $3,000.
    d. Positively skewed. The median and the mean are greater than the mode.

62. About 118, found by drawing a line from 50 percent on the *Y*-axis to the curve and then dropping vertically to the *X*-axis.

63. 8.7% found by:

		DISPLAY
17000000 ÷ 22000		772.72727
Depress 2nd y^x		
Depress 0.0125 =		1.0866766
Depress − 1 =		.0866766

64. 8.4% found by:

		DISPLAY
3013090000 ÷ 6225900		48.396055
Depress 2nd y^x		
Depress .0208333 =		1.0841769
Depress − 1 =		.0841769

65. *a.* 6.23% found by:

		DISPLAY
126900 ÷ 88300		1.4371461
Depress 2nd y^x		
Depress .166667		1.0623074
Depress − 1		.0623074

   b. 6.12%

66. *a.* 5.49% found by:

		DISPLAY
119900 ÷ 78200		1.5332481
Depress 2nd y^x		
Depress .125		1.0548763
Depress − 1		.0548763

   b. 5.14%

67. *a.* Mean = $166,670, median = $160,000.
From MINITAB:
MTB > describe c1

	N	MEAN	MEDIAN	TRMEAN	STDEV	SEMEAN
Price	75	166.67	160.00	165.82	35.68	4.12

	MIN	MAX	Q1	Q3
Price	92.60	255.80	140.30	190.50

b. 3.0 bedrooms (median)
c. 2.0 baths (mean and mode)
d. 14.9 miles (mean), 15.0 miles (median)

	N	MEAN	MEDIAN	TRMEAN	STDEV	SEMEAN
Bedrooms	75	3.720	3.000	3.627	1.494	0.172

	N	MEAN	MEDIAN	TRMEAN	STDEV	SEMEAN
Baths	75	2.0867	2.0000	2.0672	0.3974	0.0459

	N	MEAN	MEDIAN	TRMEAN	STDEV	SEMEAN
Distance	75	14.893	15.000	14.746	4.892	0.565

68. *a.* mean is 11,141, median 6604.
b. mean is 620, median 427.5.

69. Using MINITAB:

	N	MEAN	MEDIAN	TRMEAN	STDEV	SEMEAN
Salary	26	24.24	23.75	24.28	6.51	1.28

	N	MEAN	MEDIAN	TRMEAN	STDEV	SEMEAN
Attend	26	2.186	2.220	2.161	0.662	0.130

a. mean = $24,240,000
median = $23,750,000
b. Either mean or median, so about $24,000,000.
c. Mean 2,186,000 fans.
Median 2,220,000 fans.
d. Either mean or median, so about 2.2 million fans.

CHAPTER 4: MEASURES OF DISPERSION AND SKEWNESS

1. *a.* 7, found by 10 − 3.
   b. 6, found by 30/5.
   c. 2.4, found by 12/5.
   d. The difference between the highest number sold (10) and the smallest number sold (3) is 7.

2. *a.* 24, found by 52 − 28.
   b. 38.
   c. 6.25, found by 50/8.
   d. The difference between 28 and 52 is 24.

3. *a.* 30, found by 54 − 24.
   b. 38, found by 380/10.
   c. 7.2 found by 72/10.
   d. On the average the number minutes required to install a door deviates 7.2 minutes from the mean of 38 minutes.

4. *a.* 7.6%, found by 18.2 − 10.6.
   b. 13.85 percent.
   c. 2%, found by 16/8.
   d. On the average the return on investment deviates 2 percent from the mean of 13.85%.

5. *a.* 15, found by 41 − 26.
   b. 33.9, found by 339 ÷ 10.
   c. 4.12, found by 41.2 ÷ 10. The ratings deviate 4.12 from the mean of 33.9 on the average.
   d. Since 8 < 15 and 1.9 < 4.12, we conclude that there is more dispersion in the first group.

6. *a.* 10 days, found by 10 − 0.
   b. 3.5 days found by 28/8.
   c. 2.375 days, found by 19/8. Days lost deviate 2.375 days from the mean.
   d. The measures of dispersion are almost identical. Therefore the two groups are spread out about the same.

7. *a.* 4.4, found by 22/5 using formula 4 − 3.
   b. 4.4, found by 29.4 − 25 using formula 4 − 4.

8. *a.* 15.556
   b. 15.556, found by $616/6 - (56/6)^2$

9. *a.* \$2.770, found by \$13.85/5.
   b. 1.2586, found by 6.2928/5.

10. *a.* 11.76%, found by 58.8/5.
    b. 16.89%, found by 84.452/5.

11. *a.* Range: 7.3, found by 11.6 − 4.3.
    Arithmetic mean: 6.94, found by 34.7/5.
    Variance: 6.5944, found by 32.972/5.
    Standard deviation: 2.568, found by $\sqrt{6.5944}$.
    b. Dennis has a higher mean return (11.76 > 6.94). However, Dennis has greater spread in their returns on equity (16.89 > 6.59).

12. *a.* 18, found by 90 − 72. (in \$000).
    b. \$79.6, found by \$398/5 (in \$000).
    c. Variance = 40.24, found by 201.2/5.
    Standard deviation = \$6.3435.
    d. Means about same, but less dispersion in salary for TMV vice presidents.

13. *a.* 2.3452, found by $\sqrt{22/4}$.
    b. 5.5, found by (102 − 400/5)/4.

14. *a.* 2.3452, found by $\sqrt{22/4}$.
    b. 2.3452, found by $\sqrt{(342 - 1{,}600/5)/4}$

15. *a.* 82.667, found by 744/9.
    b. 82.667.
    c. 9.09, found by $\sqrt{82.667}$.

16. *a.* 6.0086, found by 42.06/7.
    b. 6.0086, found by $\dfrac{1576.64 - 12276.64/8}{7}$
    c. 2.4512, found by $\sqrt{6.0086}$.

17. *a.* 7, found by 127 − 120.
    b. 124 grams, found by 1,240/10.
    c. 4.667, found by 42/(10−1).
    d. 2.1602 grams, found by $\sqrt{4.667}$.

18. AB4 yields a higher mean weight with less spread.

19. *a.* 24 found by 24 − 0. (or 25 if true limits are used.
    b. 5.331 found by
    $$\sqrt{\frac{5{,}265 - 133{,}225/30}{29}}$$

20. _a._ 49, found by 69 − 20 (or 50 if true limits are used)
    _b._ 12.1788, found by

$$\sqrt{\frac{163,457.5 - \frac{(3,275)^2}{70}}{70 - 1}}$$

21. _a._ 17 minutes, using the stated class limits (18 − 1 = 17). Using the true class limits, the range is 18 minutes, found by 18.5 − 0.5.
    _b._ 3.8938 minutes, found by:

$$\sqrt{\frac{3,759 - \frac{(363)^2}{42}}{42 - 1}}$$

    _c._ 15.162, found by $(3.8938)^2$.

22. _a._ $1.99 found by $2.49 − $0.50 (or $2.00 if the true limits are used).
    _b._ .3641, found by

$$\sqrt{\frac{170.367 - \frac{(113.1)^2}{80}}{79}}$$

    _c._ .1326, found by $(.3641)^2$.

23. About 69%, found by

$$1 - \frac{1}{(1.8)^2}$$

24. About 84%. Each income levels lie 2.5 standard deviations from the mean. Then

$$1 - \frac{1}{(2.5)^2} = .84.$$

25. _a._ About 95%.
    _b._ 47.5%, 2.5%.

26. _a._ 85, halfway between the end points of 140 and 30.
    _b._ About 18, found by (140 − 30)/6.
    _c._ 103 and 67, found by 85 ± (1) 18.
    _d._ 121 and 49, found by 85 ± (2) 18.

27. _a._ 8.429, found by $4.50 + \dfrac{30/4 - 2}{7}$ (5).
    _b._ 15.75
    _c._ 7.321, found by 15.75 − 8.429.
    _d._ 5.214.
    _e._ 19.50,

$$\text{found by } 19.50 + \frac{\frac{(90)(30)}{100} - 27}{3} (5).$$

28. _a._ 38.25
    _b._ 56.44, found by $49.5 + \dfrac{3(70) - 40}{18}$ (10).
    _c._ 18.19, found by 56.44 − 38.25
    _d._ 29.5, found by $19.5 + \dfrac{\frac{700}{100} - 0}{7}$ (10).
    _e._ 63.667.

29. _a._ about $1,281.32, found by:

$$\$1,199.5 + \frac{\frac{120}{4} - 21}{22} (\$200)$$

    _b._ About $1,657.83, found by:

$$\$1,599.5 + \frac{\frac{(3)(120)}{4} - 83}{24} (\$200)$$

    _c._ About $376.51, found by $1,657.83 − $1,281.32. It is the difference between the third and first quartiles.
    _d._ $188.26, found by $376.51 ÷ 2. It is half the distance between the third and first quartiles.

30. _a._ 65.125, found by

$$59.50 + \frac{150/4 - 24}{24} (10).$$

    _b._ 87.00.
    _c._ 21.875.
    _d._ 10.9375.
    _e._ 10th is $53.875.
    90th is $102. 2273 found by

$$99.5 + \frac{\frac{(90)(150)}{100} - 132}{11} (10).$$

    10–to–90 range is $48.352. It is the distance between the 10th and 90th percentile.

31. _a._ 26,299.89.
    _b._ 13,149.95.
    _c._ 32,350.147 found by 69,640.845 − 37,290.698.

32. 8.06%, found by (.25/3.10) (100).

33. Domestic 21.28%, found by (10/47) 100.
    Overseas 19.23.
    There is slightly less relative dispersion in the weights of luggage for overseas passengers.

34. _a._ Because the two series are in different units of measurement.
    _b._ P.E. ratio 16.51%.
    ROI 20.8% Less spread in the P.E. ratios.

35. The relative dispersion in stocks under $10 is 28.95%. For stocks over $60, 5.71%. Less relative dispersion in stocks over $60.

36. Symmetrical because mean, median, and mode are equal. The coefficient of skewness is zero.

37. 1.3498, found by

$$\frac{3(673,000 - 345,000)}{729,000}$$

Positively skewed.

38. *a.* Positively skewed.
    b. 2.949.

39. *a.* negatively skewed.
    b. − 1.8, found by

$$\frac{3(2.1 - 2.4)}{.5}$$

40. Advantage: Easy to compute (high minus the low value). Also, gives an approximation of the dispersion in the data. Disadvantage: An extreme value distorts the spread in the data. And, only two values are considered (highest, lowest). Thus, all the other observations are ignored.

41. For a sample, $n - 1$ is substituted for N in the denominator of the formula for the sample variance. This substitution prevents the underestimation of the population variance.

42. The minus in the coefficient of skewness indicates that the distribution is negatively skewed. The arithmetic mean is the smallest of the three averages, the median the next smallest and the mode the largest value.

43. The distribution with the C.V. of 30% has more relative dispersion than the distribution with a 20% C.V.

44. *a.* 4, found by 12 − 8.
    b. 1.0, found by 8/8.
    c. 1.31, found by

$$\sqrt{\frac{12}{8-1}}$$

    d. 1.3093, found by

$$\sqrt{\frac{734 - \frac{(76)^2}{8}}{7}}$$

45. *a.* 55, found by 72 − 17.
    b. 14.4, found by 144/10. $\bar{X}$ = 43.2.
    c. 17.6245.

46. *a.* 9, found by 12 − 3.
    b. 2.72, found by 13.6/5 where mean = 7.6.
    c. 3.5071.

47. *a.* population.
    b. 183.4734.
    c. 94.92%.

48. *a.* We can consider this a population because it includes only the 5 starters.
    b. 2.4166.
    c. 3.08%, found by (2.4166/78.40) 100.

49. *a.* $29, found by $109 − $80.
    b. $6.5138, considering this a sample.
    c. 9.289, where Q_3 = $100.854 and Q_1 = $91.565.
    d. $17.712 where P_{90} = $104.292 and P_{10} = $86.58.

50. *a.* 24 found by 24 − 0.
    b. 5.1182.
    c. 7.306, found by 16.306 − 9.0.
    d. 9.445, found by 17.278 − 7.833.

51. *a.* 28.1625, found by 2,253/80. Median is 27.6.
    b. 5.7576.
    c. 20.44%, found by (5.7576/28.1625) (100).
    d. .2931, found by

$$\frac{3 (28.1625 - 27.6)}{5.7576}$$

    Positively skewed.

52. *b.*

53. *a.*

54. *c.*

55. *b.*

56. *a.* Q_1 = 37.09, Q_3 = 54.43.
    b. 17.34.
    c. P_{10} = 29.944, P_{90} = 62.957.
    d. 33.013.

57. *a.* Q_1 = 18.151, Q_3 = 23.618
    b. QD = 5.467/2 = 2.7335.

58. *a.* Q_1 = 7.738, Q_3 = 19.241 found by:

$$9.5 + \frac{\frac{3(150)}{4} - 56}{58} (10).$$

    b. QD = 11.503/2 = 5.75
    c. P_{30} = 8.452, P_{70} = 17.948.
    d. 9.456.
    e. The middle 40% of the overweight pounds lie between 8.452 pounds and 17.948 pounds.

59. *a.* Q_1 = \$13,113, Q_3 = \$44,331.
    b. \$15,609. found by (\$44,331 − \$13,113)/2.
    c. P_{20} = \$10,755. P_{80} = \$48,692.
    d. \$37,937.14.
    e. The middle 60% of the incomes lie between \$10,755. and \$48,692.

60. *a.* 84%. Since 19 and 98 are both 2.5 standard deviations from the mean,

    $$1 - \frac{1}{(2.5)^2} = .84$$

    b. C.V. = 27.01%, found by (15.8/58.5) 100.
    c. Sk = − .9494 found by 3(58.5 − 63.5)/15.8.

61. *a.* 55.56%. Both 21 and 27 are 1.5 standard deviations from the mean.
    b. C.V. = 8.33% found by (.02/.24) 100.
    c. Sk. = − 2.25, found by 3(24 − 25.5)/2.

62. *a.* 6.06, found by:

    $$4.5 + \frac{138/2 - 64}{16} (5).$$

    b. 16.41 found by:

    $$9.5 + \frac{\frac{(75)(138)}{100} - 80}{34} (10).$$

    c. 16.41 found by 16.41 − 0.

63. *a.* From MINITAB: (Answers in \$000)

	N	MEAN	MEDIAN	TRMEAN	STDEV	SEMEAN
Price	75	166.67	160.00	165.82	35.68	4.12

	MIN	MAX	Q1	Q3
Price	92.60	255.80	140.30	190.50

   s = 35.68
   C.V. = 21.41%, found by (35.68/166.67) 100.
   Sk = .5608, found by 3(166.67 − 160.0)/35.68.
   Positive skewness because mean > median. Observations are spread out 21.41% from the mean.

b.

	N	MEAN	MEDIAN	TRMEAN	STDEV	SEMEAN
Distance	75	14.893	15.000	14.746	4.892	0.565

	MIN	MAX	Q1	Q3
Distance	6.000	28.000	11.000	19.000

s = 4.892

C.V. = 32.85%, found by (4.892/14.893)(100).

Sk = − .066, found by 3(14.893 − 15.000)/4.892.
Slight negative skewness because mean < median. Values spread out 32.85% from mean.

64.

	N	MEAN	MEDIAN	TRMEAN	STDEV	SEMEAN
Sales	200	11141	6604	8868	14388	1017

	MIN	MAX	Q1	Q3
Sales	299	107197	3714	12410

a. s = 14.388

C.V. = 129.14% found by (14388/11141) 100

Sk = .946 found by 3(11,141 − 6604)/14,388.
Positive skewness with very large relative dispersion. Values are spread out 129.14% from mean.

b.

	N	MEAN	MEDIAN	TRMEAN	STDEV	SEMEAN
Profit	200	620.0	427.5	538.7	802.4	56.7

	MIN	MAX	Q1	Q3
Profit	− 1985.0	6020.0	242.7	754.8

s = 802.4

C.V. = 129.42%, found by (802.4/620.0) 100.

Sk = .7197, found by 3(620.0 − 427.5)/802.4.
Positive skewness, profits dispersed 129.42% from the mean.

65.   From MINITAB:

	N	MEAN	MEDIAN	TRMEAN	STDEV	SEMEAN
Salary	26	24.24	23.75	24.28	6.51	1.28

	MIN	MAX	Q1	Q3
Salary	11.20	36.30	19.13	29.30

a.   s = 6.51
C.V. = 26.86%, found by (6.51/24.24) 100
Sk = .226, found by 3(24.24 − 23.75)/6.51.
Salaries are dispersed 26.86% from the mean. Positive skewness because mean > median.

b.

	N	MEAN	MEDIAN	TRMEAN	STDEV	SEMEAN
Attend	26	2.186	2.220	2.161	0.662	0.130

	MIN	MAX	Q1	Q3
Attend	0.980	4.000	1.785	2.475

s = 0.662
C.V. = 30.28% found by (.662/2.186)(100).
Sk = −.154, found by 3(2.186 − 2.220)/.662.
Slight negative skewness because mean < median. Values dispersed from mean 30.28%.

CHAPTER 5: A SURVEY OF PROBABILITY CONCEPTS

1. An experiment is the observation of some activity or the act of taking some measurement, whereas an event is the collection of several outcomes from the experiment.

2. An event is the collection of one or more outcomes from an experiment.

3. *a.* A probability may range from 0 to 1.00 inclusive.
   b. It cannot be greater than 1.
   c. It cannot be less than 0.
   d. A probability close to 1.00 indicates the event is likely to occur.

4. Yes. A probability of 0 means the event cannot happen.

5. *a.* The experiment is asking the 500 citizens whether they favor or oppose widening Indiana Avenue to three lanes.
   b. Possible events include 321 favor the widening, 387 favor the widening, 444 favor the widening, and so on.
   c. Answers will vary, but two possibilities are: a majority favor the widening, which would be 251 or more, and more than 300 favor the widening.

6. *a.* The experiment is counting the number of stockholders who favor the merger.
   b. The possible events include one through six favoring the merger.
   c. Two possible outcomes would include: more than half favor the merger or all oppose the merger.

7. *a.* Relative frequency.
   b. Classical.
   c. Classical.
   d. Subjective, because this is someone's opinion.

8. In the event one outcome occurs another outcome cannot occur.

9. *a.* 13/52 = .25.
   b. 1/52 = .019.
   c. Classical.

10. *a.* 1/6 = .167.
    b. classical.
    c. Yes, the events are equally likely. The probability that a 1, 2, 3, 4, 5, or 6 spot will occur is the same. The events are mutually exclusive, because, for example, a two-spot and a five-spot cannot occur at the same time.

11. *a.* The survey of 40 people about abortion.
    b. 26 or more, for example.
    c. 10/40 = .25.
    d. Relative frequency.
    e. The events are not equally likely but they are mutually exclusive.

12. *a.* Recording the number of violations.
    b. at least one ticket, for example.
    c. 18/2000 = .009.
    d. Relative frequency.

13. P(A or B) = P(A) + P(B)
    　　　　　 = .30 + .20
    　　　　　 = .50
    P(neither) = 1 − .50 = .50.

14. P(X or Y) = P(X) + P(Y)
    　　　　　 = .05 + .02
    　　　　　 = .07
    P(neither) = 1 − .07 = .93.

15. *a.* 102/200 = .51
    b. .49, found by 61/200 + 37/200 = .305 + .185.
    Special rule of addition.

16. *a.* Recording the opinions of the designers with respect to the color.
    b. Any color but red, for example.
    c. .4575, found by 92/400 + 91/400.
    d. .885, found by 1 − 46/400.
    e. Yes. An opinion cannot be red and, say, indigo at the same time.

17. P(A or B) = P(A) + P(B) − P(A and B)
    　　　　　 = .20 + .30 − .15
    　　　　　 = .35

18. P(X or Y) = P(X) + P(Y) − P(X and Y)
    　　　　　 = .55 + .35 − .20
    　　　　　 = .70

19. When two events are mutually exclusive it means that if one occurs the other event cannot not occur. Therefore, the probability of their joint occurrence is zero.

20. $P(H \text{ or } M) = P(H) + P(M) - P(H \text{ and } M)$
    $= .60 + .70 - .50.$
    $= .80$

21. *a.* .65 found by $.35 + .40 - .10.$
    b. A joint probability.
    c. No, an executive might read both magazines.

22. *a.* .55, found by $.50 + .40 - .35.$
    b. Joint probability.
    c. No. A vacationer can visit both attractions.

23. *a.* A joint probability is the occurrence of two events at the same time.
    b. A conditional probability is the probability of one event occurring, given another event has already occurred.

24. A contingency table shows events by cross-classifying over several categories of descriptive data. This type of table shows where each response fits into a two-way classification of data.

25. *a.* Venn diagram.
    b. Sample space.
    c. No. There is an overlapping of events D and H.
    d. $P(D \text{ or } H) = P(D) + P(H) - P(D \text{ and } H).$

26. $P(A \text{ and } B) + P(A) \times P(B|A)$
    $= .40 \times .30$
    $= .12$

27. $P(X_1 \text{ and } Y_2) = P(X_1) \times P(Y_2|X_1)$
    $= .75 \times .40$
    $= .30$

28. *a.* $P(A_1) = 3/10 = .30$
    b. $P(B_1|A_2) = 1/3 = .33$
    c. $P(B_2 \text{ and } A_3) = 1/10 = .10$, or $(.40)(.25)$

29. *a.* 6/380 or .01579, found by $3/20 \times 2/19$.
    b. 272/380 or .7158, found by $17/20 \times 16/19$.

30. *a.* A contingency table.
    b. .27, found by $300/500 \times 135/300$.
    c. The tree diagram would appear as:

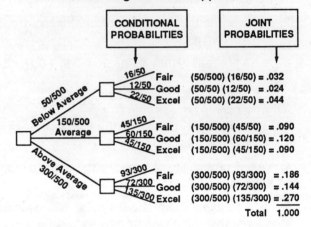

31. .4286, found by:

$$P(A_1|B_1) = \frac{P(A_1) \times P(B_1|A_1)}{P(A_1) \times P(B_1|A_1) + P(A_2) \times P(B_1|A_2)}$$
$$= \frac{.60 \times .05}{(.60 \times .05) + (.40 \times .10)}$$

32. .3636, found by:

$$P(A_3|B_1) = \frac{.40 \times .10}{(.20 \times .25) + (.40 \times .05) + (.40 \times .10)}$$

33. .5645, found by:

$$P(night|win) = \frac{P(night)\ P(win|night)}{P(night)\ P(win|night) + P(day)\ P(win|day)}$$
$$= \frac{(.70)(.50)}{[(.70)(.50)] + [(.30)(.90)]}$$

34. .8571, found by:

$$= \frac{(.80) \times (.90)}{(.80 \times .90) + (.20 \times .60)}$$

35. .1053, found by:

$$P(cash)| > \$50) = \frac{P(cash)\ P(>\$50|cash)}{P(cash)\ P(>\$50|cash) + P(check)\ P(>\$50|check) + P(charge)\ P(>\$50|charge)}$$
$$= \frac{(.30)(.20)}{[(.30)(.20)] + [(.30)(.90)] + [(.40)(.60)]}$$

36. .1667, which is the probability of purchasing a product from Asmus given that it was defective. Found by:

$$\frac{(.20 \times .0175)}{(.20 \times .0175) + (.30 \times .0250) + (.25 \times .0300) + (.25 \times .0100)}$$

37.   *a.* A permutation is the number of arrangements of r objects selected from n possible objects. Order is important.
    b. A combination is the number of ways to select r objects from a group of n objects without regard to order.

38.   *a.* 78,960,960
    b. 840, found by (7) (6) (5) (4). That is 7!/3!
    c. 10 found by 5!/3!2!

39.   *a.* 6,840
    b. 504
    c. 21

40. 210, found by: (10) (9) (8) (7)/(4) (3) (2)

41. 10,000, found by: $(10)^4$

42. 120, found by 5!

43. 3003, found by $_{15}C_{10} = (15 \times 14 \times 13 \times 12 \times 11)/(5 \times 4 \times 3 \times 2)$

44. 10,897,286,400, found by $_{15}P_{10} = (15)(14)(13)(12)(11)(10)(9)(8)(7)(6)$.

45.   *a.* Asking teenagers their reactions to a newly developed soft drink.
    b. More than half of the respondents like it.

46. Relative frequency.

47. Subjective.

48. No. Probability would be .00.

49. 3/6 or 1/2, found by 1/6 + 1/6 + 1/6. Classical.

50.   *a.* .10, found by 50/500.
    b. Yes. Mutually exclusive, because at the same time an envelope cannot contain, for example, a total offering of $2 and a total offering of $56.
    c. 1.00
    d. .60, found by 300/500.
    e. .90, found by 450/500 or 1 − (50/500).

51.   *a.* The likelihood an event will occur, assuming that another event has already occurred.
    b. The collection of one or more outcomes of an experiment.
    c. A measure of the likelihood that two or more events will happen concurrently.

52. *a.* 4/52, or .077.
     b. 3/51, or .059.
     c. .0045, found by (4/52)(3/51).

53. *a.* .8145, found by $(.95)^4$, or (.95)(.95)(.95)(.95).
     b. Special rule of multiplication.
     c. P(A and B and C and D) = P(A) × P(B) ×
          P(C) × P(D)

54. *a.* Venn diagram.
     b. A sample space.
     c. Complement rule.
     d. 1.00.

55. *a.* .08, found by .80 × .10.
     b.

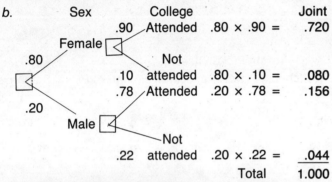

Sex	College	Joint
.90 Attended	.80 × .90 =	.720
Female		
.80	Not	
.10 attended	.80 × .10 =	.080
.78 Attended	.20 × .78 =	.156
.20		
Male		
Not		
.22 attended	.20 × .22 =	.044
	Total	1.000

     c. Yes, because all the possible outcomes are
          shown on the tree diagram.

56. *a.* 1/16 or .0625, found by 1/2 × 1/2 × 1/2 ×
          1/2.
     b. P(A and B and C and D) = P(A) × P(B) ×
          P(C) × P(D)
     c. 1/2 or .50.

57. *a.* 0.062, found by 100/400 × 99/399.
     b. .7538 found by 300/398.
     c. .2462 found by 1 − .7538.

58. .99, found by 57/100 + 40/100 + 2/100.

59. *a.* P(A and B) = P(A) × P(B/A).
     b. 6/2,450 or .0024, found by 3/50 × 2/49.

60. *a.* .0292, found by $(.308)^3$.
     b. .3314, found by $(1 − .308)^3$.

61. All hit = .4096, found by $(.80)^4$. None hit =
     .0016, found by $(.20)^4$.

62. .3059, found by (50/90) × (49/89).

63. *a.* .3818, found by (9/12)(8/11)(7/10).
     b. .6182, found by 1 − .3818.

64. *a.* .40, found by 200/500.
     b. .60, found by 100/500 + 200/500.
     c. .60, found by (200/500) + (200/500) −
          (100/500). General rule of addition.
     d. .33, found by 100/300.
     e. .1595, found by (200/500) × (199/499).

65. *a.* .5467, found by 82/150.
     b. .76, found by (39/150) + (75/150).
     c. .6267, found by 82/150 + 39/150 − 27/150.
          General rule.
     d. .3293, found by 27/82.
     e. .2972, found by (82/150)(81/149).

66. *a.* .42, found by (.60)(.70).
     b. .28, found by (.40)(.70).
     c. .88, found by (.40)(.70) + (.30)(.60) +
          (.60)(.70).

67. .0294, found by:

$$P(\text{poor}|\text{profit}) = \frac{P(\text{poor})\,P(\text{profit}|\text{poor})}{P(\text{poor})\,P(\text{profit}|\text{poor}) + P(\text{good})P(\text{profit}|\text{good}) + P(\text{fair})\,P(\text{profit}|\text{fair})}$$

$$= \frac{(.10)(.20)}{[(.10)(.20)] + (.60)(.80)] + [(.30)(.60)])}$$

68. .0009766, found by $(.25)^5$.

69. 45 matches, found by $\dfrac{10!}{2!\,(10-2)!}$

70. 24, found by $\dfrac{4!}{(4-4)!}$

71. .70, found by $= P(A) + P(B) - P(A \text{ and } B)$
$= .60 + .40 - .30$
$= .70$

72. .4545, found by:

$$\frac{(.50)\,(.625)}{(.50)\,(.625) + (.50)\,(.75)} = \frac{.3125}{.6875}$$

73. .5454, found by applying Bayes' theorem.

$$\frac{(.50)\,(.75)}{(.50)\,(.75) + (.50)\,(.625)}$$

74. .60, found by:

$$\frac{(.50)\,(.375)}{(.50)\,(.375) + (.50)\,(.25)}$$

75. .40, found by applying Bayes' theorem.

$$\frac{(.50)\,(.25)}{(.50)\,(.25) + (.50)\,(.375)}$$

76. 4320 different meals, found by $4 \times 3 \times 12 \times 6 \times 5$.
4104 early bird different meals, found by $(12 \times 4 \times 3 \times 6) + (12 \times 4 \times 3 \times 5) + (12 \times 4 \times 6 \times 5) + (12 \times 3 \times 6 \times 5)$.

77. Yes. 256 is found by 2^8.

78. 15, found by 5×3.

79. 2,520, found by,

$$_7P_5 = \frac{7!}{(7-5)!}$$

80. 45, found by

$$_nC_r = \frac{10!}{2!\,(10-2)!}$$

81. .4437, found by $(.85)^5$.

82. .9744, found by $1 - (.40)^4$.

83. 17,576,000, found by (26)(26)(26)(10)(10)(10).

84. *a.* .185, found by (.15)(.95) + (.05)(.85).
b. .0075, found by (.15)(.05).

85. *a.* .333, found by: (6/10) × (5/9).
b. .9286, found by: $1 - [(6/10)(5/9)(4/8)(3/7)]$.
c. dependent.

86. *a.* $P(F \text{ and } >60) = .25$, found by solving with the general rule of addition
$1 = P(F) + P(>60) + P(F \text{ and } >60)$
$1 = .75 + .50 + P(F \text{ and } >60)$
$P(F \text{ and } >60) = 1.25 - 1.00 = .25$
b. 0
c. .3333, found by 1/3.

87. *a.* 2024, found by:

$$_{24}C_3 = \frac{24!}{3!\,(24-3)!}$$

b. .125, found by: $1 - [(23/24)(22/23)(21/22)]$.

88. *a.* .216, found by: $(.60)^3$.
b. .936, found by: $1 - (.40)^3$.
c. .648, found by:
(.40)(.60)(.60) + (.60)(.40)(.60) + (.60)(.60)(.40) + (.60)(.60)(.60).

89. *a.* .3284, found by: 220/670
b. .1045, found by: 70/670
c. .4030, found by: (220/670) + (70/670) − (20/670)
d. .2857, found by: 20/70
e. .1111, found by: 50/450

90. *a.* .3041, found by: 19,001/62,488
    b. .7042, found by: (5,830/62,488) +
        (43,487/62,488) − (5,311/62,488)
    c. .3353, found by:

    $$\frac{4{,}344 + 2{,}596 + 1{,}719}{12{,}590 + 8{,}038 + 5{,}193}$$

    d. .6647, found by:

    $$\frac{8{,}246 + 5{,}442 + 3{,}474}{12{,}590 + 8{,}038 + 5{,}193}$$

    e. .4839, found by: [(43,467/62,488) ×
        (43,466/62,487)]

91. *a.* The overall percent defective is 5.175, found
        by
        .20(.03) + .30(.04) + .25(.07) + .25(.065)
            = .05175
    b. Using Bayes Rule:

    $$P(\text{Tyson/Defective}) = \frac{.20(.03)}{.20(.03) + .30(.04) + .25(.07) + .25(.065)}$$
    $$= .1159$$

    c.

Supplier	Joint Probability	Revised
Tyson	.00600	.1159
Fuji	.01200	.2319
Kirkpatricks	.01750	.3382
Parts	.01625	.3140
Total	.05175	1.0000

92. For the system to operate both components in
    the series must work. The probability they both
    work is 0.81, found by P(A) · P(B) = (.90)(.90).

93. .99, found by 1 − [(.90)(.90) + .90(.10) + .10
    (.90)]

94. 1/3,628,800

95. The following tree diagram lists the probabilities

    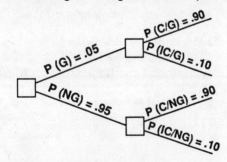

    P(G) = Probability of guilty = .05
    P(NG) = Probability of not guilty = .95
    P(C/G) = Probability of correct assessment if
            guilty = .90
    P(C/NG) = Probability of correct assessment if
            not guilty = .90

    a. George will fire all those that fail the lie detec-
        tor test, whether they are guilty or not.
        P(Fire) = .05(.90) + .95(.10) = .14
        These are guilty but not fired.
    b.

    $$P(G/F) = \frac{.05(.90)}{.05(.90) + .95(.10)} = .3214$$

    c.

    $$P(G/N) = \frac{.05(.10)}{.05(.10) + .95(.90)} = .0058$$

    d. George's policy is not very effective. About
        2/3 of the time innocent people are fired. (The
        complement of part b.)

96. *a.* Using MINITAB:

ROWS: Pool 0 = no pool, 1 = pool COLUMNS: Twnship

	1	2	3	4	5	ALL
0	7	6	6	8	2	29
1	5	9	13	10	9	46
ALL	12	15	19	18	11	75

1. 70.67%, found by 12/75 + 46/75 − 5/75.
2. 68.42%, found by 13/19.
3. 17.33% found by 13/75.

   b. From MINITAB:

ROWS: Twnship 0 = no garage, 1 = garage
COLUMNS: Garage

	0	1	ALL
1	4	8	12
2	4	11	15
3	7	12	19
4	7	11	18
5	2	9	11
ALL	24	51	75

1. 68%, found by 51/75.
2. 18.18%, found by 2/11.
3. 16.0%, found by 12/75.
4. 46.67%, found by 24/75 + 15/75 − 4/75.

97. *a.* From MINITAB:

	Winning	Losing	Record Total
Attendance 1	1	3	4
Attendance 2	10	6	16
Attendance 3	5	1	6
Total	16	10	26

1. 61.54%, found by 16/26.
2. 65.38%, found by 16/26 + 6/26 − 5/26.
3. 83.33%, found by 5/6.
4. 11.54%, found by (10/26)(3/10).

97. *b.* MINITAB:

	Win	Loss	Total
Turf	6	4	10
Grass	10	6	16
Total	16	10	26

1. 38.46%, found by 10/26.
2. Grass 10/16 is larger than 6/16.
3. 76.92%, found by 16/26 + 10/26 − 6/26.

CHAPTER 6:   DISCRETE PROBABILITY DISTRIBUTIONS

1. A discrete distribution can assume only certain values and is usually found by a counting process. A continuous distribution can assume an infinite number of values within a given range. Continuous distributions are usually determined by some type of measurement.

2. A discrete distribution can assume only certain values, the probability of a particular outcome is greater than 0, and the sum of all possible outcomes is 1.00.

3. Mean = 1.3, variance = .81, found by:

$$\mu = \Sigma XP(X) = 0(.20) + 1(.40) + 2(.30) + 3(.10) = 1.3$$
$$\sigma^2 = \Sigma(X - \mu)^2 P(X)$$
$$= (0-1.3)^2(.2) + (1-1.3)^2(.4) + (2-1.3)^2(.3) + (3-1.3)^2(.10)$$
$$= .81$$

4. Mean = 5.4, variance = 12.04, found by:

$$\mu = \Sigma XP(X) = 2(.5) + 8(.3) + 10(.2) = 5.4$$
$$\sigma^2 = \Sigma(X - \mu)^2 P(X)$$
$$= (2-5.4)^2(.5) + (8-5.4)^2(.3) + (10-5.4)^2(.2)$$
$$= 12.04$$

5. Mean = 1.1, variance = .89, standard deviation = .943, found by:

$$\mu = 0(.3) + 1(.4) + 2(.2) + 3(.1)$$
$$= 1.1$$
$$\sigma^2 = (0-1.1)^2(.3) + (1-1.1)^2(.4) + (2-1.1)^2(.2) + (3-1.1)^2(.1)$$
$$= 0.89$$
$$\sigma = .943.$$

6. Mean = 1,110, variance = 24,900, standard deviation = 157.8, found by:

E(X) = 1,110 found by

X	P(X)	X•P(X)
1,000	.60	600
1,200	.30	360
1,500	.10	150
		1110

$$\sigma^2 = (1000-1110)^2(.6) + (1200-1110)^2(.3) + (1500-1110)^2(.1)$$
$$= 24,900$$
$$\sigma = 157.8.$$

7. The characteristics are:
   1. There are only two possible outcomes. That is, an outcome can be classified into one of two mutually exclusive categories.
   2. The data collected are the result of counts.
   3. The probability of success remains the same from one trial to another.
   4. Each trial is independent of another trial.

8. *a.*
$$P(1) = \frac{5!}{1!(5-1)!}\,(.20)^1(.80)^{5-1} = .4096$$

   b.
$$P(3) = \frac{5!}{3!(5-3)!}\,(.20)^3(.80)^{5-3} = .0512$$

9. *a.*
$$P(2) = \frac{4!}{2!(4-2)!}\,(.25)^2(.75)^{4-2} = .2109$$

   b.
$$P(3) = \frac{4!}{3!(4-3)!}\,(.25)^3(.75)^{4-3} = .0469$$

10. *a.*
$$P(2) = \frac{5!}{1!(5-1)!}\,(.4)^1(.6)^{5-1} = .2592$$

    b.
$$P(3) = \frac{5!}{2!(5-2)!}\,(.4)^2(.6)^{5-2} = .3456$$

11. *a.*

r	P(r)
0	.064
1	.288
2	.432
3	.216

    b.
$$\mu = np = 3(.6) = 1.8$$
$$\sigma^2 = np(1-p) = 3(.6)(.4) = 0.72$$
$$\sigma = \sqrt{0.72} = .8485$$

12. *a.*

r	P(r)
0	.168
1	.360
2	.309
3	.132
4	.028
5	.002

    b.
$$\mu = 5(.3) = 1.5$$
$$\sigma^2 = 5(.3)(.7) = 1.05$$
$$\sigma = \sqrt{1.05} = 1.0247$$

13. *a.* Number of production employees absent.

    b. Discrete because the number absent can only assume certain values, such as 1, 2, 3, and so on. There cannot be a fractional number of employees absent on a particular day.

    c. .349, found by referring to Appendix A, an n of 10, an r of 0, and a p of 0.10.

    d.

r	P(r)	r	P(r)
0	.349	6	.000
1	.387	7	.000
2	.194	8	.000
3	.057	9	.000
4	.011	10	.000
5	.001		

    e. $\mu = 1.00$, found by $np = (10)(.10)$
$\sigma^2 = .90$, found by $np(1-p) = (10)(.10)(.90)$
$\sigma = .949$, found by $\sqrt{.90}$

    f.

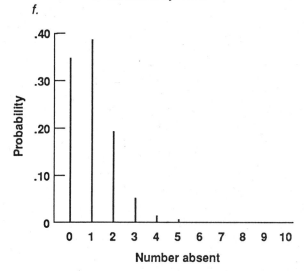

    g. (1) The outcomes can be classified only as "absent" or "not absent"; (2) the number absent is the result of counts; (3) the probability of .10 remains the same; and (4) the daily number of absences are independent.

14. *a.* 1/5 or 0.20
    b. Number of bowls of cereal.
    c. Discrete because there can only be 0, 1, 2, 3, 4, or 5 bowls identified correctly.
    d. 0.168 from Appendix A.
    e.

Number correct r	Probability of occurrence P(r)	Number correct r	Probability of occurrence P(r)
0	0.168	5	0.009
1	0.336	6	0.001
2	0.294	7	0.000
3	0.147	8	0.000
4	0.046	Total	1.000*

*slight discrepancy due to rounding.

   f. μ = 1.60 found by (8)(.20); variance = 1.28; standard deviation = 1.1314.

   g.

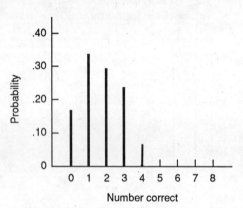

   h. They were probably not guessing. The chance that they would guess 7 out of 8 correctly is practically 0.
   i. Outcomes can only be right or wrong, probability distribution results from counts, probability of success remains the same from trial to trial. Trials are independent.

15. *a.* .296, found by using Appendix A with n of 8, p of .30, and r of 2.
    b. .552, found by using Appendix B with n of 8, p of .30, and r less than or equal to 2. It could also be determined by the special rule of addition and Appendix A. This is done by adding all the probability values of r up to seven in the .30 column for p.
    c. .448, found by P(r ≥ 3) = 1 − P(r ≤ 2) = 1 − .552.

16. *a.* .101, found from Appendix A, n = 12, r = 5.
    b. .158, found from Appendix B with n of 12, p of .60, and an of 5 or less.
    c. .842, found by P(r ≥ 6) = 1 − P(r ≤ 5) = 1 − .158.

17. *a.* .387, found from Appendix A with n of 9, p of .90, and an r of 9.
    b. .001, found in Appendix B with n of 9, p of .90, and an r of 4 or less.
    c. .992, found by 1 − .008 which is probability that 5 or less have a color TV.
    d. .947, found by 1 − .053 which is the probability that 6 or less have a color TV.

18. *a.* .358, found from Appendix A with n of 20, p of .05, and an r of 0.
    b. .642, found by 1 − .358.
    c. .076, found by 1 − [.358 + .377 + .189]

19. *a.* .50
    b. About .40.
    c. .377, found by 1 − .623.

20. *a.* .021, found by either using Appendix A and adding .015 + .005 + .001 for an n = 20, p = 50, or Appendix B and 1 − .979.
    b. .005 from Appendix A, n = 20, p = .50.
    c. .000
    d. .021
    e. .006

21. $P(2) = \dfrac{[_6C_2][_4C_1]}{_{10}C_3} = \dfrac{15(4)}{120} = .50$

22. $P(3) = \dfrac{[_{10}C_3][_5C_1]}{_{15}C_4} = \dfrac{120(5)}{1365} = .4396$

23. .4667, found by

$$\frac{\dfrac{7!}{2!5!} \times \dfrac{3!}{0!3!}}{\dfrac{10!}{2!8!}} = \frac{21}{45}$$

24. *a.* .3571 is the probability that all three are tenured, found by

$$\frac{\dfrac{6!}{3!3!} \times \dfrac{2!}{0!2!}}{\dfrac{8!}{3!5!}} = \frac{20}{56}$$

 b. .6429, found by 1 − .3571.

25. .4196. found by:

$$\frac{\dfrac{9!}{6!3!} \times \dfrac{6!}{4!2!}}{\dfrac{15!}{5!10!}} = \frac{1260}{3003}$$

26. .84615, found by:
 N = 5, S = 4, n = 5, r = 0 found by 1 − P(0).

$$P\text{ (none)} = \frac{\dfrac{4!}{0!4!} \times \dfrac{11!}{5!6!}}{\dfrac{15!}{5!10!}} = \frac{1(462)}{3003} = .15385$$

 Then 1 − .15385 = .84615, is the probability that at least one question will appear.

27. *a.* .6703, found from Appendix C with μ = .4 and X = 0.
 b. .3297, found from Appendix C with μ = .4 and X ≥ 0.

28. *a.* .1465, found from Appendix C with μ = 4 and X = 2.
 b. .2381, found from Appendix C with μ = 4 and X ≤ 2.
 c. .7619, found from Appendix C with μ = 4 and X > 2.

29. *a.* .0613, where n = 40, p = .025, and μ = 1. See Appendix C.
 b. .0803, found by .0613 + .0153 + .0031 + .0005 + .0001, from Appendix C.

30. *a.* .1353, found using Appendix C with μ = 2.
 b. .8647, found by 1 − .1353.

31. .7148, where μ = np = .005 (1200) = 6. Adding .1606 + .1606 + .1377 + . . . + .0001 = .7148.

32. .8088, found by .4493 + .3595.

33. The characteristics are:
 1. There are only two possible outcomes.
 2. The trials are not independent, so the probability of a success is not the same on each trial.
 3. The distribution results from a count of the number of successes in a fixed number of trials.

34. The binomial distribution is a discrete probability distribution where the outcomes of the experiments can take only one of two forms. A second important part is that data collected is a result of counts. Additionally, one trial is independent from the next and the chance for success remains the same from one trial to the next.

35. When n is large and p is small the Poisson and the binomial distribution will yield approximately the same results.

36. Outcomes that can assume only certain values within a range of values.

37. Mean = 2.0 units, found by 0 + .20 + .60 + 1.20. Standard deviation = 1.00, found by Σ (X − μ)^2 × P(X) = .40 + .20 + 0 + .40 = 1. The standard deviation is $\sqrt{1.0}$ = 1.

38. Mean = \$2,200, variance = 1,560,000, found by:

(X)(PX)		$(X - \mu)^2 PX$
1,000 (.25) =	250	360,000
2,000 (.60) =	1,200	24,000
5,000 (.15) =	750	1,176,000
Total	2,200	1,560,000

39. Mean = 1.30 accidents, found by .00 + .20 + .40 + .30 + .40.
 Variance = 1.81, found by $\Sigma(X - \mu)^2 P(X)$ = .676 + .018 + .098 + .289 + .729.
 Standard deviation = $\sqrt{1.81}$ = 1.3454 accidents.

40. μ = 13.2, found by 3.00 + 5.20 + 3.50 + 1.50
 σ^2 = .86, found by .36 + .016 + .16 + .324.
 $\sigma = \sqrt{.86}$ = .9274

41. Yes. μ = .0025, found by − .03 + (− .03) + 0 + .0225 + .0200 + .0200.
 σ^2 = .02905, found by .00765 + .00390 + .00000 + .00270 + .00490 + .00990.

42. *a.* 0.001
 b. 0.001

43. *a.* .0009765, found by:

$$P(5) = \frac{5!}{5!\,(5-5)!} \,(.25)^5 \,(.75)^{5-5}$$
$$= (1)\,(.0009765)\,(1)$$

b. .2373046, found by:

$$P(0) = \frac{5!}{0!\,(5-0)!} \,(.25)^0 \,(.75)^{5-0}$$
$$= (1)\,(1)\,(.2373046)$$

c. .7626954, found by $1 - .2373046$.

44. From Appendix A:
   a. 0.185, where $n = 18$, $p = 0.50$, and $r = 9$.
   b. 0.241, where $n = 18$, $p = 0.50$, and $r = $ all probabilities 11 and greater, same as 7 or less girls.
   c. 0.121, where $n = 18$, $p = 0.50$, and $r = 11$.
   d. 0.50

45. The probability of exactly two Spanish-speaking Americans on the jury is 0.168 (Appendix A, $n = 12$, $p = .3$, and $r = 2$). One might argue that this is a sufficiently large chance and agree with the government lawyer.

46. About 330 cars. $\mu = 0.4$, found by 40/100. Then $1 - 0.6703 = 0.3297$, which is about 330 out of 1,000.

47. *a.* About 6,065 doors. From Appendix C, $\mu = .5$ $X = 0$, $P(0) = .6065$.
   b. About 902 doors, found by $1 - (.6065 + .3033)$ (Appendix C).

48. *a.* Referring to Appendix C and finding $P(X < 5)$ $= 0.1353 + 0.2707 + 0.2707 + 0.1804 + 0.0902 = .9473$, which is very close to the goal of 0.95.
   b.

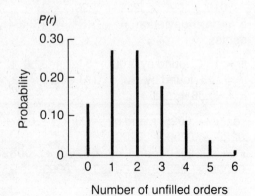

49. *a.* .8187 from Appendix C. $\mu = 0.2$, found by 100 (.002).
   b. .9824, found by $.8187 + .1637$.
   c. No. The probability that three or more machines are broken down is only .0012, found by $.0011 + .0001$.

50. *a.* $\mu = 3$, probability $= .0498$.
   b. .5768, found by $1 - (.0498 + .1494 + .2240)$.

51. $\mu = 4.0$ from Appendix C.
   a. .0183
   b. .1954
   c. .6289
   d. .5665

52. *a.* .60 found by:

$$\frac{2!}{1!1!} \times \frac{4!}{2!2!} \times \frac{3!3!}{6!} = (2)\,(6)\,(0.05)$$

   b. .20, found by:

$$\frac{2!}{2!0!} \times \frac{4!}{1!3!} \times \frac{3!3!}{6!} = (1)\,(4)\,(0.05)$$

53. *a.* .0498
   b. .7746, found by $(1 - .0498)^5$

54. .4286, found by:

$$\frac{6!}{2!4!} \times \frac{4!}{2!2!} \times \frac{4!6!}{6!}$$

55. *a.* .4506, found by:

$$\frac{20!}{3!17!} \times \frac{5!}{1!4!} \times \frac{4!21!}{25!}$$

   b. .410, found by using Appendix A with $n = 4$, $p = .2$, and $r = 1$.
   c. .3595, found by $\mu = np = 4(.2) = .8$, with $X = 1$.

56. Expected loss is $4.50, found by 999/1,000 $(-\$5)$.
   Expected gain is $.50, found by 1/1,000 ($495), so the average person will lose $4.50.

57. .8409 where $N = 12$, $S = 5$, $n = 3$, $r = 0$.

$$\left(\frac{5!}{0!5!}\right)\left(\frac{7!}{3!4!}\right)\left(\frac{3!9!}{12!}\right) = \frac{35}{220} = .1591$$

Then, $1 - .1591 = .8409$.

58. *a.* .20 found by 10/50.
   b. $0.255, found by ($.05)(.2) + ($.10)(.2) + ($.25)(.3) + ($.50)(.3).
   c. .0312, found by .0084 + .0048 + .0000 + .0180.

59. For the NASA estimate $\mu = np = 25 (1/60,000) = .0004$. Using MINITAB, the probability of no disasters is .9996. The probability of a disaster is .0004, found by $1 - .9996$.

   MTB > pdf;
   SUBC> poisson mu = .0004.
   POISSON WITH MEAN = 0.0000

K	P (X = K)
0	0.9996
1	0.0004
2	0.0000

   Using the Air Force estimates, $\mu = 25 (1/35) = 0.7143$. The probability of no disasters is 0.4895, so the probability of a disaster is .5105, found by $1 - .4895$.

   MTB > pdf;
   SUBC> poisson mu = .7143.
   POISSON WITH MEAN = 0.714

K	P (X = K)
0	0.4895
1	0.3497
2	0.1249
3	0.0297
4	0.0053
5	0.0008
6	0.0001
7	0.0000

   Thus, the probability of a disaster for NASA (.0004) is considerably less than the Air Force (.5105).

60. .1899, found by:

$$\frac{34!}{29!5!} (.8529)^{29} (.1471)^{5}$$

61. *a.* Using MINITAB: The histogram would appear as:
   Histogram of Bedrooms N = 75

Midpoint	Count
2	18
3	21
4	16
5	8
6	9
7	2
8	1

   Then 18/75 gives the probabilities .2400; 21/75 = .2800, etc.

X	P(X)	X·P(X)	$(x - \mu)^2$ P(X)
2	.2400	.4800	.7100
3	.2800	.8400	.1452
4	.2133	.8532	.0167
5	.1067	.5335	.1748
6	.1200	.7200	.6238
7	.0267	.1869	.2872
8	.0133	.1064	.2436
Total	1.0000	3.7200	2.2014

   Mean = 3.7200, standard deviation = $\sqrt{2.2014}$ = 1.4837.

   b.

X	P(X)	X·P(X)	$(X - \mu)^2$ P(X)
1.5	.1467	0.2200	.0505
2.0	.6267	1.2534	.0047
2.5	.1333	0.3333	.0228
3.0	.0933	0.2799	.0778
Total	1.0000	2.0866	.1558

   Mean = 2.0866, standard deviation = $\sqrt{.1558}$ = .3947.

CHAPTER 7:   THE NORMAL PROBABILITY DISTRIBUTION

1. The actual shape of a normal distribution depends on its mean and standard deviation. Thus, there is a normal distribution, and an accompanying normal curve, for a mean of 7 and a standard deviation of 2. There is another normal curve for a mean of $25,000 and a standard deviation of $1,742, and so on.

2. It is bell shaped and symmetrical about its mean. It is asymptotic. There is a family of normal curves.

3. *a.* 490 and 510, found by 500 ± 1(10).
   b. 480 and 520, found by 500 ± 2(10).
   c. 470 and 530, found by 500 ± 3(10).

4. *a.* about 68 percent.
   b. about 95 percent.
   c. over 99 percent.

5. *a.* 1.25, found by:

   $$z = \frac{X - \mu}{\sigma} = \frac{25 - 20}{4.0} = 1.25$$

   b. .3944, found in Appendix D.
   c. .3085, found by:

   $$z = \frac{18 - 20}{4.0} = -0.5$$

   Find .1915 in Appendix D for z = − 0.5, then .5000 − .1915 = .3085.

6. *a.* z = 0.84, found by:

   $$z = \frac{14.3 - 12.2}{2.5} = 0.84$$

   b. .2995, found in Appendix D.
   c. .1894, found by:

   $$z = \frac{10 - 12.2}{2.5} = -0.88$$

   Find .3106 in Appendix D for z = − 0.88, then .5000 − .3106 = .1894.

7. *a.* .3413, found by:

   $$z = \frac{\$20 - \$16.50}{\$3.50} = 1.00$$

   Then find .3413 in Appendix D for a z = 1.
   b. .1587, found by .5000 − .3413 = .1587.
   c. .3336, found by:

   $$z = \frac{\$15.00 - \$16.50}{\$3.50} = -0.43$$

   Find .1664 in Appendix D for a z = − 0.43, then .5000 − .1664 = .3336.

8. *a.* About .4332 from Appendix D, where z = 1.50
   b. About .1915, where z = − 0.50
   c. About .3085, found by .5000 − .1915.

9. *a.* .8276, First find z = − 1.5 ((44 − 50)/4) and z = 1.25 (55 − 50/4). The area between − 1.5 and 0 is .4332 and the area between 0 and 1.25 is .3944, both from Appendix D. Then adding the two areas we find that .4332 + .3944 = .8276.
   b. .1056, found by .5000 − .3944, where z = 1.25.
   c. .2029. Recall that the area for z = 1.25 is .3944. And the area for z = .5 ((52 − 50)/4) is .1915. Then subtract .3944 − .1915 and find .2029.
   d. X = 56.58, found by adding .5000 (the area left of the mean) and then finding a z value that forces 45% of the data to fall inside the curve. That z value is 1.645. .5000 + .4500 = .9500. Solving for X: 1.645 = (X − 50)/4 = 56.58.

10. *a.* .4017. First find z = − .36 ((75 − 80)/14) and z = .71 ((90 − 80)/14). The area between − 0.36 and 0 is .1406 and the area between 0 and 0.71 is .2611, both from Appendix D. Then adding the two areas we find .1406 + .2611 = .4107.

b. .3594, found by .5000 − .1406, where z = − 0.36.

c. .2022, found by,
z = (55 − 80)/14 = − 1.79, for which the area is .4633.
z = (70 − 80)/14 = − 0.71, for which the area is .2611. Then subtract .4633 − .2611 = .2022.

d. 68.17, found by solving for the z value that forces .3000 of the area to fall inside the curve. That z value is z = − 0.845. Then .3000 + .5000 = .8000.

11. *a.* .1525, found by subtracting .4938 − .3413, which are the areas associated with z values of 2.5 and 1, respectively.

b. .0062, found by .5000 − .4938.

c. .9710, found by recalling that the area for the z value of 2.5 is .4938. Then find z = − 2.00 found by ((6.8 − 7.0)/.1). Then add the area for z = 2.5 and z = − 2. Thus, .4938 + .4772 = .9710.

d. 7.233. Find a z value where .4900 of area is between 0 and z. That value is z = 2.33. Then solve for X: 2.33 = (X − 7)/.1 = 7.233.

12. *a.* .3085, found by z = ($80,000 − $70,000)/$20,000 = 0.50. The area is .1915. Then .5000 − .1915 = .3085.

b. .2902. found as follows.
z = (($80,000 − $70,000)/$20,000) = 0.50. The area is .1915.
z = (($65,000 − $70,000)/$20,000) = − 0.25. The area is .0987.
Adding these values together: .1915 + .0987 = .2902.

c. .5987, found by the area under the curve with a z = − 0.25. Then .0987 + .5000 = .5987.

d. $86,900. First find a z value that forces 30% of the area to fall below the z value (z = .845). Then solve for X in the equation for z 0.845 = (X − $70,000)/$20,000) = $86,900.

13. *a.* .0764, found by z = (20 − 15)/3.5 = 1.43. Then .5000 − .4236 = .0764.

b. .9236, found by .5000 + .4236, where z = 1.43.

c. .1185, found by z = (12 − 15)/3.5 = − 0.86. The area under the curve is .3051. Then z = (10 − 15/3.5) = − 1.43. The area is .4236. Finally, .4236 − .3051 = .1185.

d. 16.84 minutes, found by solving for X where z = .525. This point forces .20 of the area to fall under the curve. First multiplying .525 × 3.5 and then adding 15, we find X = 16.84.

14. *a.* 2.28%, found by (200 − 160)/20 = 2. The area is .4772. Then .5000 − .4772 = .0228.

b. 69.15%, found by (150 − 160)/20 = − 0.5. The area is .1915. Then .1915 + .5000 = .6915.

c. 143.1, found by solving for X for a z = − 0.845, which forces .30 of the area to fall under the curve. First multiplying − 0.845(20) and then adding 160, so X = 143.1.

15. *a.* μ = np = 50(.25) = 12.5
σ^2 = np(1 − p) = 12.5(1 − .25) = 9.375.
$\sigma = \sqrt{9.375}$ = 3.0619.

b. .2578, found by (14.5 − 12.5)/3.0619 = .653. The area is .2422. Then .5000 − .2422 = .2578.

c. .2578, found by (10.5 − 12.5)/3.06 = − 0.65. The area is .2422. Then .5000 − .2422 = .2578.

16. *a.* μ = np = (40)(.55) = 22
σ^2 = np(1 − p) = 9.9
σ = 3.15

b. .2148, found by (24.5 − 22)/3.15 = .79. The area is .2852. Then .5000 − .2852 = .2148.

c. .0197, found by (15.5 − 22)/3.15 = − 2.06. The area is .4803. Then .5000 − .4803 = .0197.

d. .8578, found by .4913 + .3665 = .8578.

17. *a.* .0655, found by (9.5 − 6)/2.32 = 1.51. The area is .4345. Then .5000 − .4345 = .0655.

b. .1401, found by (8.5 − 6)/2.32 = 1.08. The area is .3599. Then .5000 − .3599 = .1401.

c. .0746, found by .4345 − .3599 = .0746. This is the probability of getting exactly 9 errors.

18. *a.* 10, which is the same as μ.

b. .1894, found by ((7.5 − 10)/2.828) = − 0.88. The area is .2019. Then .5000 − .3106 = .1894.

c. .2981, found by ((8.5 − 10)/2.828) = − 0.53. The area is .2019. Then .5000 − .2019 = .2981.

d. .1087, found by .3106 − .2019.

19. *a.* Yes. (1) There are two mutually exclusive outcomes-overweight and not overweight. (2) It is the result of counting the number of successes (overweight members). (3) Each trial is independent. (4) The probability of .30 remains the same for each trial.

b. .0084, found by μ = np = 500(.30) = 150. Variance = np(1 – p) = 105. Standard deviation = 10.24695, found by $\sqrt{105}$.

$$z = \frac{X - \mu}{\sigma} = \frac{174.5 - 150}{10.24695} = 2.39$$

Area under the curve for 2.39 is .4916. Then .5000 – .4916 = .0084.

c. .8461, found by:

$$z = \frac{139.5 - 150}{10.24695} = -1.02$$

The area between 139.5 and 150 is .3461. Adding, .3461 + .5000 = .8461.

20. a. About .9599 found by:
   μ = np = 100(.38) = 38. Then σ^2 = np(1 – p) = 100(.38)(1 – .38) = 23.56. σ = $\sqrt{23.56}$ = 4.85. Then ((29.5 – 38)/4.85) = – 1.75. Area under the curve for – 1.75 is .4599. Adding, .4599 + .5000 = .9599. Note that the correction factor was applied.

   b. .6985, found by ((40.5 – 38)/4.85) = .52, for which the area is .1985. Then .5000 + .1985 = .6985.

   c. .6584, found by .4599 + .1985 = .6584.

21. a. 46.41%, found by (20.27 – 20.00)/.15 = 1.8 P(8) = .4641

   b. 3.59%, found by .5000 – .4641.

   c. 81.85%, found by .3413 + .4772.

   d. 27.43%, found by .5000 – .2257.

22. a. About 34.13%, found by (34 – 32)/2 = 1.00. The area for 1.00 is .3413.

   b. About 4.95%, found by (28.7 – 32)/2 = – 1.65. The area for – 1.65 is .4505. Then .5000 – .4505 = .0495.

   c. About 77.45%, found by (29 – 32)/2 = – 1.5. The area for – 1.5 is .4332. Then .4332 + .3413 (from part a) = .7745.

   d. About 35.29 hours, found 1.645 = (X – 32)/2.

23. a. – 0.4 for net sales, found by (170 – 180)/25. And, 2.92 for employees, found by (1,850 – 1,500)/120.

   b. Net sales are – 0.4 standard deviations below the mean. Employees are 2.92 standard deviations above the mean.

   c. 65.54% of the aluminum fabricators have greater net sales compared with Clarion, found by .1554 + .5000. Only 0.18% have more employees than Clarion, found by .5000 – .4982.

24. Only 1.92% had a mechanical aptitude score greater than Shawn. (1310 – 1000)/150 = 2.07. The area for 2.07 is .4808. Then .5000 – .4808 = .0192. About 11.51% had an IQ greater than Shawn, found by (122 – 110)/10 = 1.2. The area for 1.2 is .3849. Then .5000 – .3849 = .1151.

25. a. 15.87%, found by (15 – 20)/5 = – 1.0. The area for – 1.0 is .3413. Then .5000 – .3413 = .1587.

   b. .5403. First, the area between 18 and 20 is .1554. The area between 20 and 26 is .3849. Adding, .1554 + .3849 = .5403.

   c. About 1 person, found by z = (7 – 20)/5 = – 2.6, for which the area is .4953. Then .5000 – .4953 = .0047. Finally, 200(.0047) = 0.94, which is about 1 person.

26. a. About .82%, found by (320 – 500)/75 = – 2.4. The area under the curve for a z = 2.4 is .4918. Then .5000 – .4918 = .0082.

   b. About 563, found by:
   0.84 = (X – 500)/75.

   c. About 404, found by:
   – 1.28 = (X – 500)/75.

27. 60.06%, found by ($42,000 – $40,000)/$5,000 = 0.40. The area under the curve for 0.40 is .1554. Similarly, the area between $32,000 and $40,000 is .4452. Adding, .1554 + .4452 = .6006.

28. a. First (860 – 1,000)/50 = – 2.8. The area below 860 is .0026, found by .5000 – .4974, or .26 percent.

   b. Second, (1,055 – 1,000)/50 = 1.1. The area between 1000 and 1055 is .3643. The area between 1,000 and 1,100 is .4772. Subtracting: .4772 – .3643 gives .1192, or 11.92%.

29. a. 39.44%, found by (1,970 – 1,820)/120 = 1.25. The area for a z of 1.25 is .3944.

   b. 10.56%, found by .5000 – .3944.

   c. 3.36%, found by .5000 – .4664 = .0336.

30. About 4,099 units (rounded to the nearest unit) found by solving for X.
   1.645 = (X – 4,000)/60

31. a. About 578, found by solving for X in the equation 1.56 = (X – 500)/50.

   b. About 2.28 percent. z is = – 2.00, found by (400 – 500)/50. The area between 400 and 500 is .4772. Then .5000 – .4772 = .0228.

   c. About 39.93%. The area between 500 and 400 is .4772, and the area between 500 and 485 is .1179. Subtracting, .4772 – .1179 = .3593. About 360.

32. a. About 27.08%, found by .0793 + .1915.
   z = (296 − 300)/20 = −0.20. Area is .0793.
   z = (310 − 300)/20 = 0.50. Area is .1915.
   b. About 5.48%, found by z = (332 − 300)/20 = 1.60. Area is .4452. Then .5000 − .4452 = .0458.
   c. About 283.2 pounds, found by −0.84 = (X − 300)/20.

33. a. About .47%. (65,200 − 60,000)/2,000 = 2.60. Then .5000 − .4953 = .0047.
   b. About 22 trucks. (55,000 − 60,000)/2,000 = −2.50. Then .5000 − .4938 = .0062. Multiplying, .0062 × 3,500 = 21.7.
   c. About 2,945. (62,000 − 60,000)/2,000 = 1.00. Then .5000 + .3413 = .8413. Multiplying, .8413 × 3,500 = 2,944.55.

34. a. Only 2.28% earn more than John: ($30,400 − $28,000)/$1,200 = 2.00. Then .5000 − .4772 = .0228.
   b. Of the other supervisors, 97.72% have more service. (10 − 20)/5 = −2.00. Then .4772 + .5000 = .9772.

35. a. 26.43%, found by (30 − 35)/8 = −0.63. Then .5000 − .2357 = .2643.
   b. 26.43%, found by (40 − 35)/8 = 0.63. Then .5000 − .2357 = .2643.
   c. The normal distribution is continuous. Thus, the probability of an exact value is very small.
   d. About 4.26%. You could find the probability of 39.5 and 40.5.
   z = (39.5 − 35)/8 = .56. Area is .2123.
   z = (40.5 − 35)/8 = .69. Area is .2549.
   Subtracting: .2549 − .2123 = .0426.
   e. 45.24 minutes, found by solving for X. 1.28 = (X − 35)/8.

36. a. 15.39%, found by (8 − 10.3)/2.25 = −1.02. Then .5000 − .3461 = .1539.
   b. 17.31%, found by:
   z = (12 − 10.3)/2.25 = 0.76. Area is .2764.
   z = (14 − 10.3)/2.25 = 1.64. Area is .4495. The area between 12 and 14 is .1731, found by .4495 − .2764.
   c. Yes, but it is rather remote. Reasoning: On 99.73% of the days, returns are between 3.55 and 17.03, found by 10.3 ± 3(2.25). Thus, the chance of less than 3.55 returns is rather remote.

37. a. 6.55, found by solving for σ.
$$0.84 = \frac{45 - 39.5}{\sigma}$$
   σ = 6.55
   b. .3520, found by (42 − 39.5)/6.55. Then .5000 − .1480 = .3520.
   c. About 50.27 yards, found by solving for X. 1.645 = (X − 39.5)/6.55.
   d. Mean would decrease; standard deviation would increase; distribution would become negatively skewed.

38. a. .0262, found by:
   μ = np = 50(.20) = 10
   σ^2 = np(1 − p) = 50(.20)(.80) = 8
   $\sigma = \sqrt{8}$ = 2.83
   Then (4.5 − 10)/2.83 = −1.94, for which the area is .4738. Then .5000 − .4738 = .0262.
   b. .9441, found by (5.5 − 10)/2.83 = −1.59, for which the area is .4441. Then .5000 + .4441 = .9441.
   c. .0297, found by first subtracting .5000 − .4441 = .0559. Then .4738 − .4441 = .0297.
   d. .8882, found by adding the area between z = −1.59 and z = 1.59. Then 2(.4441) = .8882.

39. a. .9678, found by:
   μ = np = 60(.64) = 38.4
   σ^2 = np(1 − p) = 60(.64)(.36) = 13.824
   $\sigma = \sqrt{13.824}$ = 3.72.
   Then (31.5 − 38.4)/3.72 = −1.85, for which the area is .4678. Then .5000 + .4678 = .9678.
   b. .0853, found by (43.5 − 38.4)/3.72 = 1.37, for which the area is .4147. Then .5000 − .4147 = .0853.
   c. .80384, found by (32.5 − 38.4)/3.72 = −1.59. The area is .4441. And (42.5 − 38.4)/3.72 = 1.10, for which the area is .3643. Then adding the total is .8084.
   d. .0348, by finding area for less than 44.0 (44.5 − 38.4)/3.72 = 1.64. The area is .4495. And recall the area for 43 or less was .4147. Then .4495 − .4147 = .0348.

40. μ = np = 100 (.05) = 5
   σ^2 = np(1 − p) = 100(.05)(.95) = 4.75
   $\sigma = \sqrt{4.75}$ = 2.18
   a. .1251, found by (7.5 − 5)/2.18 = 1.15. The area is .3749. Then .5000 − .3749 = .1251.
   b. .1192, found by (10.5 − 5)/2.18 = 2.52. The area is .4941. Subtracting, .4941 − .3749 = .1192.

    c. .0714. Calculate the probability of 8.5 and 7.5. Then find the difference. Probability of 8.5 is .4463, 7.5 is .3749 so .4463 − .3749 = .0714.

    d. .0197, found by .5000 − .4803.

41. *a.* .8106, where μ = 10, variance = 8, standard deviation = 2.8284. z = (7.5 − 10)/2.8284 = − .88. The area is = .3106. Then .5000 + .3106 = .8106.

    b. .1087, found by: z = (8.5 − 10)/2.8284 = − .53. Then .3106 − .2019 = .1087.

    c. .2981, found by .5000 − .2019.

42. *a.* .0393, found by:
$$\mu = np = 60(.10) = 6$$
$$\sigma^2 = np(1-p) = 60(.10)(.90) = 5.4$$
$$\sigma = \sqrt{5.4} = 2.3238$$
Calculate the probability of − 2.5 (.4345) and − 1.5 (.4738). Then .4738 − .4345 = .0393.

    b. .9738, found by .5000 + .4738 = .9738.

43. .0968, found by:
$$\mu = np = 50(.40) = 20$$
$$\sigma^2 = np(1-p) = 50(.40)(.60) = 12$$
$$\sigma = \sqrt{12} = 3.4641.$$
z = (24.5 − 20)/3.4641 = 1.30. The area is .4032. Then for 25 or more, .5000 − .4032 = .0968.

44. .0150, found by:
$$\mu = np = 800(.80) = 640$$
$$\sigma^2 = np(1-p) = 800(.40)(.60) = 128$$
$$\sigma = \sqrt{128} = 11.3137.$$
z = (664.5 − 640)/11.3137 = 2.17. The area is .4850. Then .5000 − .4850 = .0150.

45. *a.* 36.775 minutes, found by solving for μ. 1.645 = (45 − μ)/5 = 36.775.

    b. 28.55 minutes, found by solving for μ. 1.645 = (45 − μ)/10 = 28.55.

    c. 55.96%, found by (30 − 28.55)/10 = .15. The area is .0596. Then .5000 + .0596 = .5596.

46. .6026, found by .5000 − .1026. Then 1 − .3794 = .6026 compared with .5105 fairly close.

47. *a.* .6687, found by: z = (2.00 − 2.80)/.40 = − 2.00 p = .4772. And, (3.00 − 2.80)/.40 = .50; p = .1915. Then .4772 + 1915 = .6687.

    b. .0228, found by: (2.00 − 2.80)/.40 = − 2.00 p = .5000 − .4772 = .0228.

    c. 122, found by: z = (3.70 − 2.80)/.40 = 2.25 p = .5000 − .4878 = .0122. Then 10,000 × .0122 = 122.

    d. 3.312, found by 1.28 = (X − 2.8)/.40 = 3.312

48. Kamie is the 88.04 percentile, George 47.89 percentile. Scores are normally distributed.

49. *a.* 21.19 percent found by z = (9.00 − 9.20)/.25 = − 0.80; p = .5000 − .2881 = .2119

    b. Increase the mean. σ = (9.00 − 9.25)/.25 = 1.00; p = .5000 − .3413 = .1587. Reduce the standard deviation. σ = (9.00 − 9.20)/.15 = 1.33; p = .5000 − .4082 = .0918. Reducing the standard deviation is better because a smaller percent of the hams will be below the limit.

50. *a.* z = ($210,000 − $166,670)/$35.68 = 1.2144 area = .3869. Then .5000 − .3869 = .1131 11.31% using normal. There are 10 homes (13.33%) over $210,000 using actual data. Normal good approximation. Normal is a reasonable approximation.

    b.

	z	Normal Probability	Actual
19 miles	.84	.7995	.840
20 miles	1.04	.8508	.880
21 miles	1.25	.8944	.930

Normal is a reasonable approximation.

51. *a.* Normal: 31.56% found by .5000 − .1844. Actual: 30.5%. Not much difference.

    b. 22.06%, found by .5000 − .2794. Not very accurate since 8 out of 200, or 4%, actually lost money.

52. *a.* 26.43%, found by z = (110 − 130.12)/32.01 = − .6286 Area = .2357. Then .5000 − .2357 = .2643. Actual: 5 out of 26 = 19.23% comparing 26.43% and 19.23 we see that the normal overestimates the number of teams hitting less than 110 home runs.

    b. 18.94%, found by (30.0 − 24.24)/6.51 Area = .3106. Then .5000 − .3106 = .1894. Actual: 6 of 26 = 23.08%. Normal underestimates the number of teams with total salaries over $30 million.

CHAPTER 8: SAMPLING METHODS AND SAMPLING DISTRIBUTIONS

1. *a.* 303 Louisiana, 5155 S. Main, 3501 Monroe, 2652 W. Central.
   b. Answers will vary.

2. *a.* 3124 Monroe, 3465 Stickney, 5555 Airport Highway, 5804 Monroe, 2124 W. Alexis.
   b. Answers will vary.

3. 630 Dixie, 835 S. McCord, 4624 Woodville.

4. 5166 Airport, 3454 Dorr St., 5804 Monroe, 1945 Woodville.

5. Answers will vary.

6. Answers will vary.

7. *a.* 6, found by the combination $_4C_2$:

$$_4C_2 = \frac{4!}{2!\,(4 \times 2)!} = \frac{4 \times 3 \times 2 \times 1}{(2 \times 1)\,(2 \times 1)} = 6$$

   b.

Sample	Values	Sum	Mean
1	12,12	24	12
2	12,14	26	13
3	12,16	28	14
4	12,14	26	13
5	12,16	28	14
6	14,16	30	15

   c. $\mu_{\bar{x}} = (12 + 13 + 14 + 13 + 14 + 15)/6 = 13.5$
   $\mu = (12 + 12 + 14 + 16)/4 = 13.5$
   They are equal.
   d. The dispersion of the population is greater than that of the sample means. The sample means vary from 12 to 15, whereas population varies from 12 to 16.

8. *a.* 10, found by the combination $_5C_2$:

$$_5C_2 = \frac{5!}{2!(5 - 2)!} = 10$$

   b.

Sample	Values	Sum	Mean
1	2,2	4	2
2	2,4	6	3
3	2,4	6	3
4	2,8	10	5
5	2,4	6	3
6	2,4	6	3
7	2,8	10	5
8	4,4	8	4
9	4,8	12	6
10	4,8	12	6

c. $\mu = (2 + 2 + 4 + 4 + 8)/5 = 4$
   $\mu_{\bar{x}} = (2 + 3 + 3 + 5 + 3 + 3 + 5 + 4 + 6 + 6)/10 = 4$
   They are equal.
d. The dispersion for the population is greater than that for the sample means. The population varies from 2 to 8, whereas the sample means only vary from 2 to 6.

9. *a.* 6, found by 4!/2!2!.
   b.

Test scores	Mean
90,86	88
90,70	80
90,80	85
86,70	78
86,80	83
70,80	75

   c.

$$\mu_{\bar{x}} = \frac{88 + 80 + 85 + 78 + 83 + 75}{6} = 81.5$$

$$\mu = \frac{90 + 86 + 70 + 80}{4} = 81.5$$

   They are equal.

   d.

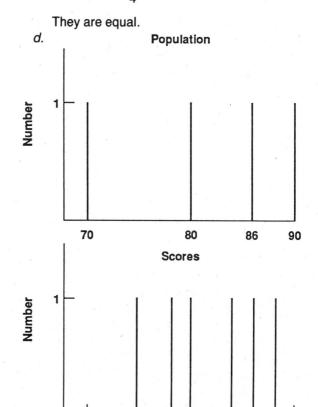

   e. More dispersion in the population than in sample means.

10. *a.* 10, found by: (5!)/3!2!

   b.

Cars sold	Sample mean	Cars sold	Sample mean
8, 6	7	6,10	8
8, 4	6	6,6	6
8, 10	9	4,10	7
8, 6	7	4,6	5
6, 4	5	10,6	8

   c. 6.8 for population, 6.8 for sample means. They are indentical.

   d.

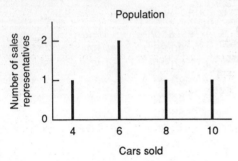

Population

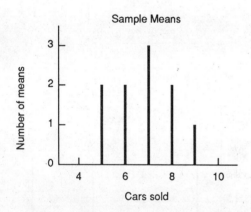

Sample Means

   e. Note that there is less dispersion the sample means compared with the population values.

11. 51.314 and 58.686, found by $55 \pm 2.58 \ (10/\sqrt{49})$.

12. 38.911 and 41.089, found by $40 \pm 1.96 \ (5/\sqrt{81})$.

13. *a.* 1.581, found by $\sigma_{\bar{x}} = \sigma/\sqrt{n} = 5/\sqrt{10} = 1.581$.

   b. The population is normally distributed and the population variance is known.

   c. 16.901 and 23.099, found by 20 ± 3.099.

14. 1.645, found in Appendix D.

15. *a.* $20. It is our best estimate of the population mean.

   b. $18.60 and $21.40, found by $\$20 \pm 1.96 \ (\$5/\sqrt{49})$.

16. *a.* $18.775 and $21.225, found by $\$20 \pm 1.96 \ (\$5/\sqrt{64})$.

   b. The confidence interval is based on the standard error computed by $s/\sqrt{n}$. As n, the sample size, increases (in this case from 49 to 64) the standard error decreases and the confidence interval becomes smaller.

17. *a.* 8.60 gallons.

   b. 7.83 and 9.37, found by $8.60 \pm 2.58 \ (2.30/\sqrt{60})$.

   c. If 100 such intervals were determined, the population mean would lie in about 99 intervals.

18. *a.* 5.29 and 6.81 errors, found by $6.05 \pm 1.96 \ (2.44/\sqrt{40})$.

19. *a.* .80, found by 80/100.

   b. .7216 and .8784, found by: $.80 \pm 1.96 \sqrt{[(.80)(.20)/100]}$

20. *a.* .75, found by 300/400.

   b. .694 and .806, found by: $.75 \pm 2.58 \sqrt{[(.75)(.25)/400]}$

   c. She is almost assured of receiving more than 50 percent of the votes.

21. *a.* .625, found by 250/400.

   b. .578 and .672, found by: $.625 \pm 1.96 \sqrt{[(.625)(.375)/400]}$

22. *a.* .15, found by 30/200.

   b. .101 and .199, found by:

$$.15 \pm 1.96 \sqrt{\frac{(.15)(.85)}{200}}$$

23. 33.465 and 36.535, found by

$$35 \pm 1.96 \ (5/\sqrt{36}) \sqrt{\frac{300-36}{300-1}}$$

24. 36.846 and 43.154, found by

$$40 \pm 2.58 \ (9/\sqrt{49}) \sqrt{\frac{500-49}{500-1}}$$

25. 3.069 and 3.411, found by

$$3.24 \pm 2.58 \ (.50/\sqrt{50}) \sqrt{\frac{400-50}{400-1}}$$

26. .43 and .77, found by:

$$.60 \pm 1.96\sqrt{[(.60)(.40)/30]} \ \sqrt{\frac{(300-30)}{(300-1)}}$$

27. 97, found by $n = ((1.96 \cdot 10)/2)^2 = 96.04$.

28. 60, found by $n = ((2.58 \cdot 15)/5)^2 = 59.91$.

29. 554, found by n = $((1.96 \cdot 3)/.25)^2$ = 553.19.

30. 25, found by n = $((1.96 \cdot .5)/0.2)^2$ = 24.01.

31. 196, found by:
    n = .15 (.85)$[1.96/.05]^2$ = 195.916

32. 165, found by:
    n = .45 (.55)$[2.58/.10]^2$ = 164.75

33. *a.* 577, found by:
    n = .60(.40)$[1.96/.04]^2$ = 576.24
    b. 601, found by:
    n = .50(.50)$[1.96/.04]^2$ = 600.25

34. *a.* 5,683, found by:
    n = .30(.70)$[1.645/.01]^2$ = 5,682.65
    b. Increase the allowable error from .01 to .05. Thus the sample size would be reduced to 228, found by:
    n = .30(.70)$[1.645/.05]^2$ = 227.31

35. *a.* It is usually not feasible to study the entire population. Thus, if we want to infer something about a characteristic of a population, a part of the population—called a sample—is needed.
    b. Contacting all the voters or all consumers would be too time-consuming and too costly. It is impossible to tag all the whales in the ocean for study. Checking all products for strength is destructive, and none would be available for sale.

36. *a.* Systematic sampling.
    b. Stratified sampling.

37. A nonprobability sample, such as a panel sample, may not give results that are representative of the population because every item or person does not have a chance of being selected for the sample.

38. It is the difference between a population parameter and a sample statistic. For example, if the mean age of all retired persons is 68.0 and the mean of the sample taken from that population is 68.3, the sampling error is 0.3 years.

39. The metropolitan area could be subdivided into precincts. Four precincts could be selected for study. Suppose there are 74 mobile home parks in the area. Eight could be selected, and the persons conducting the survey would concentrate on the residents of those eight parks.

40. National Family Opinion and other consumer opinion firms organize a group of persons, called a panel, to give opinions or test products. The panel could consist of, say, retired persons or persons owning home computers. It is nonprobability sampling because all retired persons owning a home computer does not have a chance of being selected in the sample.

41. *a.* Jeanne Fiorito, Douglas Smucker, Jeanine S. Huttner, Harry Mayhew, Mark Steinmetz, and Paul Langenkamp.
    b. One randomly selected group of numbers is 05, 06, 74, 64, 66, 55, 27, 22. The members of the sample are Janet Arrowsmith, David DeFrance, Mark Zilkoski, and Larry Johnson.

42. Francis Aona, Paul Langenkamp, Ricardo Pena, and so on.

43. Answers will vary.

44. *a.* We selected 60, 104, 75, 72, 48. Answers will vary.
    b. We selected the third observation. So the sample consists of 75, 72, 68, 82, 48. Answers will vary.
    c. Number the first 20 motels from 00 to 19. Randomly select three numbers. Then number the last five numbers 20 to 24. Randomly select two numbers from that group.

45. *a.* 10, found by 5!/3!2!.
    b.

Number correct	Mean	Number correct	Mean
4,3	3.5	3,3	3.0
4,5	4.5	3,2	2.5
4,3	3.5	5,3	4.0
4,2	3.0	5,2	3.5
3,5	4.0	3,2	2.5

c.

Sample mean	Frequency	Probability
2.5	2	.20
3.0	2	.20
3.5	3	.30
4.0	2	.20
4.5	1	.10
	10	1.00

d. $\mu_{\bar{x}}$ = (3.5 + 4.5 + ... + 2.5)/10 = 3.4
μ = (4 + 3 + 5 + 3 + 2)/5 = 3.4
The two means are equal.
e. The population values are uniform in shape. The distribution of sample means tends toward normality.

46. Use of either a proportional or nonproportional stratified random sample would be appropriate. For example, suppose the number of banks in Region 111 were as follows:

Assets	Number	Percent Of Total
$500 million and more	20	2.0
$100–499 million	324	32.4
less than $100 million	656	65.6
	1,000	100

For a proportional stratified sample, if the sample size is 100, then two banks worth assets of $500 million would be selected, 32 medium-size banks and 66 small banks. For a nonproportional sample, 10 or even all 20 large banks could be selected and fewer medium- and small-size banks and the sample results weighted by the appropriate percents of the total.

47. A simple random sample would be appropriate, but this means each 10-foot length would have to be numbered 1, 2, 3, . . . , 720. A faster method would be to (1) select a pipe from the first say, 20 pipes produced, and (2) select every 20th pipe produced thereafter and measure its inside diameter. Thus, the sample would include about 36 PVC pipes.

48. a. 15, found by 6!/2!4!
    b.
Ages	Mean	Ages	Mean
54,50	52	50,52	51
54,52	53	52,48	50
54,48	51	52,50	51
54,50	52	52,52	52
54,52	53	48,50	49
50,52	51	48,52	50
50,48	49	50,52	51
50,50	50		

   c.
Sample means	Frequency	Probability
49	2	.13
50	3	.20
51	5	.33
52	3	.20
53	2	.13

   d. $\mu = 51$
      $\mu_{\bar{x}} = 51$
   e. Population. Tending toward normal.
   f. Sample means. Somewhat normal.

49. 6.14 years to 6.86 years, found by $6.5 \pm 1.96 (1.7/\sqrt{85})$.

50. .42 and .50, found by:
$$.46 \pm 2.58 \sqrt{\frac{.46(1 - .46)}{900}}$$

51. 369, found by $n = .60(1 - .60) [1.96/.05]^2 = 368.79$.

52. .647 and .753, found by:
$$.70 \pm 2.58 \sqrt{\frac{.70(1 - .70)}{500}}$$

Note that the finite-population correction factor was not applied because n/N is less than .05.

53. 133, found by $[(1.645 \times 14)/2]^2$

54. Answers will vary.

55. a. 3.01 pounds
    b. 3.0002 and 3.0198 pounds, found by $3.01 \pm 1.96 (.03/\sqrt{36})$.
    c. About 95 percent of similarly constructed intervals would include the population mean.

56. $52.56 and $55.44, found by:
$$\$54.00 \pm 1.96 (\$.50/\sqrt{35}) \sqrt{\frac{(500 - 35)}{(500 - 1)}}$$

57. .345 and .695, found by:
$$.52 \pm 2.58 \sqrt{\frac{.52(.48)}{50}} \sqrt{\frac{(650 - 50)}{(650 - 1)}}$$

58. $1.168 and $1.190, found by $1.179 \pm 2.58(.03/\sqrt{50})$

59. .633 and .687, found by
$$.66 \pm 1.96 \sqrt{\frac{.66(.34)}{1200}}$$

60. a. The driveway, because it has the smallest standard deviation.
    b. driveway: 10.776 and 13.224 ($12 \pm 2.58(3/\sqrt{40})$)
       patio: 9.553 and 14.447 ($12 \pm 2.58(6/\sqrt{40})$)
       deck: 8.737 and 15.263 ($12 \pm 2.58(8/\sqrt{40})$)

61. It is highly likely that the estimate is accurate. If we use the actual sample as the p, the 82% estimate does fall within a 95% confidence interval.
    $.786 \pm 1.96 \sqrt{[(.786)(.214)/140]}$
    $.786 \pm .068$
    So the actual interval is from .718 to .854 and .82 is included in this interval.

62. .162 and .298, found by

$$.23 \pm 2.58 \sqrt{\frac{.23(.77)}{256}}$$

63. *a.* 708.13, rounded up to 709, found by:
 $.21(1 - .21)[1.96/.03]^2$
 b. 1,068, found by:
 $.50(.50)[1.96/.03]^2$

64. *a.* 25%, found by 25/100.
 b. .172 to .328, found by

$$.25 \pm 1.96 \left(\sqrt{\frac{(.25)(.75)}{100}}\right)\left(\sqrt{\frac{605-100}{604}}\right)$$

 No. .40 not in interval.
 c. 1.65, found by 165/100.
 d. 1.387 to 1.913, found by

$$1.65 \pm 1.96 \left(\frac{1.4659}{\sqrt{100}}\right)\left(\sqrt{\frac{505}{604}}\right)$$

 e. No, because 0 is not in the interval between 1.387 and 1.91.

65. *a.* $158.59 and $174.76 found by

$$\$166.67 \pm 1.96 \left(\frac{\$35.68}{\sqrt{75}}\right)$$

 b. 13.78 miles and 16.00 miles, found by

$$14.8933 \pm 1.96 \left(\frac{4.892}{\sqrt{75}}\right)$$

 c. $\bar{p} = 51/75 = .68$. Then

$$.68 \pm 1.96 \sqrt{\frac{(.68)(.32)}{75}}$$

 gives 57.44% to 78.56%.

66. *a.* 13.700 to 16.240, found by

$$14.97 \pm 1.96 \left(\frac{8.524}{\sqrt{173}}\right)$$

 Using the $7,900 price for Berkshire Hathaway:
 b. $16.43 to $170.57, found by

$$\$93.50 \pm 1.96 \left(\frac{\$556.10}{\sqrt{200}}\right)$$

 $93.50 \pm 1.96 ($39.32)
 Using a $79 price for Berkshire Hathaway:
 c. $49.03 to $59.69, found by

$$\$54.36 \pm 1.96 \left(\frac{\$38.431}{\sqrt{200}}\right)$$

According to the New York *Times* the actual price of a share of Berkshire Hathaway is $7900. This one price caused the standard deviation ($556.10) to be very high compared with a price of just $79. Thus the confidence limits for the actual data are quite wide ($16.43 to $170.57). And, the mean is higher ($93.50) compared with the data set having a $79 price.

CHAPTER 9: TESTS OF HYPOTHESES: LARGE SAMPLES

1. a. Two-tailed.
   b. Reject H_0 and accept H_1 where z does not fall in the region from -1.96 and 1.96.
   c. -1.2, found by:
   $$z = \frac{\bar{X} - \mu}{(\sigma/\sqrt{n})} = \frac{49 - 50}{(5/\sqrt{36})} = -1.2$$
   d. Fail to reject H_0.
   e. p = .2302, found by 2(.5000 − .3849)

2. a. One-tail.
   b. Reject H_0 when z > 2.05
   c. 4, found by:
   $$z = \frac{\bar{X} - \mu}{(\sigma/\sqrt{n})} = \frac{12 - 10}{(3/\sqrt{36})} = 4.0$$
   d. Reject H_0 and conclude that $\mu > 10$.
   e. p < .0000 given a z of 4. Area under curve is about .5000.

3. a. H_0: $\mu = 60{,}000$
      H_1: $\mu \neq 60{,}000$
   b. Reject H_0 if z < -1.96 or z > 1.96.
   c. -0.69, found by:
   $$z = \frac{59{,}500 - 60{,}000}{(5{,}000/\sqrt{48})} = -0.69$$
   d. Fail to reject H_0 at the .05 significance level. Crosset's experience is not different from that claimed by the manufacturer. The p-value is .4902, found by 2(.5000 − .2549)

4. a. H_0: $\mu = 3$
      H_1: $\mu < 3$
   b. Reject H_0 and accept H_1 if z < -1.645.
   c. -1.768, found by:
   $$z = \frac{2.75 - 3}{(1/\sqrt{50})} = -1.768$$
   d. Reject H_0 and conclude that the mean waiting time is less than 3, using the .05 significance level. p = .0384, found by .5000 − .4616.

5. a. One-tailed.
   b. Reject H_0 and accept H_1 where z > 1.645.
   c. 1.2, found by:
   $$z = \frac{\bar{X} - \mu}{(s/\sqrt{n})} = \frac{21 - 20}{(5/\sqrt{36})} = 1.2$$
   d. Fail to reject the H_0 at the .05 significance level.
   e. p = .1151, found by .5000 − .3849.

6. a. One-tailed.
   b. Reject H_0 and accept H_1 where z < -1.88.
   c. -2.67, found by:
   $$z = \frac{\bar{X} - \mu}{(s/\sqrt{n})} = \frac{215 - 220}{(15/\sqrt{64})} = -2.67$$
   d. Reject H_0 and conclude that the population mean is less than 220 at the .03 significance level.
   e. p = .0038, found by .5000 − .4962.

7. a. H_0: $\mu = 6.8$
      H_1: $\mu < 6.8$
   b. Reject H_0 if z < -1.645.
   c. -7.2, found by:
   $$z = \frac{6.2 - 6.8}{0.5/\sqrt{36}} = -7.2$$
   d. Reject H_0 and conclude that the mean number of videos watched by college students is less than 6.8 at the .05 significance level.

8. a. H_0: $\mu = \$20$
      H_1: $\mu > \$20$
   b. Reject H_0 if z > 2.33.
   c. 8.856, found by:
   $$z = \frac{\$24.85 - \$20.00}{\$3.24/\sqrt{35}} = 8.856$$
   d. Reject H_0 and conclude that the mean daily tips are greater $20.

9. a. Two-tailed test.
   b. Reject H_0 if z < -2.055 or z > 2.055.
   c. 2.59, found by:
   $$z = \frac{\bar{X}_1 - \bar{X}_2}{\sqrt{\frac{s_1^2}{n_1} + \frac{s_2^2}{n_2}}} = \frac{102 - 99}{\sqrt{\frac{5^2}{40} + \frac{6^2}{50}}} = 2.59$$
   d. Reject H_0 and accept H_1.
   e. p = .0096, found by 2(.5000 − .4952).

10. a. One-tailed test.
    b. Reject H_0 and accept H_1 if z > 1.405.
    c. .607, found by:
    $$z = \frac{\bar{X}_1 - \bar{X}_2}{\sqrt{\frac{s_1^2}{n_1} + \frac{s_2^2}{n_2}}} = \frac{2.67 - 2.59}{\sqrt{\frac{(.75)^2}{65} + \frac{(.66)^2}{50}}} = 0.607$$
    d. Fail to reject H_0.
    e. p = .2709, found by .5000 − .2291.

11. **Step 1** $H_0: \mu_1 = \mu_2$

   $H_1: \mu_1 < \mu_2$

   Step 2 The .05 significance level was chosen.

   Step 3 Reject H_0 and accept H_1 if $z < -1.645$.

   Step 4 -0.94, found by:

   $$z = \frac{7.6 - 8.1}{\sqrt{\frac{(2.3)^2}{40} + \frac{(2.9)^2}{55}}} = -0.94$$

   Step 5 Fail to reject H_0. No difference in lengths of time owner occupied his home. $p = .1736$ found by $.5000 - .3264$

12. **Step 1** $H_0: \mu_c = \mu_p$

   $H_0: \mu_c \neq \mu_p$

   Step 2 The .05 significance level was chosen.

   Step 3 Reject H_0 and accept H_1 if z less than -1.96 or greater than 1.96.

   Step 4 -1.53, found by:

   $$z = \frac{\$370 - \$380}{\sqrt{\frac{(\$30)^2}{35} + \frac{(\$26)^2}{40}}} = -1.53$$

   Step 5 Fail to reject H_0. There is no difference in the mean cost of apartments.

   The p-value is .126 found by $2(.5000 - .4370)$

13. *a.* Two-tailed test. Because we are trying to show that a difference exists between the two means.

   b. Reject H_0 if $z < -2.58$ or $z > 2.58$.

   c. -2.66, found by:

   $$z = \frac{31.4 - 34.9}{\sqrt{\frac{(5.1)^2}{32} + \frac{(6.7)^2}{49}}} = -2.66$$

   Reject H_0 at the .01 level. There is a difference in the mean turnover rate.

   $p = .0078$, found by $2(.5000 - .4961)$

14. $z = (9,922 - 9,880)/(400/\sqrt{100}) = 1.05$. Then $.5000 - .3531 = .1469$, which is the probability of a Type II error.

15. $z = (9,922 - 9,940)/(400/\sqrt{100}) = -0.45$. Then the area of $.1736 + .5000 = .6736$, which is the probability of a Type II error.

16. Reject H_0 and conclude that the mean is less than 10 pounds. Found by rejecting H_0 if $z < -1.645$. Then,

   $$z = \frac{9.0 - 10}{(2.8/\sqrt{50})} = -2.53$$

   H_0 is rejected. The mean weight loss is less than 10 pounds. p-value is .0057 found by $.5000 - .4943$.

17. $H_0: \mu = 16$

   $H_1: \mu > 16$

   Reject H_0 if $z > 1.645$.

   Computed $z = 11.78$, found by:

   $$z = \frac{16.05 - 16.0}{(0.03/\sqrt{50})} = 11.78$$

   Reject H_0. The cans are being overfilled. p-value $= .0000$.

18. $H_0: \mu = \$15,000$

   $H_1: \mu > \$15,000$

   Reject H_0 if $z > 1.645$.

   Computed $z = 5.77$, found by:

   $$z = \frac{\$17,000 - \$15,000}{\$3,000/\sqrt{75}} = 5.77$$

   Reject H_0. At the .05 level we can conclude that the mean household income is greater than \$15,000.

19. $H_0: \mu = 90$

   $H_1: \mu > 90$

   Reject H_0 if $z > 1.28$.

   Computed $z = 1.82$,

   $$z = \frac{94 - 90}{(22/\sqrt{100})} = 1.82$$

   Reject H_0. At the .10 level we can conclude that the farm selling time has increased.

20. $H_0: \mu = \$30,000$

   $H_1: \mu \neq \$30,000$

   Reject H_0 if $z < -1.645$ or $z > 1.645$.

   Computed $z = 1.83$, found by:

   $$z = \frac{\$30,500 - \$30,000}{(\$3,000/\sqrt{120})} = 1.83$$

   Reject H_0. We can conclude that the mean salary is not \$30,000.

21. $H_0: \mu = 28$
    $H_1: \mu < 28$
    Reject H_0 where $z < -2.05$
    Computed $z = -1.55$, found by:

$$z = \frac{26.9 - 28.0}{(8/\sqrt{127})} = -1.55$$

Fail to reject H_0. Changes did not reduce the wait time.

22. $H_0: \mu_1 = \mu_2$
    $H_1: \mu_1 \neq \mu_2$
    Reject H_0 if $z < -2.05$ or $z > 2.05$.
    Computed $z = -1.60$, found by

$$z = \frac{114.6 - 117.9}{\sqrt{\dfrac{(9.1)^2}{40} + \dfrac{(10.4)^2}{50}}} = -1.60$$

Fail to reject H_0. There is no difference in the test scores. The p-value is .1096, found by 2(.5000 − .4452)

23. $H_0: \mu_1 = \mu_2$
    $H_1: \mu_1 \neq \mu_2$
    Reject H_0 if $z < -1.96$ or $z > 1.96$.
    Computed $z = -1.37$, found by:

$$z = \frac{20 - 21}{\sqrt{\dfrac{4^2}{45} + \dfrac{3^2}{50}}} = -1.37$$

Do not reject the H_0. There is no difference in delivery times. p-value is .1706, found by 2 (5000 − .4147).

24. $H_0: \mu_1 = \mu_2$
    $H_1: \mu_1 \neq \mu_2$
    Reject H_0 if $z < -1.645$ or $z > 1.645$.
    Computed $z = 34.20$, found by:

$$z = \frac{2{,}175 - 2{,}050}{\sqrt{\dfrac{(12)^2}{64} + \dfrac{(20)^2}{36}}} = 34.20$$

Reject H_0. There is a significant difference in the two shifts with regard to the rpms of the motors.

25. $H_0: \mu_1 = \mu_2$
    $H_1: \mu_1 < \mu_2$
    Reject H_0 if z is < -1.645.
    Computed $z = -0.14$, found by:

$$z = \frac{\$31{,}290 - \$31{,}330}{\sqrt{\dfrac{(\$1060)^2}{45} + \dfrac{(\$1900)^2}{60}}} = -0.14$$

Fail to reject H_0. There is no difference in the starting salaries.

26. $H_0: \mu = \$1{,}010$
    $H_1: \mu > \$1{,}010$
    Reject H_0 where $z > 2.33$, Computed $z = 23.41$, found by:

$$z = \frac{\$1{,}250 - \$1{,}010}{(\$205/\sqrt{400})}$$

Reject H_0. The mean amount spent has increased.

27. $H_0: \mu = .012$
    $H_1: \mu < 0.12$
    Reject H_0 where $z < -1.645$. Computed $z = -30.0$

$$z = \frac{0.09 - 0.12}{(0.03/\sqrt{900})}$$

Reject H_0. The pollution level has declined.

28. $H_0: \mu = 200{,}000$
    $H_1: \mu < 200{,}000$
    Reject H_0 where $z < -1.645$. Computed $z = -10.0$, found by:

$$z = \frac{190{,}000 - 200{,}000}{(12{,}000/\sqrt{144})}$$

Reject H_0. The mean is less than 200,000.

29. $H_0: \mu = \$3.65$
    $H_0: \mu \neq \$3.65$
    Reject H_0 where z does not fall in the range between -1.96 and 1.96. Computed $z = 1.12$, found by:

$$z = \frac{\$3.69 - \$3.65}{(\$0.24/\sqrt{45})}$$

Fail to reject H_0. There is no difference between Northwest Ohio and the rest of the United States.

30. $H_0: \mu_1 = \mu_2$
    $H_1: \mu_1 > \mu_2$
    Reject H_0 if $z > 2.33$.
    Computed $z = 4.10$, found by:

$$z = \frac{11.00 - 8.90}{\sqrt{\dfrac{2.65^2}{36} + \dfrac{1.64^2}{40}}} = 4.10$$

Reject H_0 and conclude that the fog index is higher in scientific journals.

31. H_0: $\mu_1 = \mu_2$
H_1: $\mu_1 < \mu_2$
Reject H_0 if $z < -1.645$. Computed $z = -1.30$, found by:

$$z = \frac{345 - 351}{\sqrt{\dfrac{21^2}{54} + \dfrac{28^2}{60}}} = -1.30$$

Fail to reject H_0. There is not enough evidence to say more units are produced on the afternoon shift.

32. *a.* Reject H_0 where $z > 1.645$. Computed $z = 1.28$, found by:

$$z = \frac{24,421 - 24,000}{(1,944/\sqrt{35})} = 1.28$$

Fail to reject H_0.
b. 24,541, found by:

$$1.645 = \frac{\bar{X}_c - 24,000}{(1,944/\sqrt{35})} = 24,540.54$$

c. $z = (24,540.54 - 25,000)/(1,944/\sqrt{35}) = -1.40$
$.5000 - .4192 = .0808$

33. *a.* $9.00 + 1.645(1/\sqrt{36}) = 9.00 + 0.274$
So the limits are 8.726 and 9.274.
b. $z = (8.726 - 8.900)/(1/\sqrt{36}) = -1.04$
So the probability is $.3508 + .5000 = .8508$
c. $z = (9.274 - 9.300)/(1/\sqrt{36}) = -0.16$
So the probability is $.5000 - .0636 = .4364$

34. *a.* H_0: $\mu = .75$, H_1: $\mu > .75$. Critical value is 1.645

$$z = \frac{.80 - .75}{\dfrac{.1}{\sqrt{45}}} = 3.35$$

Reject H_0. The shoppers are now spending more than an average of .75 hours in the mall.
b. $\bar{X}_c = .7745$, found by

$$1.645 = \frac{\bar{X}_c - .75}{\dfrac{.1}{\sqrt{45}}}$$

$z = .302$ found by $\dfrac{.7745 - .77}{\dfrac{.1}{\sqrt{45}}}$

area $= .1179$. Then $.5000 + .1179 = .6179$.
c. Increase level of significance to say 0.10.

35.

$$50 + (2.33)\left(\frac{10}{\sqrt{n}}\right) = 55 - (.525)\left(\frac{10}{\sqrt{n}}\right)$$

$$50 + \frac{23.3}{\sqrt{n}} = 55 - \frac{5.25}{\sqrt{n}}$$

$$\frac{28.55}{\sqrt{n}} = 5$$

$$n = (5.71)^2 = 32.6 = 33$$

36. *a.* H_0: $\mu = 180$, H_1: $\mu < 180$ H_0 is rejected if $z < -1.645$

$$z = \frac{166.67 - 180.0}{35.68/\sqrt{75}} = -3.235$$

H_0 is rejected. The mean selling price is less than \$180,000. The p-value is .0000.
b. H_0: $\mu = 2000$, H_1: $\mu > 2000$ H_0 is rejected if $z > 1.645$

$$z = \frac{2154.8 - 2000}{207.4/\sqrt{75}} = 6.464$$

H_0 is rejected. The mean size is greater than 2000 square feet.

37. *a.* Critical values are 1.96 and -1.96
$z = -2.177$ found by $\dfrac{10,304 - 12,000}{\dfrac{11017.55}{\sqrt{200}}}$

Reject H_0: p $= .02971$
b. Critical values are 1.96 and -1.96
$z = 3.793$. Reject H_0. The mean sales are different from \$15,000 million.

CHAPTER 10: TESTS OF HYPOTHESES: PROPORTIONS

1. *a.* H_0 is rejected if $z > 1.645$.
   b.
   $$z = \frac{.75 - .70}{\sqrt{\dfrac{.70\,(.30)}{100}}} = \frac{.0500}{.0458} = 1.09$$

   c. H_0 is not rejected.

2. *a.* H_0 is rejected if $z < -1.96$ or $z > 1.96$.
   b.
   $$z = \frac{.30 - .40}{\sqrt{\dfrac{.40\,(.60)}{120}}} = \frac{-.1000}{.0490} = -2.236$$

   c. H_0 is rejected.

3. *a.* $H_0{:}p = .52$, $H_1{:}p > .52$
   b. H_0 is rejected if $z > 2.33$.
   c.
   $$z = \frac{.5667 - .52}{\sqrt{\dfrac{.52\,(.48)}{300}}} = \frac{.0467}{.0288} = 1.620$$

   d. H_0 is not rejected. The proportion of men driving on the Ohio Turnpike is not larger than .52.

4. *a.* $H_0{:}p = .33$, $H_1{:}p > .33$
   b. H_0 is rejected if $z > 2.05$.
   c.
   $$z = \frac{.40 - .3333}{\sqrt{\dfrac{.3333\,(.6667)}{200}}} = \frac{.0667}{.0332} = 2.001$$

   d. H_0 is not rejected. The proportion of students with jobs is not larger at your school.

5. *a.* $H_0{:}p = .90$, $H_1{:}p < .90$
   b. H_0 is rejected if $z < -1.28$.
   c.
   $$z = \frac{.82 - .90}{\sqrt{\dfrac{.90\,(.10)}{100}}} = \frac{-.08}{.03} = -2.667$$

   d. H_0 is rejected. Less than 90% of the customers receive their orders in less than 30 minutes.

6. *a.* $H_0{:}p = .50$, $H_1{:}p < .50$
   b. H_0 is rejected if $z < -1.645$.
   c.
   $$z = \frac{.48 - .50}{\sqrt{\dfrac{.50\,(.50)}{100}}} = \frac{-.02}{.05} = -0.40$$

   d. H_0 is not rejected. The proportion of students changing their major has not changed.

7. *a.* H_0 is rejected if $z > 1.645$
   b.
   $$\bar{p}_c = \frac{70 + 90}{100 + 150} = .64$$

   c.
   $$z = \frac{.70 - .60}{\sqrt{\dfrac{.64\,(.36)}{100} + \dfrac{.64\,(.36)}{150}}} = 1.614$$

   d. H_0 is not rejected.

8. *a.* H_0 is rejected if $z < -1.96$ or $z > 1.96$
   b.
   $$\bar{p}_c = \frac{170 + 110}{200 + 150} = .80$$

   c.
   $$z = \frac{.85 - .7333}{\sqrt{\dfrac{.80\,(.20)}{200} + \dfrac{.80\,(.20)}{150}}} = = 2.701$$

   d. H_0 is rejected.

9. *a.* $H_0{:}p_1 = p_2$ $H_1{:}p_1 \neq p_2$
   b. H_0 is rejected if $z < -1.96$ or $z > 1.96$
   c.
   $$\bar{p}_c = \frac{24 + 40}{400 + 400} = .08$$

   d.
   $$z = \frac{.06 - .10}{\sqrt{\dfrac{.08\,(.92)}{400} + \dfrac{.08\,(.92)}{400}}} = -2.085$$

   e. H_0 is rejected. The proportion infested is not the same in the two fields.

10. *a.* $H_0 : p_1 = p_2 \qquad H_1 : p_1 < p_2$

    b. H_0 is rejected if $z < -1.645$

$$\bar{p}_c = \frac{2010 + 1530}{3000 + 3000} = .59$$

    c.

$$z = \frac{.51 - .67}{\sqrt{\dfrac{.59\,(.41)}{3000} + \dfrac{.59\,(.41)}{3000}}} = -12.60$$

    d. H_0 is rejected. The proportion of women who think men are thoughtful has declined.

11. $H_0 : p_d = p_r \qquad H_1 : p_d > p_r$
    H_0 is rejected if $z > 2.05$

$$\bar{p}_c = \frac{168 + 200}{800 + 1000} = .2044$$

$$z = \frac{.21 - .20}{\sqrt{\dfrac{.2044\,(.7956)}{800} + \dfrac{.2044\,(.7956)}{1000}}} = 0.523$$

H_0 is not rejected. There is no difference in the proportion of Democrats and Republicans who favor lowering the standards.

12. $H_0 : p_s = p_m \qquad H_1 : p_s \neq p_m$
    H_0 is rejected if $z < -1.96$ or $z > 1.96$.

$$\bar{p}_c = \frac{120 + 150}{400 + 600} = .27$$

$$z = \frac{.30 - .25}{\sqrt{\dfrac{.27\,(.73)}{400} + \dfrac{.27\,(.73)}{600}}} = 1.745$$

H_0 is not rejected. There is no difference in the proportion of married and single drivers that have accidents.

13. $H_0 : p = .60 \qquad H_1 : p > .60$
    H_0 is rejected if $z > 2.33$

$$z = \frac{.70 - .60}{\sqrt{\dfrac{.60\,(.40)}{200}}} = \frac{.10}{.0346} = 2.887$$

H_0 is rejected. Ms. Dennis is correct. More than 60% of the accounts are more than 3 months old.

14. $H_0 : p = .55 \qquad H_1 : p > .55$
    H_0 is rejected if $z > 1.645$

$$z = \frac{.60 - .55}{\sqrt{\dfrac{.55\,(.45)}{70}}} = \frac{.05}{.0595} = 0.841$$

H_0 is not rejected. We cannot conclude that more than 55% of the commuters would use the route.

15. $H_0 : p = .20 \qquad H_1 : p < .20$
    H_0 is rejected if $z < -1.645$

$$z = \frac{.195 - .20}{\sqrt{\dfrac{.20\,(.80)}{2000}}} = \frac{-.005}{.0089} = -0.559$$

He is not rejected. We cannot conclude that less than 20% of the population will watch the show.

16. $H_0 : p = .44 \qquad H_1 : p > .44$
    H_0 is rejected if $z > 1.645$

$$z = \frac{.480 - .44}{\sqrt{\dfrac{.44\,(.56)}{1000}}} = \frac{.04}{.0157} = 2.548$$

H_0 is rejected. We conclude that there has been an increase in the proportion of people traveling to Europe.

17. $H_0 : p_n = p_o \qquad H_1 : p_n > p_o$
    H_0 is rejected if $z > 1.645$.

$$\bar{p}_c = \frac{180 + 261}{200 + 300} = .882$$

$$z = \frac{.90 - .87}{\sqrt{\dfrac{.882\,(.118)}{200} + \dfrac{.882\,(.118)}{300}}} = 1.019$$

H_0 is not rejected. There is no difference in the proportions that found relief in the new and the old drugs.

18. $H_0 : p_a = p_f \qquad H_1 : p_a \neq p_f$
    H_0 is rejected if $z < -1.96$ or $z > 1.96$.

$$\bar{p}_c = \frac{198 + 117}{1000 + 500} = .21$$

$$z = \frac{.198 - .234}{\sqrt{\dfrac{.21\,(.79)}{1000} + \dfrac{.21\,(.79)}{500}}} = -1.614$$

H_0 is not rejected. There is no difference in the proportion of Americans born citizens and foreign born citizens who favor resumption of diplomatic relations with Cuba.

19. $H_0: p = .40 \qquad H_1: p < .40$
H_0 is rejected if $z < -1.645$

$$z = \frac{.38 - .40}{\sqrt{\frac{.40\,(.60)}{80}}} = \frac{-.02}{.0548} = -0.365$$

H_0 is not rejected. We conclude that the .02 difference could be due to chance. Production cutbacks are not needed.

20. $H_0: p_w = p_{nw} \qquad H_1: p_w > p_{nw}$
H_0 is rejected if $z > 1.645$.

$$\bar{p}_c = \frac{70 + 90}{100 + 150} = .64$$

$$z = \frac{.70 - .60}{\sqrt{\frac{.64\,(.36)}{100} + \frac{.64\,(.36)}{150}}} = 1.614$$

H_0 is not rejected. There is no difference in the proportion of meals eaten outside the home for those couples where the wife works full-time outside the home and those where the wife does not work full-time outside the home.

21. $H_0: p_m = p_w \qquad H_1: p_m \neq p_w$
H_0 is rejected if $z < -1.96$ or $z > 1.96$

$$\bar{p}_c = \frac{70 + 72}{500 + 400} = .1578$$

$$z = \frac{.14 - .18}{\sqrt{\frac{.1578\,(.8422)}{500} + \frac{.1578\,(.8422)}{400}}} = -1.636$$

H_0 is not rejected. There is no difference in the proportion of meals eaten outside the home for those couples where the wife works full-time outside the home and those where the wife does not work full-time outside the home.

22. a. $H_0: p = .76 \qquad H_1: p < .76$
H_0 is rejected if $z < -2.33$

$$z = \frac{.75 - .76}{\sqrt{\frac{.71\,(.24)}{1060}}} = \frac{-.01}{.0131} = -.762$$

We cannot conclude that less than .76 will like the cereal.

b. $H_0: p_e = p_w \qquad H_1: p_e \neq p_w$
H_0 is rejected if $z < -2.58$ or $z > 2.58$

$$\bar{p}_c = \frac{468 + 327}{632 + 428} = .75$$

$$z = \frac{.7405 - .7640}{\sqrt{\frac{.75\,(.25)}{632} + \frac{.75\,(.25)}{428}}} = -0.867$$

23. a. $H_0: p = .5, \; H_1: p > .5$ Reject H_0 if $z > 1.645$

$$z = \frac{.6133 - .50}{\sqrt{\frac{.50\,(.50)}{75}}} = \frac{.1133}{.0577} = 1.962$$

H_0 is rejected. More than half of the homes have a pool.

b. $H_0: p = .5, \; H_1: p > .5$ Reject H_0 if $z > 1.645$

$$\bar{p} = \frac{51}{75} = .68$$

$$z = \frac{.68 - .50}{\sqrt{\frac{(.50)\,(.50)}{75}}} = \frac{.18}{.0577} = 3.118$$

H_0 is rejected. More than half of the homes have a garage.

CHAPTER 11: STUDENT'S t TEST: SMALL SAMPLES

1. *a.* Reject H_0 where t > 1.833
   b.
   $$t = \frac{\bar{X}-\mu}{(s/\sqrt{n})} = \frac{12-10}{(3/\sqrt{10})} = 2.108$$
   c. Reject H_0. The mean is greater than 10.

2. *a.* Reject H_0 if t < − 3.106 or t > 3.106.
   b.
   $$t = \frac{\bar{X}-\mu}{(s/\sqrt{n})} = \frac{407-400}{(6/\sqrt{12})} = 4.0415$$
   c. Reject H_0. The mean does not equal 400.

3. H_0: $\mu = 40$
   H_1: $\mu > 40$
   Reject H_0 if t > 1.703.
   $$t = \frac{42-40}{(2.1/\sqrt{28})} = 5.04$$
   Reject H_0 and conclude that the mean number of calls is greater than 40 per week.

4. H_0: $\mu = 42.3$
   H_1: $\mu < 42.3$
   Reject H_0 if t < − 1.319.
   $$t = \frac{40.6-42.3}{(2.7/\sqrt{24})} = -3.084$$
   Reject H_0. The mean assembly time is less than 42.3 minutes.

5. H_0: $\mu = 22,100$
   H_1: $\mu > 22,100$
   Reject H_0 if t > 1.740.
   $$t = \frac{23,400-22,100}{(1,500/\sqrt{18})} = 3.68$$
   Reject H_0. The mean life of the spark plug is greater than 22,100 miles.

6. H_0: $\mu = 15$
   H_1: $\mu > 15$
   Reject H_0 if t > 1.725.
   $$t = \frac{18-15}{(1/\sqrt{21})} = 13.75$$
   Reject H_0. The mean service time is greater than 15 minutes.

7. *a.* Reject H_0 if t < − 3.747.
   b. $\bar{X} = 17$ and s = $\sqrt{(1495-(85)^2/5)/(5-1)}$
      = 3.536
   $$t = \frac{17-20}{3.536/\sqrt{5}} = -1.90$$
   c. Do not reject H_0. We can not conclude the population mean is less than 20.
   d. Between .05 and .10, about .065

8. *a.* Reject H_0 if t < −2.571 or t > 2.571.
   b.
   $$t = \frac{111.667-100}{6.055/\sqrt{6}} = 4.72$$
   c. Reject H_0. The population mean is not equal to 100.
   d. less than .01 (between .001 and .01)

9. H_0: $\mu = 4.35$
   H_1: $\mu > 4.35$
   Reject H_0 if t > 2.821.
   $$t = \frac{4.368-4.35}{(0.0339/\sqrt{10})} = 1.68$$
   Do not reject H_0. The additive did not increase the mean weight of the chickens.

10. *a.* H_0: $\mu = 2,160$
    H_1: $\mu > 2,160$
    Reject H_0 if t > 2.306.
    $$t = \frac{2,172.44-2,160}{(9.3823/\sqrt{9})} = 3.98$$
    Reject H_0. The mean chlorine shelf life has increased.

11. *a.* H_0: $\mu = 4.0$
    H_1: $\mu > 4.0$
    Reject H_0 if t > 1.796.
    $$t = \frac{4.50-4.0}{(2.68/\sqrt{12})} = 0.65$$
    Do not reject H_0. Mean number of fish caught has not been shown to be greater than 4.0.

12. *a.* H_0: $\mu = 53$
    H_1: $\mu > 53$
    Reject H_0 if t > 1.761.
    $$t = \frac{56.4-53.0}{(3.7378/\sqrt{15})} = 3.52$$
    Reject H_0. The mean number of surveys conducted is greater than 53.

13. *a.* Reject H_0 if $t < -2.120$ or $t > 2.120$.

  b.

  $$s_p^2 = \frac{(10-1)4^2 + (8-1)5^2}{10 + 8 - 2}$$

  $$= 19.9375$$

  c.

  $$t = \frac{23 - 26}{\sqrt{19.9375(1/10 + 1/8)}} = -1.416$$

  d. Do not reject H_0.

14. *a.* Reject H_0 if $t < -1.697$ or $t > 1.697$.

  b.

  $$s_p^2 = \frac{(15-1)\,12^2 + (17-1)15^2}{15 + 17 + -2} = 187.20$$

  c.

  $$t = \frac{350 - 342}{\sqrt{187.20(1/15 + 1/17)}} = 1.65$$

  d. Do not reject H_0.

15. H_0: $\mu_1 = \mu_2$
  H_1: $\mu_1 < \mu_2$
  Reject H_0 if $t < -2.624$.

  $$s_1^2 = \frac{55{,}476 - (702)^2/9}{9 - 1} \qquad s_2^2 = \frac{43{,}971 - (553)^2/7}{7 - 1}$$

  $$= 90 \qquad\qquad\qquad = 47.33$$

  $$s_p^2 = \frac{(9-1)(90) + (7-1)(47.33)}{9 + 7 - 2} = 71.71$$

  $$t = \frac{78 - 79}{\sqrt{71.71(1/9 + 1/7)}} = -0.234$$

  Do not reject H_0. There is no difference in the mean grades.

16. H_0: $\mu_1 = \mu_2$
  H_1: $\mu_1 \neq \mu_2$
  Reject H_0 if $t < -2.052$ or $t > 2.052$.

  $$s_p^2 = \frac{(16-1)(20) + (13-1)(18)}{16 + 13 - 2} = 19.1111$$

  $$t = \frac{300 - 305}{\sqrt{19.111(1/16 + 1/13)}} = -3.06$$

  Reject H_0. There is a difference in the mean scores.

17. H_0: $\mu_1 = \mu_2$
  H_1: $\mu_1 > \mu_2$
  Reject H_0 if $t > 1.301$.

  $$t = \frac{89 - 87}{\sqrt{26.667(1/22 + 1/25)}} = 1.325$$

  Reject H_0. The mean pollen count in the valley is greater than in the mountains.

18. H_0: $\mu_1 = \mu_2$
  H_1: $\mu_1 \neq \mu_2$
  Reject H_0 if $t < -3.012$ or $t > 3.012$
  $s_p^2 = 44.35$

  $$t = \frac{66.0 - 65.5}{\sqrt{44.3457(1/5 + 1/10)}} = 0.137$$

  Do not reject H_0. There is no difference in the mean speeds.

19. *a.* Reject H_0 if $t > 2.353$.
  b. $\bar{d} = 3.000$
     $s_d = 0.816$
  c.

  $$t = \frac{\bar{d}}{s_d/\sqrt{n}} = \frac{3}{.816/\sqrt{4}} = 7.353$$

  d. Reject H_0. The review session was effective.

20. *a.* Reject H_0 if $t < -2.776$ or $t > 2.776$.
  b. $\bar{d} = 4.60$
     $s_d = 1.517$
  c.

  $$t = \frac{\bar{d}}{s_d/\sqrt{n}} = \frac{4.60}{1.517/\sqrt{5}} = 6.780$$

  d. Reject H_0. The movie affected their knowledge of the outdoors.

21. H_0: $\mu_d = 0$
  H_1: $\mu_d > 0$
  Reject H_0 if $t > 2.764$.
  $\bar{d} = 7.3636$, $s_d = 8.3699$.

  $$t = \frac{7.3636}{(8.3699/\sqrt{11})} = 2.92$$

  Reject H_0. The weights have increased.

22. H_0: $\mu_d = 0$
  H_1: $\mu_d > 0$
  Reject H_0 if $t > 1.796$.
  $\bar{d} = 25.917$, $s_d = 40.791$.

  $$t = \frac{25.917}{40.791/\sqrt{12}} = 2.20$$

  Reject H_0. The incentive plan resulted in an increase in daily income. The p-value is about .025.

23. H_0: $\mu_d = 0$
 H_1: $\mu_d > 0$
 Reject H_0 if t > 2.821.
 $\bar{d} = .10$, $s_d = 4.28$.

 $t = \dfrac{0.10}{4.28/\sqrt{10}} = 0.07$

 Fail to reject H_0. There has been no reduction.

24. H_0: $\mu_d = 0$
 H_1: $\mu_d < 0$
 Reject H_0 if t < -2.998.
 $\bar{d} = -3.625$, $s_d = 4.8346$.

 $t = \dfrac{-3,625}{4.8346/\sqrt{8}} = -2.12$

 Do not reject H_0. The p-value is about .035.

25. H_0: $\mu = 87$
 H_1: $\mu < 87$
 Reject H_0 if t < -1.895.

 $s = \sqrt{\dfrac{55,244 - (664)^2/8}{8-1}} = 4.3425$

 $\bar{X} = \dfrac{664}{8} = 83.0$

 $t = \dfrac{83-87}{4.3425/\sqrt{8}} = -2.61$

 Reject H_0. The mileage is less than advertised.

26. H_0: $\mu = 235$
 H_1: $\mu > 235$
 Reject H_0 if t > 2.821.

 $t = \dfrac{240-235}{(11/\sqrt{10})} = 1.44$

 Do not reject H_0. The mean weight has not increased from 235 pounds.

27. H_0: $\mu = 42$
 H_1: $\mu > 42$
 Reject H_0 if t > 1.796.

 $t = \dfrac{51-42}{8/\sqrt{12}} = 3.90$

 Reject H_0. The mean time for delivery is more than 42 days.

28. H_0: $\mu = 9$
 H_1: $\mu > 9$
 Reject H_0 if t > 2.998.
 $\bar{X} = 9.488$, s = .467.

 $t = \dfrac{9.488-9.00}{.467/\sqrt{8}} = 2.95$

 Do not reject H_0. The mean prime rate for small banks is 9.0 percent.

29. H_0: $\mu = 2.25$
 H_1: $\mu \neq 2.25$
 Reject H_0 if t < -2.201 or t > 2.201.
 $\bar{X} = 2.087$, s = .4048.

 $t = \dfrac{2.087-2.25}{0.4048/\sqrt{12}} = -1.403$

 Do not reject H_0. There is not a difference in the amount of coffee consumed at Northwestern State.

30. H_0: $\mu_1 = \mu_2$
 H_1: $\mu_1 \neq \mu_2$
 Reject H_0 if t < -2.060 or t > 2.060.

 $s_p^2 = \dfrac{(15-1)(2.6)^2 + (12-1)(3.3)^2}{15+12-2} = 8.5772$

 $t = \dfrac{17.6-16.2}{\sqrt{8.5772(1/15 + 1/12)}} = 1.23$

 Do not reject H_0. There is no difference in the mean percent of the two health packages.

31. $H_0: \mu_1 = \mu_2$
    $H_1: \mu_1 > \mu_2$
    Reject H_0 if $t > 2.567$.

    $$s_p^2 = \frac{(8-1)(2.2638)^2 + (11-1)(2.4606)^2}{8 + 11 - 2} = 5.672$$

    $$t = \frac{10.375 - 5.636}{\sqrt{5.672\,(1/8 + 1/11)}} = 4.28$$

    Reject H_0. The mean number of transactions by the young adults is more for than the senior citizens.

32. $H_0: \mu_1 = \mu_2$
    $H_1: \mu_1 > \mu_2$
    Reject H_0 if $t > 2.056$.

    $$s_p^2 = \frac{(15-1)(0.25)^2 + (13-1)(0.20)^2}{15 + 13 - 2} = .0521$$

    $$t = \frac{0.29}{\sqrt{0.0521\,(1/15 + 1/13)}} = 3.35$$

    Reject H_0. The 10-10-40 group has greater mean height.

33. $H_0: \mu_1 = \mu_2$
    $H_1: \mu_1 \neq \mu_2$
    Reject H_0 if $t < -2.528$ or $t > 2.528$.

    $$t = \frac{160 - 162}{\sqrt{2.30\,(1/10) + 1/12}} = -3.08$$

    Reject H_0. The mean ratings are not the same.

34. $H_0: \mu_d = 0$
    $H_1: \mu_d \neq 0$
    Reject H_0 if $t < -2.201$ or $t > 2.201$.
    $\bar{d} = 0.0833$, $s_d = 5.143$.

    $$t = \frac{0.0833}{5.143/\sqrt{12}} = 0.056$$

    Do not reject H_0. There is no difference in output between the two.

35. $H_0: \mu_d = 0$
    $H_1: \mu_d < 0$
    Reject H_0 if $t < -2.998$.
    $\bar{d} = -2.50$, $s_d = 2.928$.

    $$t = \frac{-2.5}{2.928/\sqrt{8}} = -2.42$$

    Do not reject H_0. The mean number of accidents has not changed.

36. $H_0: \mu_1 - \mu_2 = \$10$; $\mu_1 - \mu_2 > \$10$. $df = 15 + 10 - 2 = 23$. Let population 1 be Saturday shoppers. H_0 is rejected if $t > 1.714$. $s_1 = 22.34$, $\bar{X}_1 = 67.36$. $s_2 = 24.26$, $\bar{X}_2 = 50.35$. $s_p^2 = 534.0863$.

    $$t = \frac{7.01}{\sqrt{534.0863\left(\frac{1}{15} + \frac{1}{10}\right)}} = 0.74$$

    The null hypothesis is not rejected. Shoppers are not spending $10 more on Saturdays than on weekdays.

37. $H_0: \mu = 3.5$, $H_1 \ \mu < 3.5$ $df = 16$, critical value $= -1.746$.
    computed $t = \dfrac{2.9553 - 3.5}{.55955/\sqrt{16}} = -4.01$

    Reject H_0. Games last less than 3.5 hours on the average.

38. $H_0: \mu = 10$, $H_1: \mu > 10$ $df = 14$. Reject H_0 if $t > 1.761$.
    $t = .9878$, found by

    $$\frac{12.4 - 10}{9.40972/\sqrt{15}}$$

    Do not reject H_0. The justices spend 10 years on the bench.

39. *a.* μ_1 = without pool, μ_2 = with pool. Critical value = ± 2.000, df = 73. $\bar{X}_1$ = 152.697, s_1 = 26.5137.
$\bar{X}_2$ = 175.487, s_2 = 38.0921. Computed t = −2.817, p = .006.
Reject H_0 indicating that the mean selling price of a home with a pool is significantly greater than one without a pool.

b. $\bar{X}_1$ = 138.071 without a garage, 180.135 with garage, critical value = ± 2.000, computed value of t = 5.680. Reject H_0. p = .000. Home with garage costs more.

c. H_0:$\mu_1 = \mu_2$, H_1:$\mu_1 \neq \mu_2$, df = $n_1 + n_2 - 2$ = 12 + 15 − 2 = 25. Reject H_0 if t < −2.060 or t > 2.060. $\bar{X}_1$ = 148.64, s_1 = 24.61, $\bar{X}_2$ = 172.69, and s_2 = 34.29

$$s_p^2 = \frac{(11)(24.61)^2 + 14(34.29)^2}{12 + 15 - 2} = 924.94$$

$$t = \frac{148.64 - 172.69}{\sqrt{924.94\left(\frac{1}{12} + \frac{1}{15}\right)}} = -2.042$$

Do not reject H_0.

40. *a.* H_0:$\mu_n = \mu_t$, H_1:$\mu_n < \mu_t$. Reject H_0 if t < −1.711.
$\bar{X}_n$ = 115.9, s_n = 28.9, $\bar{X}_t$ = 139.0, and s_t = 31.4
t = −1.88
H_0 is rejected. Natural surface teams hit fewer home runs than team playing on turf.

b. H_0:$\mu_n = \mu_a$ H_1 $\mu_n > \mu_a$. Reject H_0 if t > 1.711
t = 1.95. Reject H_0. National League teams steal more bases.

c. H_0:$\mu_n = \mu_a$; H_1:$\mu_n \neq \mu_a$. Reject H_1 if t < −2.064 or t < −2.064. t = 0.28. H_0 is not rejected. Salaries per team do not differ.

d. H_0:$\mu_n = \mu_a$ H_1:$\mu_n \neq \mu_a$. Reject H_1 if t < −2.064 or t > 2.064. t = 0.88. H_0 is not rejected. There is no difference in the mean attendance.

CHAPTER 12:   ANALYSIS OF VARIANCE

1. 9.01 from Appendix G.

2. 9.78

3. Reject H_0 if $F > 10.5$, where df in numerator are 7 and 5 in the denominator. Computed $F = 2.04$, found by:

$$F = \frac{s_1^2}{s_2^2} = \frac{(10)^{2)}}{(7)^2} = 2.04$$

Do not reject H_0. There is no difference in the variations of the two populations.

4. Reject H_0 where $F > 9.15$, where df in numerator are 4 and 6 in the denominator. Computed $F = 2.94$, found by:

$$F = \frac{s_1^2}{s_2^2} = \frac{(12)^{2)}}{(7)^2} = 2.94$$

Do not reject H_0. There is no difference in the variations of the two populations.

5. $H_0: \sigma_1^2 = \sigma_2^2$
$H_1: \sigma_1^2 \neq \sigma_2^2$
Reject H_0 where $F > 3.10$. (3.10 is about halfway between 3.14 and 3.07.) Computed $F = 1.44$, found by:

$$F = \frac{(12)^2}{(10)^2} = 1.44$$

Do not reject H_0. There is no difference in the variations of the two populations.

6. $H_0: \sigma_1^2 = \sigma_2^2$
$H_1: \sigma_1^2 \neq \sigma_2^2$
Reject H_0 when $F > 3.68$. Computed $F = 1.24$, found by:

$$F = \frac{(3.9)^2}{(3.5)^2} = 1.24$$

Do not reject H_0. The variation in the stocks is the same.

7. a. $H_0: \mu_1 = \mu_2 = \mu_3 = \mu_4$
        H_1: The treatment means are not the same.
    b. Reject H_0 when $F > 3.49$.
    c. SST = 63.19, SSE = 13.75, and SS total = 76.94.
    d. | Source | SS | df | MS | F |
        |---|---|---|---|---|
        | Treatment | 63.19 | 3 | 21.06 | 18.38 |
        | Error | 13.75 | 12 | 1.15 | |
        | Total | 76.94 | 15 | | |
    e. Reject H_0: $18.38 > 3.49$.

8. *a.* $H_0: \mu_1 = \mu_2 = \mu_3$
   H_1: Not all treatment means are the same.
   b. Reject H_0 where $F > 3.68$
   c. SST = 66.34, SSE = 90.16, SS total = 156.5
   d.

Source	SS	df	MS	F
Treatment	66.34	2	33.17	5.52
Error	90.16	15	6.01	
Total	156.50	17		

   e. Reject H_0. The treatment means differ.

9. $H_0: \mu_1 = \mu_2 = \mu_3$; H_1: Not all treatment means are the same. H_0 is rejected if $F > 4.26$.

   $$\text{SS total} = 20{,}783 - \frac{(495)^2}{12} = 364.25$$

   $$\text{SST} = \frac{(142)^2}{4} + \frac{(164)^2}{4} + \frac{(189)^2}{4} - \frac{(495)^2}{12} = 276.5$$

   SSE = 364.25 − 276.50 = 87.75

Source	SS	df	MS	F
Treatment	276.50	2	138.25	14.18
Error	87.75	9	9.75	
Total	364.25	11		

   Since 14.18 > 4.26, H_0 is rejected. Not all treatment means are the same.

10. $H_0: \mu_1 = \mu_2 = \mu_3$
    H_1: Not all means are the same.
    Reject H_0 where $F > 3.89$.

    $$\text{SS total} = 1{,}280 - \frac{(136)^2}{15} = 46.93$$

    $$\text{SST} = \frac{(54)^2}{5} + \frac{(40)^2}{5} + \frac{(42)^2}{5} - \frac{(136)^2}{15} = 22.93$$

    SSE = 46.93 − 22.93 = 24.00

Source	SS	df	MS	F
Treatment	22.93	2	11.4650	5.7325
Error	24.00	12	2.0	
Total	46.93			

    Reject H_0, 5.7325 > 3.89. The mean number of hours spent on a terminal are not all equal.

11. *a.* $H_0: \mu_1 = \mu_2 = \mu_3$
    H_1: Not all means are the same.
    b. Reject H_0 where $F > 4.26$.
    c. SST = 107.20, SSE = 9.47, SS total = 116.67
    d.

Source	SS	df	MS	F
Treatment	107.20	2	53.600	50.96
Error	9.47	9	1.052	
Total	116.67	11		

e. Since 50.96 > 4.26, H_0 is rejected. At least one of the means differ.

f. $(\bar{X}_1 - \bar{X}_2) \pm t\sqrt{MSE(1/n_1 + 1/n_2)}$
$(9.667 - 2.20) \pm 2.262\sqrt{1.052(1/3 + 1/5)}$
7.467 ± 1.69
[5.777, 9.157] Yes, we can conclude that the treatments 1 and 2 are different.

12. a. $H_0: \mu_1 = \mu_2 = \mu_3$
H_0: Not all means are the same
b. Reject H_0 where $F > 3.47$.
c. SST = 46.96, SSE = 53.00, SS total = 99.96.

d.
Source	SS	df	MS	F
Treatment	46.96	2	23.48	9.30
Error	53.00	21	2.52	
Total	99.96	23		

e. Since 9.30 > 3.47, reject H_0. At least one of the means differ.

f. $(\bar{X}_1 - \bar{X}_2) \pm t\sqrt{MSE(1/n_1 + 1/n_2)}$
$(6.0 - 4.25) \pm 2.080\sqrt{2.52(1/10 + 1/8)}$
1.75 ± 1.57
[0.18, 3.32] Yes, we can conclude that treatments 2 and 3 are different.

13. $H_0: \mu_1 = \mu_2 = \mu_3 = \mu_4$; H_1: Not all means are equal. H_0 is rejected if $F > 3.71$.

$$SS\ total = 2{,}444 - \frac{(182)^2}{14} = 78.00$$

$$SST = \frac{(48)^2}{4} + \frac{(46)^2}{4} + \frac{(46)^2}{3} + \frac{(42)^2}{3}$$

$$- \frac{(182)^2}{14} = 32.33$$

SSE = 78.00 − 32.33 = 45.67

Source	SS	df	MS	F
Treatment	32.33	3	10.77	2.36
Error	45.67	10	4.567	
Total	78.00	13		

Since 2.36 is less than 3.71, H_0 is not rejected. There is no difference in the mean number of weeks.

14. $H_0: \mu_1 = \mu_2 = \mu_3$; H_1: At least one mean differs. H_0 is rejected if $F > 3.81$
SS total = 129.44. SST = 86.49. SSE = 42.95

Source	SS	df	MS	F
Treatment	86.49	2	43.245	13.09
Error	42.95	13	3.3038	
Total	129.44	15		

Since 13.09 > 3.81, H_0 is rejected. At least one mean rate of return differs.

b. $(17.40 - 11.62) \pm 2.160$
$\sqrt{3.3038(1/5 + 1/5)} = 5.78 \pm 2.48$
[3.30, 8.26] These treatment means differ.

15. a. $H_0: \mu_1 = \mu_2$
H_1: Not all treatment means are equal.
b. Reject H_0 where $F > 18.5$
c. $H_0: \mu_1 = \mu_2 = \mu_3$; H_0: Not all block means are equal.
H_0 is rejected if $F > 19.0$.

$$SST = \frac{(127)^2}{3} + \frac{(92)^2}{3} - \frac{(219)^2}{6} = 204.167$$

$$SSB = \frac{(77)^2}{2} + \frac{(63)^2}{2} + \frac{(79)^2}{2} - \frac{(219)^2}{6} = 76$$

SS total = 8,283 − (219)²/6 = 289.5
SSE = 289.5 − 204.167 − 76 = 9.333

e.
Source	SS	df	MS	F
Treatment	204.167	1	204.167	43.75
Blocks	76.000	2	38.000	8.14
Error	9.333	2	4.667	
Total	289.5000	5		

f. 43.75 > 18.5, so reject H_0. There is a difference in the treatments. 8.14 < 19.0, so fail to reject H_0 for blocks. There is no difference between blocks.

16. a. $H_0: \mu_1 = \mu_2 = \mu_3$
H_1: Not all treatment means are equal.
b. Reject H_0 when $F > 6.94$
c. $H_0: \mu_1 = \mu_2 = \mu_3$
H_1: Not all block means are equal.
Reject H_0 where $F > 6.94$

$$SST = \frac{(28)^2}{3} + \frac{(33)^2}{3} + \frac{(25)^2}{3} - \frac{(86)^2}{9} = 10.889$$

$$SSB = \frac{(34)^2}{3} + \frac{(29)^2}{3} + \frac{(23)^2}{3} - \frac{(86)^2}{9} = 20.222$$

SS total = 864 − (86)²/9 = 42.222
SSE = 42.222 − 20.222 − 10.889 = 11.111

e.
Source	SS	df	MS	F
Treatment	10.889	2	5.444	1.96
Blocks	20.222	2	10.111	3.64
Error	11.111	4	2.778	
Total	42.222	8		

f. 1.96 < 6.94, so fail to reject H_0. There is no difference in the treatments. 3.64 < 6.94, so fail to reject H_0. There is no difference between blocks.

17. For treatment

$H_0: \mu_1 = \mu_2 = \mu_3$

H_1: Not all means equal

Reject if $F > 4.46$

For blocks

$H_0: \mu_1 = \mu_2 = \mu_3 = \mu_4 = \mu_5$

H_1: Not all means equal

Reject if $F > 3.84$

SS total = 139.73, SST = 62.53, SSB = 33.73, SSE = 43.47.

e.

Source	SS	df	MS	F
Treatment	62.53	2	31.265	5.75
Blocks	33.73	4	8.4325	1.55
Error	43.47	8	5.4338	
Total	139.73			

There is a difference in shifts, but not by employee.

18. For treatment

$H_0: \mu_1 = \mu_2 = \mu_3$

H_1: Not all means equal.

For blocks

$H_0: \mu_1 = \mu_2 = \mu_3 = \mu_4 = \mu_5$

H_1: Not all means equal.

Rejection rules:

H_0 where $F > 4.46$ H_0 where $F > 3.84$

SS total = $6{,}172 - (298)^2/15 = 251.73$

SST = $[(88)^2/5] + [(112)^2/5] + [(98)^2/5] - [(298)^2/15]$

    = 58.13

SSB = $(56)^2/3 + \ldots + (72)^2/3 - (298)^2/15$

75.73

SSE = $251.73 - 58.13 - 75.73 = 117.87$

Source	SS	df	MS	F
Treatment	58.13	2	29.0650	1.97
Blocks	75.73	4	18.9325	1.29
Error	117.87	8	14.73	
	251.73	14		

Since $1.96 < 4.46$ the H_0 for treatments is not rejected. Likewise, since $1.29 < 3.84$ H_0 for blocks is not rejected. There is no difference in the mean number of surgeries by hospital or by day of the week.

19. $H_0: \mu_1 = \mu_2 = \mu_3$; H_1: Not all means are equal. H_0 is rejected if $F > 3.89$.

SS total = 37.73, SST = 26.13, SSE = 11.60

Source	SS	df	MS	F
Treatment	26.13	2	13.067	13.52
Error	11.60	12	0.967	
Total	37.73	14		

Reject H_0 since $13.52 > 3.89$. There is a difference in the mean weight loss among the three diets.

20. $H_0: \mu_1 = \mu_2 = \mu_3 = \mu_4$; H_1: Not all means are equal. Reject H_0 if $F > 3.10$

Source	df	SS	MS	F
Factor	3	87.79	29.26	9.12
Error	20	64.17	3.21	
Total	23	151.96		

Since computed F of $9.12 > 3.10$, the null hypothesis of no difference is rejected at the .05 level. At least one mean differs.

21. a. $H_0: \mu_1 = \mu_2 = \mu_3$; H_1: Not all means are equal. H_0 is rejected if $F > 3.68$.

SS total $= 16{,}608 - \dfrac{(542)^2}{18} = 287.7778$

SST $= \dfrac{(233)^2}{7} + \dfrac{(167)^2}{6} + \dfrac{(142)^2}{5} - \dfrac{(542)^2}{18}$

    = 116.3187

SSE = $287.7778 - 116.3187 = 171.4591$

$F = 5.09$. Therefore, H_0 is rejected because $5.09 > 3.68$. Perfectionism scores differ depending on the size of the city.

b. Yes, because both endpoints are positive. $(33.29 - 28.4) \pm 2.131 \sqrt{11.43(1/7 + 1/5)} = 0.67$ and 9.11.

The mean perfectionism score for those from a rural bakground differs from those from urban areas.

22. a. $H_0: \mu_1 = \mu_2 = \mu_3$; H_1: At least one mean differs. SS total = 9.09. SST = 6.45. SSE = 2.64. H_0 is rejected if $F > 4.26$.

Source	SS	df	MS	F
Treatment	6.45	2	3.225	10.99
Error	2.64	9	0.2933	
Total	9.09	11		

H_0 is rejected. At least one mean differs.

b. Giorgio East and Giorgio West do not differ. Giorgio East and Giorgio South differ. Giorgio West and Giorgio South differ, found by:

$(2.5 - 4.24) \pm 2.262 \sqrt{0.2933\left(\dfrac{1}{3} + \dfrac{1}{5}\right)}$

    $= -1.74 \pm .89$

23.

Source	SS	df	Mean square	F
Treatment	320	2	160	8.00
Error	180	9	20	
Total	500	11		

a. 3.

b. 12.

c. 4.26.

d. $H_0: \mu_1 = \mu_2 = \mu_3$; H_1: Not all means are equal.

e. H_0 is rejected. The treatment means differ.

24. $H_0: \mu_1 = \mu_2$; $H_1: \mu_1 \neq \mu_2$. Critical value of $F = 4.75$. SS total $= 333.4286$. SST $= 219.4286$. SSE $= 114.0000$.

Source	SS	df	Mean Square	F
Treatment	219.4286	1	219.4286	23.10
Error	114.0000	12	9.5	
	333.4286	13		

$$t = \frac{19-27}{\sqrt{9.51\left(\frac{1}{6} + \frac{1}{8}\right)}} = -4.80$$

Then $t^2 = F$. That is $(-4.80)^2 \approx 23.10$ (actually 23.04. Difference due to rounding)

25. a. Recall that $\bar{X} = \Sigma X/n$, so $\bar{X}(n) = \Sigma X$. For the first treatment $\bar{X}(n) = 51.32(10)$, so $\Sigma X = 513.2$. SST is 300.65 found by

$$SST = \frac{(513.2)^2}{10} + \frac{(446.4)^2}{10} + \frac{(472.0)^2}{10} + \frac{(508.5)^2}{10} - \frac{(1940.1)^2}{40}$$

$= 300.645$

b. $650.75 - 300.645 = 350.105$

c.
Source	SS	df	MS	F
Treatment	300.645	3	100.215	10.304
Error	350.105	36	9.725	
Total	650.750			

d. $10.304 > 2.89$, so reject H_0. There is a difference in the treatment means.

e. $(51.32 - 50.85) \pm 2.03 \sqrt{9.725(1/10 + 1/10)}$
0.470 ± 2.831
$[-2.361, 3.301]$ We can not conclude that the number of minutes of music differ between $\bar{X}_1$ and $\bar{X}_4$.

26. $H_0: \mu_1 = \mu_2 = \mu_3 = \mu_4$
H_1: Not all means are the same
Reject H_0 where $F > 2.92$ (or 2.89 interpolated)
SS total $= 127.75$
SST $= 29.80$
SSE $= 97.96$

Source	SS	df	MS	F
Treatment	29.80	3	9.93	3.35
Error	97.96	33	2.97	
	127.75	36		

Reject H_0, $3.35 > 2.92$. There is a difference in the mean amount spent by the groups.

27. SS total $= 22.59$ SST $= 3.92$,
    SSB $= 10.21$,   SSE $= 8.46$

For cars	For gasoline
$H_0: \mu_1 = \mu_2 = \mu_3$	$H_0: \mu_1 = \mu_2 = \mu_3 = \mu_4$
H_1: Means not equal	H_1: Means not equal
H_0: is rejected if $F > 5.14$	H_0: is rejected if $F > 4.76$

Source	SS	df	Mean square	F
Treatment	3.92	2	1.96	1.39
Blocks	10.21	3	3.40	2.41
Error	8.46	6	1.41	
Total	22.59	11		

a. There is no difference between the types of gasoline because 2.41 is less than 4.76.
b. There is no difference in the cars because 1.39 is less than 5.14.

28. For color the critical value of F is 4.76, for size it is 5.14

Source	SS	df	Mean Square	F
Treatment	25.0	3	8.3333	5.88
Blocks	21.5	2	10.75	7.59
Error	8.5	6	1.4167	
Total	55.0	11		

H_0 for both treatments and blocks (color and size) is rejected. At least one mean differs for color and at least one mean differs for size.

29. *a.* $H_0: \mu_1 = \mu_2 = \mu_3 = \mu_4$. Reject if $F > 3.29$
Do not reject H_0 because computed F (2.865) is less than 3.29.
b. $H_0: \mu_1 = \mu_2 = \mu_3 = \mu_4 = \mu_5 = \mu_6$. Reject if $F > 2.90$.

Source	SS	df	MS	F
Treat	31533.00	3	10511	2.865
Blocks	35402.83	5	7080.57	1.930
Error	55033.5	15	3668.90	
Total	121969.5	23		

For a and b, do not reject H_0. There is no difference in the mean by location or by week.

30. *a.* Critical value of F is 3.49. Computed F is .668. Do not reject H_0.
b. Critical value of F is 3.26. Computed F value is 100.204. Reject H_0 for block means.

31. $H_0: \mu_1 = \mu_2 = \mu_3$; H_1: The means are not all equal. Critical value of $F = 3.44$.
From MINITAB:
ANALYSIS OF VARIANCE

Source	df	SS	MS	F
Factor	2	3872	1936	10.18
Error	22	4182	190	
Total	24	8054		

Since the computed value of 10.18 exceeds the critical value of 3.44, the null hypothesis is rejected and the alternate is accepted. At least one mean is different. The mean salary for those with high school or less is $49,000, it is $74,670 for those with an undergraduate degree, and $78,330 for those with a Master's degree or more. The salary for those with only high school differs from both the other groups. The salaries for those with college work do not differ. The confidence interval for the difference between high school and undergraduate is computed as follows.

$$(49.00 - 74.67) \pm 2.074 \sqrt{190\left(\frac{1}{4} + \frac{1}{9}\right)}$$

$$= -25.67 \pm 14.41$$

for $\bar{X}_1$ and $\bar{X}_3$: $(\bar{X}_1 - \bar{X}_3) \pm 2.074 \sqrt{190\left(\frac{1}{7} + \frac{1}{9}\right)} =$

$$-29.333 \pm 14.41$$

32. $H_0: \mu_1 = \mu_2 = \mu_3 = \mu_4$; H_1: The means are not all equal. Critical value of $F = 2.90$.
From MINITAB:
ANALYSIS OF VARIANCE

Source	df	SS	MS	F
Factor	3	34.6	11.5	0.71
Error	34	555.5	16.3	
Total	37	590.1		

H_0 is not rejected. There is no difference in the mean salaries.

33. $H_0: \mu_1 = \mu_2 = \mu_3 = \mu_4 = \mu_5$. H_1: At least one mean differs. H_0 is rejected if computed $F > 3.83$, or 3.78 if interpolated.
ANALYSIS OF VARIANCE

Source	df	SS	MS	F
Factor	4	2.68	0.67	0.11
Error	45	281.40	6.25	
Total	49	284.08		

The null hypothesis is not rejected. There is no difference in the mean age.

34. *a.* $H_0: \sigma_p^2 = \sigma_{np}^2$, $H_1: \sigma_p^2 \neq \sigma_{np}^2$. Reject H_0 if F is greater than 2.28 based on 45 and 28 degrees of freedom. The computed value of F is 2.064, found by $(38.09)^2/(26.51)^2$. H_0 is not rejected. The sample size and standard deviations are computed as follows using MINITAB.

```
MTB    > table c4;
 SUBC> standard c1;
 SUBC> n c1.
 ROWS: Pool
           Price    Price
          STD DEV    N
   0      26.51     29
   1      38.09     46
  ALL     35.68     75
```

b. $H_0: \sigma_g^2 = \sigma_{ng}^2$. $H_1: \sigma_g^2 \neq \sigma_{ng}^2$. Reject H_0 if $F > 2.50$ (50,23 degrees of freedom). The computed F is 2.614, found by $(33.34)^2/(20.62)^2$. H_0 is rejected. There is a difference in the variation of the selling price of homes with a garage and those without a garage.

```
MTB    > table c7;
 SUBC> standard c1;
 SUBC> n c1.
 ROWS: Garage
           Price    Price
          STD DEV    N
   0      20.62     24
   1      33.34     51
  ALL     35.68     75
```

c. H_0: $\mu_1 = \mu_2 = \mu_3 = \mu_4 = \mu_5$. H_1: means not all equal. Critical value $F_{4,70} = 2.28$. Computed value of $F = 1.65$. Do not reject H_0. There is no difference in the mean selling price in the few townships.

ANALYSIS OF VARIANCE ON Price

SOURCE	DF	SS	MS	F	p
Twnship	4	5322	1330	1.05	0.389
ERROR	70	88895	1270		
TOTAL	74	94217			

35. Comparing the 200 companies on assets.
H_0 $\mu_1 = \mu_2 = \mu_3$; H_1: Not all means are equal. Reject if $F > 3.00$. There are 8 companies that lost money, 141 that made up to $750 million, and 51 that made more than $750 million. The MINITAB output is as follows:

Source	SS	df	MS	F
Effect	23.2489	2	11.689	12.046
Error	190.0889	197	.9689	
Total	213.3289	199		

36. a. Winning percent. H_0: $\mu_1 = \mu_2 = \mu_3$. H_1: means not all equal. Critical value of $F = 3.42$, computed value $= 4.737$. H_0 is rejected.

b. For home runs: Critical value $= 3.42$, Computed value 4.171. Reject H_0.

c. For stolen bases: Critical value of $F = 3.42$ Computed value of $F = .1827$

Source	SS	df	MS	F
Effect	645.84	2	322.922	.1827
Error	40657.27	23	1767.71	
Total	41303.11	25		

It would seem that the teams that win more frequently or hit more home runs have greater attendance. However, stolen bases does not relate to attendance.

CHAPTER 13:   SIMPLE CORRELATION ANALYSIS

1. | X | Y | X^2 | XY | Y^2 |
|---|---|---|---|---|
| 4 | 4 | 16 | 16 | 16 |
| 5 | 6 | 25 | 30 | 36 |
| 3 | 5 | 9 | 15 | 25 |
| 6 | 7 | 36 | 42 | 49 |
| 10 | 7 | 100 | 70 | 49 |
| 28 | 29 | 186 | 173 | 175 |

$$r = \frac{5(173) - (28)(29)}{\sqrt{[5(186) - (28)^2][5(175) - (29)^2]}}$$

$$= \frac{53}{\sqrt{(146)(34)}} = 0.75$$

The 0.75 coefficient indicates a rather strong positive correlation between X and Y.

2. | X | Y | X^2 | XY | Y^2 |
|---|---|---|---|---|
| 5 | 13 | 25 | 65 | 169 |
| 3 | 15 | 9 | 45 | 225 |
| 6 | 7 | 36 | 42 | 49 |
| 3 | 12 | 9 | 36 | 144 |
| 4 | 13 | 16 | 52 | 169 |
| 4 | 11 | 16 | 44 | 121 |
| 6 | 9 | 36 | 54 | 81 |
| 8 | 5 | 64 | 40 | 25 |
| 39 | 85 | 211 | 378 | 983 |

$$r = \frac{8(378) - (39)(85)}{\sqrt{[8(211) - (39)^2][8(983) - (85)^2]}}$$

$$= \frac{-291}{\sqrt{(167)(639)}} = -0.89$$

The -0.89 indicates a very strong negative relationship between X and Y.

3. *a.* Sales.
   b.

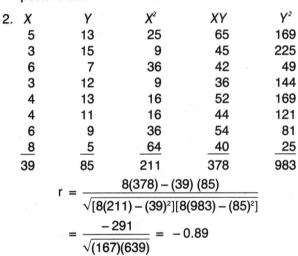

   c. Yes. There is a strong positive correlation.
   d. .93
   e. .93 indicates a strong positive correlation between the number of times the advertisement was aired and sales.

4. *a.*

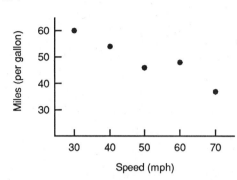

   b. Yes. A strong negative correlation. As speed increases miles per gallon decreases.
   c. r = $-.949$ indicating a very strong negative relationship between X and Y.

5. *a.* Efficiency rating.
   b.

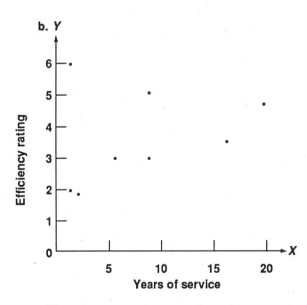

   c. There seems to be a weak positive correlation.
   d. .35, found by:

$$\frac{8(254) - (61)(30)}{\sqrt{[8(795) - (61)^2]\ [8(128) - (30)^2]}}$$

   e. .35 indicates a weak relationship.

6. *a.*

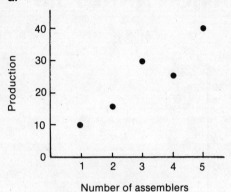

b. Yes. As the number of assemblers increases so does production. It appears that the relationship is linear.

c. $r = .927$, found by

$$\frac{5(430) - (15)(120)}{\sqrt{[5(55) - (15)^2][5(3,450) - (120)^2]}}$$

$$= \frac{350}{\sqrt{[50][2,850]}} = \frac{350}{377.49}$$

d. Very strong positive relationship.

7. $r^2 = (.75)^2 = .56$
coefficient of nondetermination $= 1 - .56 = .44$

8. $r^2 = (-.89)^2 = .79$
coefficient of nondetermination $= 1 - .79 = .21$

9. *a.* $r^2 = (.93)^2 = .86$
$1 - r^2 = 1 - .86 = .14$
b. The coefficient of determination of .86 is the proportion of the variation in sales explained by the number of advertisements; .14 is the proportion of the variation in sales not explained by the number of advertisements.

10. *a.* $r^2 = (-.949)^2 = .9006 = .90.$
$1 - r^2 = 1 - .90 = .10.$
b. .90 is the proportion of miles per gallon accounted for by the speed, .10 is the proportion not explained.

11. *a.* $r^2 = (.35)^2 = .12$
$1 - r^2 = 1 - .12 = .88$
b. .12 is the proportion of the variation in the efficiency rating that is accounted for by years of service; .88 is the proportion of the variation not accounted for by the years of service.

12. *a.* $r^2 = (.93)^2 = .86$
$1 - r^2 = 1 - .86 = .14$
b. .86 is the proportion of the variation that is explained by the number of assemblers; .14 is the proportion not explained by the number of assemblers.

13. Reject H_0 if $t > 1.812$.

$$t = \frac{.32\sqrt{12 - 2}}{\sqrt{1 - (.32)^2}} = 1.07$$

Do not reject H_0.

14. Reject H_0 if $t < -1.771$.

$$t = \frac{-.46\sqrt{15 - 2}}{\sqrt{1 - (-.46)^2}} = -1.86$$

Reject H_0.

15. $H_0: \rho = 0$
$H_1: \rho > 0$
Reject H_0 if $t > 2.552$. $df = 18$.

$$t = \frac{.78\sqrt{20 - 2}}{\sqrt{1 - (.78)^2}} = 5.28$$

Reject H_0. There is a positive correlation between gallons sold and the pump price.

16. $H_0: \rho = 0$
$H_1: \rho > 0$
Reject H_0 if $t > 1.734$. $df = 18$.

$$t = \frac{.86\sqrt{20 - 2}}{\sqrt{1 - (.86)^2}} = 7.15$$

Reject H_0. There is a correlation between assets and pretax profit.

17. *a.*

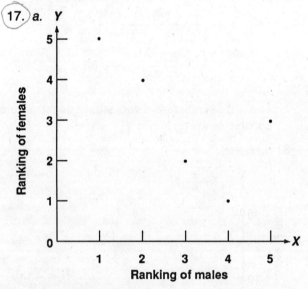

b. $-.70$, found by

$$1 - \frac{(6)(34)}{5(5^2 - 1)}$$

There is a rather strong, but inverse, relationship.

18. *a.*

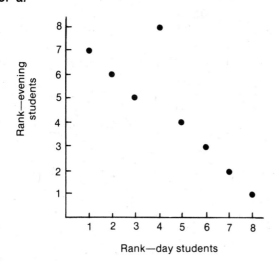

b. – .86, found by

X	Y	d	d²
6	3	3	9
7	2	5	25
2	6	– 4	16
5	4	1	1
1	7	– 6	36
4	8	– 4	16
3	5	– 2	4
8	1	7	49
		0	156

$$r_s = 1 - \frac{6(156)}{8(8^2 - 1)} = 1 - \frac{936}{504} = -.8571428$$

There is a strong (inverse) relationship between the two sets of ranks.

19. *a.* $r_s = -0.488$, found by

$$r_s = 1 - \frac{6(245.5)}{10(10^2 - 1)}$$

b. There is a moderate, but inverse, relationship.

20. *a.* $r_s = .842$, found by

$$r_s = 1 - \frac{6(26)}{10(10^2 - 1)}$$

b. There is a strong positive correlation.

21. *a.*

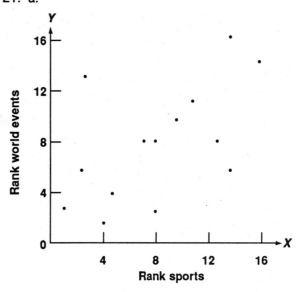

b. .49, found by

$$1 - \frac{6(234)}{14[(14)^2 - 1]}$$

c. No, the correlation in the population is not 0. Computed *t* = 1.95, found by

$$.49\sqrt{\frac{14 - 2}{1 - (.49)^2}}$$

Since 1.95 lies beyond the critical value of 1.782 (from appendix F), the null hypothesis that r_s in the population is 0 is rejected at the .05 level. (*df* = 12).

22. The activity rank, the error rank, the difference and the difference squared for the first five observations are:

a.
Activity Rank	Error Rank	Difference d	d²
1	4.0	– 3.0	9.0
2	1.0	1.0	1.0
3	2.0	1.0	1.0
4	9.5	– 5.5	30.25
5	5.0	0	0

$\Sigma d = 0. \ \Sigma d^2 = 1,049.50$

b.

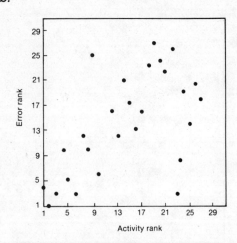

c. There is a moderate to strong relationship between the two sets of ranks.

d.
$$r_s = 1 - \frac{6(1,049.50)}{27[(27)^2 - 1]}$$

$$= 1 - 0.32$$

$$= .68$$

e. computing *t*:

$$t = .68\sqrt{\frac{27 - 2}{1 - (.68)^2}}$$

$$= 4.6$$

The null hypothesis that the rank correlation in the population = 0 is rejected at the .05 level because 4.6 lies in the rejection area beyond the critical value of 1.708.

f. The .68 indicates that there is a moderate to somewhat strong relationship between the degree of activity a warehouse has and error rate. That is, generally speaking the more active the warehouse the higher the error rate.

23. *a.* r = 0.589, found by MINITAB.
    b. $r^2 = 0.347$
    c. $H_0: \rho = 0$
       $H_1: \rho > 0$
       Reject H_0 if $t > 1.860$

$$t = \frac{.589\sqrt{10 - 2}}{\sqrt{1 - (.589)^2}} = 2.06$$

Reject H_0. Larger families spend more money on food.

24. *a.* r = 0.307.
    b. $r^2 = 0.094$
    c. $H_0: \rho = 0$
       $H_1: \rho > 0$
       Reject H_0 if $t > 1.812$, *df* = 10.

$$t = \frac{.307\sqrt{12 - 2}}{\sqrt{1 - (.094)}} = 1.02$$

Do not reject H_0. There is no correlation in the population.

25. $H_0: \rho = 0$
    $H_1: \rho < 0$
    Reject H_0 if $t < -1.701$, *df* = 28.

$$t = \frac{-.45\sqrt{30 - 2}}{\sqrt{1 - .2025}} = -2.67$$

Reject H_0. There is a negative correlation between the selling price and the number of miles driven.

26. $H_0: \rho = 0$.
    $H_1: \rho < 0$
    Reject H_0 if $t < -1.697$.

$$t = \frac{-.363\sqrt{32 - 2}}{\sqrt{1 - .1318}} = -2.13$$

Reject H_0. There is a negative association between square feet and rental rate.

27. *a.* r = .181, found by MINITAB
    b. $r^2 = .0328$.

28. *a.*

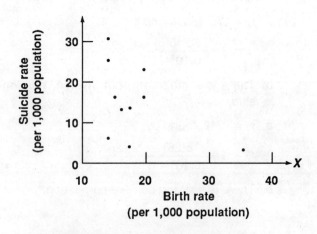

b. Rather weak negative relationship.
c. $r = -.47$; $r^2 = .22$; $1 - .22 = .78$.
d. Only 22 percent of the variation in suicide rate is explained by birth rate; 78 percent is not explained.

e. $t = -1.506$, found by

$$\frac{-.47\sqrt{10-2}}{\sqrt{1-(-.47)^2}}$$

Using the .01 level, and a two-tailed test, the critical value of t for 8 degrees of freedom is plus and minus 3.355. Since -1.506 lies in the acceptance region, we accept the null hypothesis that r in the population is zero.

29. a. $r = 0.291$
    b. $H_0: \rho = 0$
       $H_1: \rho > 0$
    Reject H_0 if $t > 1.684$

$$t = \frac{.291\sqrt{45-2}}{\sqrt{1-.085}} = 1.995$$

Reject H_0. Positive correlation exists between age and GPA.

30. a.

Academic performance	Rating for advancement	d	d²
2	1.5	0.5	0.25
7.5	8.5	-1.0	1.00
5.5	1.5	4.0	16.00
4	4.5	-0.5	0.25
9	7	2.0	4.00
7.5	4.5	3.0	9.00
2	4.5	-2.5	6.25
2	4.5	-2.5	6.25
5.5	8.5	-3.0	9.00
		0.0	52.00

b.

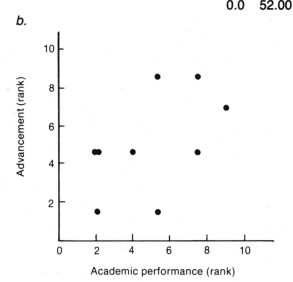

c. It appears that there is only a moderate relationship.

d.

$$1 - \frac{6(52)}{9(9^2-1)} = 1 - \frac{312}{720} = .5667,$$

or .532 using MINITAB and CSS STATISTICA

e. and f. H_0: The rank correlation in the population is zero; H_1: The rank correlation in the population is greater than zero. H_0 is rejected if $r_s > .60$ (.05 level) and $r_s > .783$ (.01 level). Since $r_s = .57$ H_0 is not rejected at either significance level. The rank correlation in the population could be zero.

31.

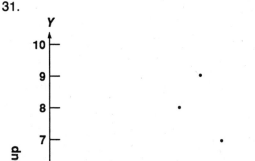
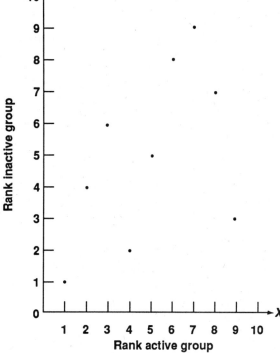

b. There is a moderate strong relationship.
c. .62, found by

$$1 - \frac{(6)(62)}{10[(10)^2-1]}$$

d. At the .01 level we accept H_0 because .62 is less than .746. We conclude that the correlation is 0.

   At the .05 level we reject H_0 because .62 is greater than .564. We conclude that the rank correlation in the population is not 0.

e. This illustrates that we accept H_0 at one level (.01), but we reject H_0 at the .05 level. The level of significance should be chosen before the experiment is conducted.

32. *a.* The correlation between starting position (a rank) and final position (also a rank) is 0.261.
    b. The correlation between the rank of the qualifying speed and order of finish is −0.231.
    c. For the rank correlation between starting position and final position.
    $H_0: \rho = 0$
    $H_1: \rho > 0$
    Reject H_0 if $t > 1.697$

    $$t = \frac{.261\sqrt{33-2}}{\sqrt{1-.068}} = 1.51$$

    Do not reject H_0. No positive rank correlation is shown.
    For the rank correlation between the rank of qualifying speed and the order of finish.
    $H_0: \rho = 0$
    $H_1: \rho < 0$
    Reject H_0 if $t < -1.697$

    $$t = \frac{-.231\sqrt{33-2}}{\sqrt{1-.053}} = -1.32$$

    Do not reject H_0. No negative rank correlation is shown. Note: If you interpret these as a two-tailed test, the decision rules change but not the decision.
    d. No positive association is shown between the ranks of the finish and the order of start. Further, the rank of the speeds and the order of finish are not shown to be associated.

33. $r = .9564$ (computed by CSS STATISTICA) $H_0: \rho = 0$; $H_1: \rho > 0$; df 18 critical value = 1.734 using the .05 level of significance. Computed $t = 13.83$. Reject H_0. There is a positive correlation between the number of calls and orders.

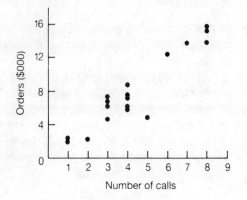

34. *a.* From MINITAB:
    MTB > corr c1 c3
    Correlation of Price and Size = 0.535. p-value = .0000.
    $H_0: \rho = 0$, $H_1: \rho > 0$ $df = 73$. Critical value of t is 1.668. Computed $t = 5.405$. Reject H_0. There is a positive relationship.
    b. MTB > corr c1 c5
    Correlation of Price and Distance = −0.373. Critical value is −1.668; p-value = .001. Reject H_0. There is an inverse relationship, $t = -3.75$.
    c. Not meaningful because township is a qualitative variable (nominal scale) with only 5 values.

35. *a.* MTB > corr c2 c3
    Correlation of Sales and Profit = 0.681. Critical value is approximately 1.98 using a two-tailed test.
    Reject H_0. There is a positive correlation between profit and sales, $t = 13.09$.
    b. MTB > corr c3 c6
    Correlation of Profit and Share = −0.011. Critical value is approximately 1.98 using a two-tailed test. Accept H_0. There is no correlation between profit and share price.
    c. Profit and value is .86; otherwise, all other correlations are weak. (Profit vs. ROI is .134, profit vs. assets .285, profit vs. turnover = −.16, profit vs. % return = .013.)

36. *a.* MTB > corr c10 c11
    Correlation of Salary and Attend = 0.353, Critical value is 1.711 for a one-tailed test, p-value .0766 (2-tail) or .0383 (1 tail).
    Yes, one possible explanation is as attendance increases, players try to negotiate higher salaries. H_0 is rejected, $t = 1.848$.

b. MTB > corr c4 c11
Correlation of Fraction and Attend = 0.557, *t* = 1.412, critical value is 1.711 for a one-tailed test. H_o is not rejected
MTB > corr c4 c10
Correlation of Fraction and Salary = 0.277, p-value .085 (one tail). H_o is not rejected. There is no correlation between winning percent (fraction) and salaries.

MTB > plot c10 c4

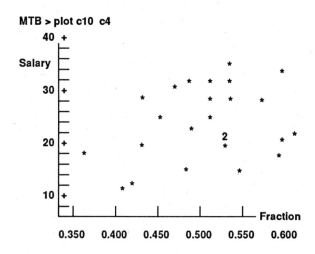

MTB > plot c11 c4

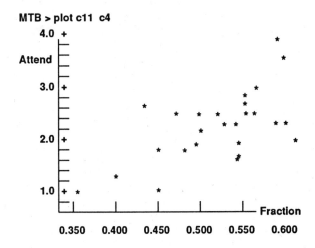

c. Here are the correlations between all the components of the problem. For example, the correlation between home runs (HR) and the fraction of games won is 0.212.
MTB > corr c4 c5 c6 c7 c8 c9 c13

	Fraction	Average	HR	ERA	SB	E
Average	0.439					
HR	0.212	0.149				
ERA	−0.497	0.025	0.487			
SB	0.266	−0.184	−0.296	−0.419		
E	−0.349	−0.206	−0.407	−0.135	0.237	
Turf	0.095	0.057	−0.358	−0.345	0.380	0.087

None of the correlations between batting average and fraction of games won (0.439) home runs and fraction of games won (0.212) and so on are very strong. The correlation between teams' batting average and games won is .439. That represents the hitting component. The earned run average of −0.497 represents the pitching component. The two coefficients of correlation are about equal. Therefore, we cannot say whether pitching is more important than hitting, or vice versa.

CHAPTER 14: SIMPLE REGRESSION ANALYSIS

1. *a.* $Y' = 3.7671 + .3630X$

   $b = \dfrac{5(173) - (28)(29)}{5(186) - (28)^2}$ $a = \dfrac{29}{5} - (0.363)\dfrac{28}{5}$

   $\quad = \dfrac{53}{146}$ $= 3.7671$

   $\quad = 0.3630$

   b. 6.3082, found by $Y' = 3.7671 + 0.3630(7)$.

2. *a.* $19.1198 - 1.7425X$

   $b = \dfrac{8(378) - (39)(85)}{8(211) - (39)^2}$ $a = \dfrac{85}{8} - (-1.74)\dfrac{39}{8}$

   $\quad = -1.7425$ $= 19.1198$

   b. 6.9222, found by $19.1198 - 1.7425(7)$

3. *a.*

   $b = \dfrac{10(718) - (91)(74)}{10(895) - (91)^2} = \dfrac{446}{669} = 0.667$

   $a = \dfrac{74}{10} - .667\left(\dfrac{91}{10}\right) = 1.333$

   b. $Y' = 1.333 + .667(6) = 5.335$

4. *a.*

   $b = \dfrac{10(26,584) - (334)(611)}{10(13,970) - (334)^2} = \dfrac{61,766}{28,144} = 2.1946$

   $a = \dfrac{611}{10} - 2.1946\left(\dfrac{334}{10}\right) = -12.201$

   b. $Y' = -12.201 + 2.1946(40) = 75.583$

5. *a.* .99198, found by MINITAB, or using the formula:

   $$\sqrt{\dfrac{175 - 3.767(29) - 0.363(173)}{5-2}}$$

   b. $Y' \pm 1s_{y \cdot x} = Y' \pm 1(.99198) = Y' \pm .99198$

6. *a.* 1.65786 using MINITAB or

   $$S_{y \cdot x} = \sqrt{\dfrac{983 - 19.1197(85) - (-1.7425)(378)}{8-2}}$$

   $\qquad = 1.65786$

   b. $Y' \pm 2s_{y \cdot x} = Y' \pm 2(1.65786) = Y' \pm 3.31572$

7. *a.* .91287, found by MINITAB or

$$\sqrt{\frac{584 - 1.33(74) - 0.667(718)}{10 - 2}}$$

b. $Y' \pm 2 (.91287) = Y' \pm 1.82574$

8. *a.* 9.31045, found by MINITAB or

$$\sqrt{\frac{51,581 - (-12.201)(611) - 2.1946(26,584)}{10 - 2}}$$

b. $Y' \pm 2 (9.31045) = Y' \pm 18.6209$

9. *a.* $6.3082 \pm (3.182)(.99198)\sqrt{.2 + \frac{(7 - 5.6)^2}{186 - (784/5)}}$

    $= 6.308 \pm 1.633$
    $= [4.6768 \text{ to } 7.9396]$

    b. $6.3082 \pm (3.182)(.99198)\sqrt{1 + 1/5 + .0671}$
    $= [2.755, 9.8613]$

10. *a.* $6.9222 \pm (2.447)(1.6578)\sqrt{\frac{1}{8} + \frac{(7.0 - 4.875)^2}{211 - (39)^2/8}}$

    $= 6.9222 \pm 2.37007$
    $= [4.5522, 9.2923]$

    b. $6.9222 \pm (2.447)(1.6578)\sqrt{1 + \frac{1}{8} + \frac{(7.0 - 4.875)^2}{211 - (39)^2/8}}$

    $= 6.9222 \pm 4.6982$
    $= [2.2238, 11.6208]$

11. *a.* [4.2939, 6.3721]
    b. [2.9854, 7.6806]

12. *a.* [68.2887, 82.8805]
    b. [52.9089, 98.2603]

13. Coefficient of correlation r = .8944, found by:

$$\frac{(5)(340) - (50)(30)}{\sqrt{[(5)(600) - (50)^2][(5)(200) - (30)^2]}}$$

Then, $(.8944)^2 = .80$, the coefficient of determination.

14. *a.*

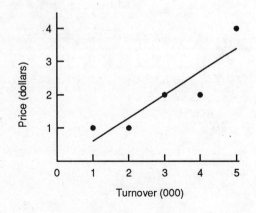

Turnover (000)

b. .8167, found by, (6 − 1.1)/6
c.

$$r = \frac{(5)(37) - (15)(10)}{\sqrt{[(5)(55) - (15)^2][(5)(26) - (10)^2]}}$$

$= .9037$ and $r^2 = .8167$

d. Turnover accounts for 81.67 percent of the variation in price.

15. *a.* Efficiency rating.
    b. **Y**

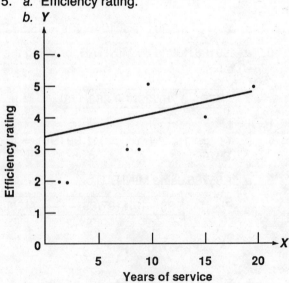

Years of service

c. Some, but a rather weak relationship.

d. $Y' = a + bX = 3.166352 + 0.076544X$

$$b = \frac{8(254) - 61(30)}{8(795) - (61)^2}$$

$$a = \frac{30}{8} - 0.076544 \left(\frac{61}{8}\right)$$

e. 3.778704, found by $Y' = 3.166352 + 0.076544(8)$.

f.
X	Y'
0	3.166352
6	3.625616
10	3.931792

16. a.

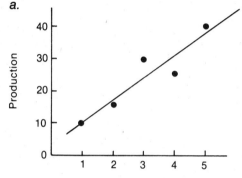

Number of assemblers

b. Yes, a rather high correlation (computed in Chapter 13 to be 0.927).

c. $Y' = a + bX = 3 + 7X$, found by

$$b = \frac{5(430) - (15)(120)}{5(55) - (15)^2} = \frac{350}{50} = 7$$

$$a = \frac{120}{5} - 7\left(\frac{15}{5}\right) = 3$$

d. 24, found by $Y' = 3 + 7(3)$

e. For
X	Y'
0	3
1	10
2	17
3	24
4	31
5	38

17. Problem solved by MINITAB.

a. Amount spent = 60.35862 + 11.2759 (size)

b. 20.818, found by:

$$S_{y \cdot x} = \sqrt{\frac{SSE}{n - 2}} = \sqrt{\frac{3467.3}{8}}$$

c. $105.46

d. The 95% confidence interval for the mean amount spent by a family of four: [$89.02, $121.90]

e. For a particular family of four: [$54.70, $156.22]

18. Using MINITAB:

a. $Y' = 67.18 + 2.564X$

b.

$$S_{y \cdot x} = \sqrt{\frac{2460.3}{10}} = 15.685$$

c. $92.82

d. 79.69 to 105.95

e. 55.48 to 130.16

19. a. 2.357, found by:

$$\sqrt{\frac{SSE}{n - 2}} = \sqrt{\frac{100}{20 - 2}}$$

b. $r^2 = .75$, found by:

$$r^2 = 1 - \frac{SSE}{SS \text{ total}} = 1 - \frac{100}{400}$$

c. $-.87$, found by $\sqrt{.75} = .87$. Then, add the negative sign because the sign of the slope is negative.

20. a.
Source	df	SS	MS	F
Regression	1	50	50	2.556
Error	23	450	19.565	
Total	24	500		

b. 25

c. 4.423, found by $\sqrt{450/(25 - 2)}$.

d. 0.10, found by 50/500.

21. a. 25.08, found by $17.08 + 0.16(50)$

b. [10.92, 39.24], found by:

$$25.08 \pm 3.182(4.05) \times$$

$$\sqrt{1 + 1/5 + \frac{(50 - 42)^2}{9850 - 210^2/5}}$$

$$25.08 \pm 14.48$$

[10.60, 39.56]

22. Using MINITAB:

a. Bid = 1.1029 + .7381 (bidders), more bidders causes the winning bid to increase.

b. $6.270 million.

c. [$5.238, $7.301] million.

d. $r^2 = .90$. This indicates that 90% of the variation the winning bid is explained by the regression equation.

23. Solved by MINITAB:
    a. Price = 10.6665 + 0.00302 (size)
    b. r^2 = .2172. No, by using size of the offering as the independent variable, the regression equation only explains 21.7% of the variation in price per share.

24. Problem solved by MINITAB
    a. Attendance = −0.355 + 4.01 (winning percentage). Yes, as winning increases so does home attendance.
    b. 2.0519 million fans
    c. r^2 = .297, only 29.7% of the variation in winning percent is explained by the regression equation.

25. a.

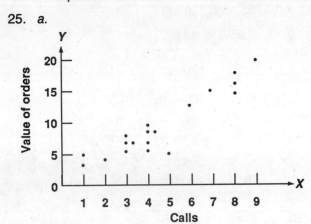

b. Y′ = −.10463 + 1.8476X
    c. 9.133
    d. 9.133 ± 3.1268 found by

$$9.133 \pm 2.101(1.4503)\sqrt{1 + \frac{1}{20} + \frac{(5-4.4)^2}{506 - \frac{(88)^2}{20}}}$$

= [6.0062, 12.2598]
    e. 91.46%

26. a. Y′ = −31.527 + .09198X for an X of 2,200, Y′ = $170,831
    $s_{x \cdot y}$ = 30.36125, then 95% confidence interval for mean = $170,831 ± $7,160 = [$163,671, $177,991]
    for individual $170,831 ± $60,992 = [$109,839, $231,823]
    b. Y′ = 207.212 − 2.72185X
    When X = 20, Y′ = 152.775
    $s_{x \cdot y}$ = 33.33014
    for mean: $152,775 ± $11,138.2
    for individual: $152,775 ± $67,420

27. a. Y′ = 197.2238 + .03795X
    when X = $12,000, Y′ = 652.6624
    for mean: 652.6024 ± 81.828
    for individual: 652.6024 ± 1158.05
    b. Y′ = 621.05 − .0155 (share)
    $s_{x \cdot y}$ = 804.3 r^2 = 0.0
    confidence interval [508.2, 773.0]
    for individual [−969.9, 2211.1]
    caution: The 7900 for company #60 greatly distorts this analysis.

28. a. Y′ = −.19358 + 2.71868X
    when X = .270, Y′ = .540467
    $s_{x \cdot y}$ = .054746, r^2 = .1928
    for Texas: .5405 ± .11528 = [.42522, .65578]
    No. Since .5000 is within the confidence interval, a winning season may not result.
    b. Y′ = .79728 − .07621X
    when X = 3.00, Y′ = .5686
    (Padres) .5686 ± .12207 = [.44653, .69067]
    No. Since .5000 (a winning season) is in the interval between .44653 and .69067, a winning season may not result.

CHAPTER 15: MULTIPLE REGRESSION AND CORRELATION ANALYSIS

1. a. Multiple regression equation.
   b. The y-intercept.
   c. $374,748, found by
   $$y' = 64,100 + 0.394(796,000) + 9.6(6,940) - 11,600(6.0)$$

2. a. Multiple regression equation.
   b. One dependent, four independent.
   c. A regression coefficient.
   d. .0002
   e. 105.014, found by
   $$y' = 11.6 + 0.4(6) + 0.286(280) + 0.112(97) + 0.002(35)$$

3. a. 465.256, found by
   $$\begin{aligned} y' = &-16.24 + 0.017(18) \\ &+ 0.0028(26,500) + 42(3) \\ &+ 0.0012(156,000) \\ &+ 0.19(141) + 26.8(2.5) \end{aligned}$$
   b. Two more social activities. Income added only 28 to the index; social activities added 53.6.

4. a. 30.69 cubic feet.
   b. A decrease of 1.86 cubic feet, down to 28.83 cubic feet.
   c. Yes. Logically, as the amount of insulation increases and outdoor temperature increases, the consumption of natural gas decreases.

5. a. $28,000 a day.
   b. .5809 found by
   $$R^2 = \frac{SSR}{SStotal} = \frac{3,050}{5,250}$$
   c. 9.199 found by $\sqrt{84.62}$.
   d. H_0 is rejected if $F > 2.97$ (approximately).
   $$\text{Computed } F = \frac{762.50}{84.62} = 9.01$$
   H_0 is rejected. At least one regression coefficient is not zero.
   e. If computed t is to the left of -2.056 or to the right of 2.056, the null hypothesis in each of these cases is rejected. Computed t for X_2 and X_3 exceed the critical value. Thus, "population" and "advertising expenses" should be retained and "number of competitors," X_1, dropped.

6. $H_0: \beta_1 = \beta_2 = \beta_3 = \beta_4 = \beta_5 = 0$
   $H_1:$ Not all β_is equal zero.
   $df_1 = 5$. $df_2 = 20 - (5 + 1) = 14$, so H_0 is rejected if $F > 2.96$.

Source	SS	df	MSE	F
Regression	448.38	5	89.656	17.58
Error	71.40	14	5.10	
Total	519.68	19		

   So H_0 is rejected. Not all the regression coefficients equal zero.

7. a. $n = 40$
   b. 4
   c.
   $$R^2 = \frac{750}{1250} = .60$$
   d.
   $$s_{y \cdot 1234} = \sqrt{500/35} = 3.7796$$
   e. $H_0: \beta_1 = \beta_2 = \beta_3 = \beta_4 = 0$
   $H_1:$ Not all the β's equal zero.
   H_0 is rejected if $F > 2.65$.
   $$F = \frac{750/4}{500/35} = 13.125$$
   H_0 is rejected. At least one β_i does not equal zero.

8. $H_0: \beta_1 = 0$ $H_0: \beta_2 = 0$
   $H_0: \beta_1 \neq 0$ $H_1: \beta_2 \neq 0$
   H_0 is rejected if $t < -2.074$ or $t > 2.074$.
   $$t = \frac{2.676}{0.56} = 4.779 \quad t = \frac{-0.880}{0.710} = -1.239$$
   The second variable can be deleted.

9. a. $n = 26$.
   b. $R^2 = 100/140 = .7143$
   c. 1.4142, found by $\sqrt{2}$
   d. $H_0: \beta_1 = \beta_2 = \beta_3 = \beta_4 = \beta_5 = 0$
   $H_1:$ Not all the βs are 0.
   $H_0:$ is rejected if $F > 2.71$.
   Computed $F = 10.0$. Reject H_0. At least one regression coefficient is not zero.
   e. H_0 is rejected in each case if $t < -2.086$ or $t > 2.086$. X_1 and X_5 should be dropped.

10. *a.* The strongest relationship is between sales and income (0.964). A problem could occur if both "cars" and "outlets" are part of the final solution. Also, outlets and income are strongly correlated (0.825). This is called multicollinearity.

b.

$$R^2 = \frac{1{,}593.81}{1{,}602.89} = 0.9943$$

c. H_0 is rejected. At least one regression coefficient is not zero.

$$F = \frac{318.76}{2.27} = 140.42$$

d. Delete "outlets" and "bosses."

e.

$$R^2 = \frac{1{,}593.66}{1{,}602.89} = 0.9942$$

There was little or no change in the coefficient of determination.

f. The normality assumption appears reasonable.

g. There is nothing unusual about the plots.

11. *a.* The strongest correlation is between GPA and legal. No problem with multicollinearity.

b.

$$R^2 = \frac{4.3595}{5.0631} = .8610$$

c. H_0 is rejected if $F > 5.41$.

$$F = \frac{1.4532}{0.1407} = 10.328.$$

At least one coefficient is not zero.

d. Any H_0 is rejected if $t < -2.571$ or $t > 2.571$. It appears that only GPA is significant. Verbal and math could be eliminated.

e.

$$R^2 = \frac{4.2061}{5.0631} = .8307.$$

R^2 has only been reduced .0303.

f. The residuals appear slightly skewed (positive), but acceptable.

g. There does not seem to be a problem with the plot.

12. *a.* Using MINITAB:

	salary	years	rating
years	0.868		
rating	0.547	0.187	
master	0.311	0.208	0.458

Years has the strongest correlation with salary. There does not appear to be a problem with multicollinearity.

b. The regression equation is
$y' = 9.92 + .899\,X_1 + .154\,X_2 - .67\,X_3$
$y' = 23.655$, or \$23,655.

c. H_0 is rejected if $F > 3.24$.

$$\text{Computed } F = \frac{301.06}{5.71} = 52.72$$

H_0 is rejected. At least one regression coefficient is not zero.

d. A regression coefficient is dropped if computed t is to the left of -2.120 or right of 2.120. Keep "years" and "rating"; drop "masters."

e. Dropping "masters," we have
Salary $= 10.1157 + .8926$ (years)
$+ .1464$ (rating)

f. The stem-and-leaf display and the histogram revealed no problem with the assumption of normality. Again using MINITAB:

Midpoint	Count	
-4	1	•
-3	1	•
-2	3	•••
-1	3	•••
0	4	••••
1	4	••••
2	0	
3	3	•••
4	0	
5	1	•

g. There does not appear to be a pattern to the residuals according to the following MINITAB plot.

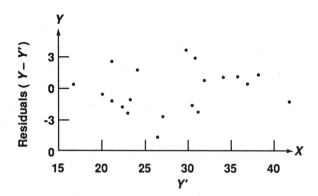

13. a. Using MINITAB the correlation matrix is:

	cars	adv	sales
adv	0.808		
sales	0.872	0.537	
city	0.639	0.713	0.389

Size of sales force (0.872) has strongest correlation with cars sold. Fairly strong relationship between location of dealership and advertising (0.713). Could be a problem.

b. The regression equation is:
cars = 31.1328 + 2.1516 adv + 5.0140 sales + 5.6651 city
$y' = 31.1328 + 2.1516(15) + 5.0140(20) + 5.6651(1) = 169.352$.

c. $H_0: \beta_1 = \beta_2 = \beta_3 = 0$; H_1: Not all βs are 0.
Reject H_0 if computed $F > 4.07$
Analysis of Variance

Source	DF	SS	MS
Regression	3	5504.4	1834.8
Error	8	420.2	52.5
Total	11	5924.7	

$F = 1,834.8/52.5 = 34.95$. Reject H_0. At least one regression coefficient is not 0.

d. H_0 is rejected in all cases if $t < -2.306$ or if $t > 2.306$. Advertising and sales force should be retained, city dropped. (Note that dropping city removes the problem with multicollinearity.)

Predictor	Coef	Stdev	t-ratio	P
Constant	31.13	13.40	2.32	0.049
adv	2.1516	0.8049	2.67	0.028
sales	5.0140	0.9105	5.51	0.000
city	5.665	6.332	0.89	0.397

e. The new output is
The regression equation is
cars = 25.2952 + 2.6187 adv + 5.0233 sales

Predictor	Coef	Stdev	t-ratio
Constant	25.30	11.57	2.19
adv	2.6187	0.6057	4.32
sales	5.0233	0.9003	5.58

$s = 7.167$ R-sq $= .922$
$R - sq\ (adj) = .905$
Analysis of Variance

Source	DF	SS	MS
Regression	2	5462.4	2731.2
Error	9	462.3	51.4
Total	11	5924.7	

f. Stem-and-leaf of C12 $N = 12$
Leaf Unit = 1.0

1	-1	6
1	-1	
2	-0	5
5	-0	110
(5)	0	01224
2	0	58

The normality assumption is reasonable.

g.

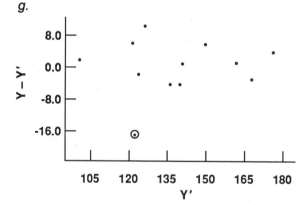

The circled value could be a problem. However, with a small sample the residual plot is acceptable.

14. a. Using MINITAB:

The variable "percent employed" has the largest correlation. The relationship between income and education is quite low.

b. $y' = 31.928 - 1.2263 (12) + .1087(15) = 18.844$ or \$18,844.

c. H_0 is rejected if computed F is > 3.63. $F = 32.43/11.11 = 2.92$, so H_0 is not rejected. Both regression coefficients could be zero.

d. Reject H_0 if computed $t < -2.120$ or $t > 2.120$. "Percent employed in agriculture" is significant; "education" is not.

e. Income $= 33.007 - 1.1875$ (% employed).

f. The normality assumption is met. The histogram of the residuals is:

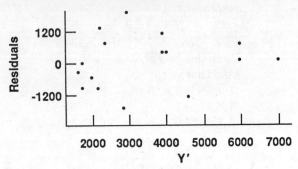

g. The plots did not reveal any violations.

h. The amount of explained variation is very low. Other independent variables should be considered.

15. a. Using MINITAB:
The regression equation is
Profit $= 965.2809 + 2.8653$ workers $+ 6.7538$ divid $+ .2873$ inv
\$2,458,780

b. Analysis of Variance

Source	DF	SS	MS
Regression	3	45510096	15170032
Error	12	12215892	1017991
Total	15	57725984	

$$F = \frac{15170032}{1017991} = 14.902$$

H_0 is rejected because computed F of 14.9 is greater than the critical value of 3.49. At least one of the regression coefficients is not zero.

c. $H_0:\beta_1 = 0 \qquad \beta_2 = 0 \qquad \beta_3 = 0$
$H_1:\beta_1 \neq 0 \qquad \beta_2 \neq 0 \qquad \beta_3 \neq 0$
The H_0s are rejected if $t < -2.179$ or $t > 2.179$.

Both workers and dividends are not significant variables. Inventory is significant. Stepwise suggests inventory and workers be used.

d. The regression equation (if we used X_1 and X_3) is: profit $= 1135 + 3.26$ workers $+ 0.310$ inv. If we used only X_3 (inventory) the equation is $y' = 1676.02 + .4738 X_3$

Predictor	Coef	Stdev	t-ratio
Constant	1134.8	418.6	2.71
Workers	3.258	1.434	2.27
inv	0.3099	0.1033	3.00

$s = 986.7 \qquad R-sq = 78.1\%$
$R-sq(adj) = 74.7\%$
Analysis of Variance

Source	DF	SS	MS
Regression	2	45070624	22535312
Error	13	12655356	973489
Total	15	57725968	

e. MTB > hist c12
Histogram of $C12 \qquad N = 16$

Midpoint	Count	
-1500	1	*
-1000	3	***
-500	1	*
0	6	******
500	2	**
1000	2	**
1500	0	
2000	1	*

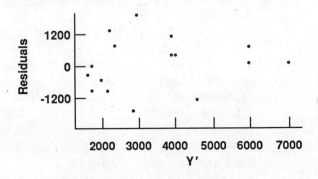

The plot of the residuals is acceptable.

16. a. $y' = -5.7328 + 0.00754 X_1 + 0.0509 X_2 + 1.0974 X_3$

b. $H_0: \beta_1 = \beta_2 = \beta_3 = 0$
H_1: not all β's equal zero.
H_0 is rejected if $F > 3.07$.
$F = 35.38$

Analysis of Variance

SOURCE	DF	SS	MS	F	p
Regression	3	11.3437	3.7812	35.38	0.000
Error	21	2.2446	0.1069		
Total	24	13.5883			

c. All coefficients are significant. Do not delete any.

d. The residuals appear to be random. No problem.

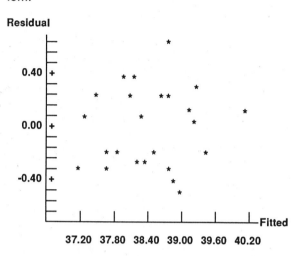

e. The histogram appears to be normal. No problem.

Histogram of Residual N = 25

Midpoint	Count	
−0.6	1	*
−0.4	3	***
−0.2	6	******
−0.0	6	******
0.2	6	******
0.4	2	**
0.6	1	*

17. Using MINITAB:

MTB > regr c1 6 c2 c3 c4 c5 c7 c8

a. The regression equation is

Price = − 8.9 + 3.90 Bedrooms + 0.0500 Size + 11.9 Pool − 1.15 Distance + 25.7 Garage + 21.9 Baths

Predictor	Coef	Stdev	t-ratio	p
Constant	− 8.92	33.17	− 0.27	0.789
Bedrooms	3.902	2.111	1.85	0.069
Size	0.05002	0.01456	3.43	0.001
Pool	11.893	5.454	2.18	0.033
Distance	− 1.1460	0.5553	− 2.06	0.043
Garage	25.681	5.921	4.34	0.000
Baths	21.853	7.084	3.08	0.003

  b. s = 22.24 R–sq = 64.3% R–sq (adj) = 61.2%

Analysis of Variance

SOURCE	DF	SS	MS	F	p
Regression	6	60588	10098	20.42	0.000
Error	68	33629	495		
Total	74	94217			

  c. Reject H_0 if F > 2.24. As given above, computed F is 20.42 so we reject H_0. Not all coefficients are 0.

  d. Reject H_0 if t < – 2.000 or t > 2.000. Accept H_0 for bedrooms because computed t = 1.85 (see above) omit bedrooms. Reject all other H_0 because all these ratios are either < – 2.000 or > 2.000 (see above).

  e. MTB > regr c1 4 c3 c5 c7 c8
  The regression equation is
  Price = – 29.3 + 0.0652 Size – 1.28 Distance + 27.7 Garage + 26.7 Baths

Predictor	Coef	Stdev	t-ratio	p
Constant	– 29.29	32.74	– 0.89	0.374
Size	0.06520	0.01342	4.86	0.000
Distance	– 1.2838	0.5735	– 2.24	0.028
Garage	27.659	6.093	4.54	0.000
Baths	26.729	6.959	3.84	0.000

  s = 23.07 R–sq = 60.5% R–sq (adj) = 58.2%
  Analysis of Variance

SOURCE	DF	SS	MS	F	p
Regression	4	56976	14244	26.77	0.000
Error	70	37241	532		
Total	74	94217			

  f.

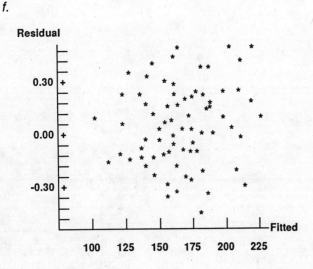

g.
```
MTB > hist c32
Histogram of Residual     N = 75
Midpoint              Count
   -50                 1   *
   -40                 4   ****
   -30                 7   *******
   -20                 7   *******
   -10                14   **************
     0                 9   *********
    10                14   **************
    20                 8   ********
    30                 6   ******
    40                 3   ***
    50                 2   **
```

18. From MINITAB:

    MTB > regr c3 6 c1 c2 c5 c6 c7 c8

    a. The regression equation is
    Profit = − 20.1 + 0.0537 Value + 0.0143
    Sales − 0.00303 Assets − 0.0073 Share
    + 0.195 Turnover − 1.19 Return%

Predictor	Coef	Stdev	t-ratio	p
Constant	− 20.07	54.74	− 0.37	0.714
Value	0.053689	0.003683	14.58	0.000
Sales	0.014282	0.003132	4.56	0.000
Assets	− 0.003028	0.001091	− 2.77	0.006
Share	− 0.00727	0.05001	− 0.15	0.885
Turnover	0.1946	0.5284	0.37	0.713
Return%	− 1.190	1.139	− 1.04	0.297

b. s = 390.5   R−sq = 77.0%   R−sq(adj) = 76.3%

Analysis of Variance

SOURCE	DF	SS	MS	F	p
Regression	6	98686376	16447729	107.87	0.000
Error	193	29428446	152479		
Total	199	128114824			

c. Reject H_0 if computed F > 2.10. F = 107.87 (see above). Reject H_0, accept H_1. Not all coefficients = 0.

d. Reject H_0 if t > 1.96 or < − 1.96. Accept H_0 for share, turnover, return %, because respective t values are − 0.15, 0.37 and 1.04 (see above). Delete these variables.

    MTB > regr c3 3 c1 c2 c5

e. The regression equation is
    Profit = − 31.0 + 0.0523 Value + 0.0150
    Sales − 0.00277 Assets

Predictor	Coef	Stdev	t-ratio	p
Constant	− 30.95	38.70	− 0.80	0.425
Value	0.052275	0.003373	15.50	0.000
Sales	0.015047	0.003035	4.96	0.000
Assets	− 0.002768	0.001054	− 2.63	0.009

s = 388.6   R−sq = 76.9%   R−sq(adj) = 76.5%

Analysis of Variance

SOURCE	DF	SS	MS	F	p
Regression	3	98509896	32836632	217.40	0.000
Error	196	29604926	151046		
Total	199	128114824			

f. See plot below. It appears there are some problems with homoscedasticity. Observation number 1, 4, 18, 35, 48, and 107 among others are causing problems.

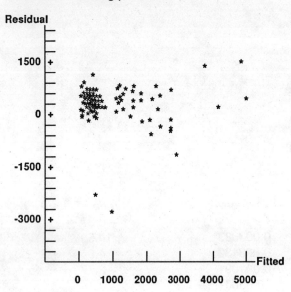

g. Residuals seem about normal.

Residual   N =   200
Midpoint Count

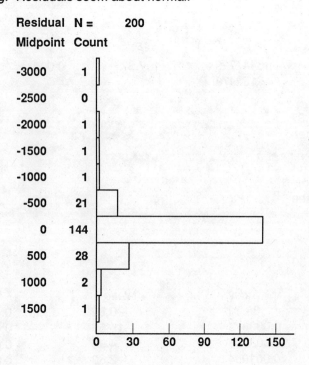

Midpoint	Count
-3000	1
-2500	0
-2000	1
-1500	1
-1000	1
-500	21
0	144
500	28
1000	2
1500	1

19. MTB > regr c4 5 c5 c6 c7 c8 c9

a. The regression equation is
   Fraction = 0.229 + 2.39 Average + 0.000843 HR − 0.100 ERA + 0.000372 SB − 0.000849 E

Predictor	Coef	Stdev	t-ratio	p
Constant	0.2292	0.2275	1.01	0.326
Average	2.3908	0.7341	3.26	0.004
HR	0.0008433	0.0002666	3.16	0.005
ERA	−0.10002	0.02151	−4.65	0.000
SB	0.0003720	0.0001910	1.95	0.066
E	−0.0008485	0.0004666	−1.82	0.084

b. s = 0.03410 R−sq = 73.9% R−sq(adj) = 67.4%

Analysis of Variance

SOURCE	DF	SS	MS	F	p
Regression	5	0.065859	0.013172	11.33	0.000
Error	25	0.023255	0.001163		
Total	25	0.089114			

c. H_0: all regression coefficients = 0. H_1: Not all are zero. Reject H_0 if computed F > 2.71. F = 11.33 (above) so we reject H_0.

d. Reject H_0 if t > 2.086 or t < −2.086. Accept for stolen bases and errors because the computed t values are 1.95 and −1.82 respectively (see above).

e. y′ = .2292 + 2.3489 average + .00098 HR − .1170 ERA.

f. Oakland and Cincinnati seem to be causing problems.

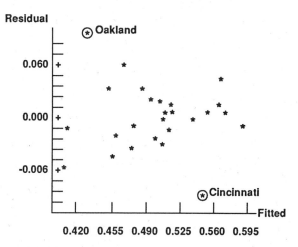

g. Residuals are approximately normal.

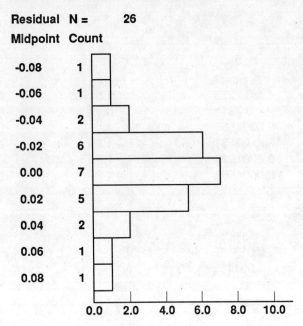

Residual N =   26
Midpoint Count

Midpoint	Count
-0.08	1
-0.06	1
-0.04	2
-0.02	6
0.00	7
0.02	5
0.04	2
0.06	1
0.08	1

0.0   2.0   4.0   6.0   8.0   10.0

CHAPTER 16: ANALYSIS OF NOMINAL-LEVEL DATA: THE CHI-SQUARE DISTRIBUTION

1. a. There are $k - 1 = 3 - 1 = 2$ degrees of freedom. The critical value is 5.991. Reject H_0 if the computed value of χ^2 is greater than 5.991. Otherwise, do not reject H_0.

   b. Computed value of x^2 is 10.

f_0	f_e	$f_0 - f_e$	$(f_0 - f_e)^2$	$\dfrac{(f_0 - f_e)^2}{f_e}$
10	20	−10	100	5
20	20	0	0	0
30	20	10	100	5
60	60	0		10 ←χ^2

   c. Since $10 > 5.991$, reject H_0 and accept H_1.

2. a. Reject H_0 if computed $\chi^2 > 9.210$.

   b. $\chi^2 = 2.500$, found by

   $$\frac{(30-24)^2}{24} + \frac{(20-24)^2}{24} + \frac{(10-12)^2}{12}$$

   c. Do not reject H_0

3. H_0: Shoplifting accounts for half of the loss, employee theft 25 percent, and poor inventory control 25 percent.

   H_1: Shoplifting does not account for 50 percent of the loss, employee theft does not account for 25 percent and poor inventory control does not account for 25 percent of the loss.

   Computed $\chi^2 = 12.00$

f_0	f_e	$f_0 - f_e$	$(f_0 - f_e)^2$	$\dfrac{(f_0 - f_e)^2}{f_e}$
60	50	10	100	2.0
30	25	5	25	1
10	25	−15	225	9.0
100	100	0		12.0 ←χ^2

   12.0 > is greater than the critical value of 7.824, so H_0 is rejected. Shoplifting does not account for twice the losses compared to theft or inventory control.

4. H_0: There is no difference. H_1: There is a difference. Critical value = 9.488. Reject if $\chi^2 > 9.488$. Computed $\chi^2 = 15.308$. Reject H_0. There is a difference. df = 4. All $f_e = 104$.

5. H_0: There is no difference between the opinions. H_1: There is a difference between the opinions. H_0 is rejected if computed chi-square is greater than 15.086. There are 5 degrees of freedom, found by $6 - 1$.

   Computed chi-square is 3.400. H_0 is not rejected. The differences are due to chance.

6. H_0: there is no difference. H_1: There is a difference. df = 7. Reject H_0 if $\chi^2 > 18.475$. All $f_e = 10$. Computed $\chi^2 = 24.6$. Reject H_0, accept H_1. Accidents not evenly distributed.

7. H_0: The sample responses are representative of the population.
   H_1: The responses are not representative of the population.
   There are $7 - 1 = 6$ degrees of freedom. The critical value of chi-square is 12.592. Reject H_0 if the computed value is greater than 12.592.

College	f_0	Proportion	f_e	$\dfrac{(f_0 - f_e)^2}{f_e}$
A & S	90	.27	81	1.00
Business	45	.14	42	.21
Education	60	.19	57	.16
Engineering	30	.08	24	1.50
Law	15	.05	15	0
Pharmacy	15	.07	21	1.71
University	45	.20	60	3.75
				8.33

   Computed $\chi^2 = 8.33$. H_0 is not rejected. The sample is representative of the population since $8.33 < 12.592$.

8. df = 7. Reject H_0 if $\chi^2 > 14.067$. Computed $\chi^2 = 2.730$. H_0 is not rejected. There is no difference.

9. There are $k - 1 = 5 - 1 = 4$ degrees of freedom. The critical value is 9.488, and computed chi-square is 19.60.

f_0	f_e	$f_0 - f_e$	$(f_0 - f_e)^2$	$\dfrac{(f_0 - f_e)^2}{f_e}$
67	56.4	10.6	112.36	1.99
22	37.6	−15.6	243.36	6.47
51	37.6	13.4	179.56	4.78
24	37.6	−13.6	184.96	4.92
24	18.8	5.2	27.04	1.44
188	188	0		19.60

Reject H_0 since $19.60 > 9.488$. The observed distribution of M&M colors does not match the expected distribution.

10. H_0: Distribution is normally distributed.
H_1: It is not normally distributed.
Reject H_0 if $\chi^2 > 11.070$

Time	z areas	f_0	f_e	$\dfrac{(f_0 - f_e)^2}{f_e}$
Up to 4	.0764	7	6.9	.001
4 to 5	.1625	14	14.6	.025
5 to 6	.2611	25	23.5	.096
6 to 7	.2611	22	23.5	.096
7 to 8	.1625	16	14.6	.134
8 or more	.0764	6	6.9	.117
Total	1.000	90	90	.469

Computed $\chi^2 = .469$. Do not reject H_0.

11. Reject H_0 if $\chi^2 > 15.086$. $df = 5$
To compute f_e:

Commission	z values	Area
Less than $900	Under −2.00	.0228
$900 to $1,200	−2.00 to −1.00	.1359
1,200 to 1,500	−1.00 to 0	.3413
1,500 to 1,800	0 to 1.00	.3413
1,800 to 2,100	1.00 to 2.00	.1359
$2,100 or more	Over 2.00	.0228
		1.000

To compute chi-square:

f_0	f_e	$\dfrac{(f_0 - f_e)^2}{f_e}$
9	11.40	0.51
63	67.95	0.36
165	170.65	0.19
180	170.65	0.51
71	67.95	0.14
12	11.40	0.03
500	500	1.74

There are $k - 1 = 6 - 1 = 5$ degrees of freedom. Critical value is 15.086. Since $1.74 < 15.086$, we fail to reject H_0. The commissions are normally distributed.

12. H_0: No relationship between income level and employment status.
H_1: They are related.
$df = 6$. Reject H_0 if $\chi^2 > 12.592$. Computed $\chi^2 = 0.776$. Do not reject H_0.

13. H_0: Age is not related to the degree of pressure.
H_1: Age is related to the degree of pressure.
$df = (4 - 1)(3 - 1) = 6$. H_0 is rejected if $\chi^2 > 16.812$.
$\chi^2 = 0.016 + 0.282 + 0.168 + \ldots + 0.178$
$= 2.191$
Since $2.191 < 16.812$, H_0 is not rejected. Age and pressure are not related.

14. $df = 4$. Reject H_0 if $\chi^2 > 9.488$. Computed $\chi^2 = 7.34$. Do not reject H_0.

15. H_0: There is no relationship between the manufacturer and the quality of the light bulbs.
H_1: There is a relationship between the quality of the light bulbs and the manufacturer:
$df = (r - 1)(c - 1) = (2 - 1)(4 - 1) = 3$.
Reject H_0 if $\chi^2 > 7.815$
$\chi^2 = 3.66$, found by:
$(12 - 9)^2/9 + (8 - 9)^2/9 + \ldots + (89 - 91)^2/91$
$= 1.0 + 0.11 + 1.78 + 0.44 + 0.10 + 0.01 + 0.18 + 0.04$
Do not reject H_0 because $3.66 < 7.815$.

16. H_0: No relationship between age and opinion. H_1: There is a relationship. $df = 12$. Reject H_0 if $\chi^2 > 21.026$. Computed $\chi^2 = 269.191$. Reject H_0, accept H_1. There is a relationship between age and opinion.

17. a. H_0: Unpaid balances are uniformly distributed by size.
H_1: Unpaid balances are not uniformly distributed by size.
b.

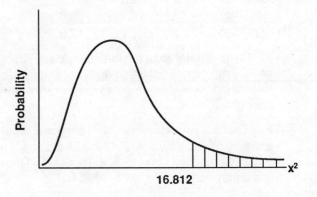

c. df $= 7 - 1 = 6$. H_0 is rejected if $\chi^2 > 16.812$. Computed chi-square $= 2.332$, found by:

Size	f_0	f_e	$\dfrac{(f_0 - f_e)^2}{f_e}$
<$20	13	12	0.083
$20 but under $40	10	12	0.333
40 but under 60	15	12	0.750
60 but under 80	14	12	0.333
80 but under 100	9	12	0.750
100 but under 150	12	12	0
150 and over	11	12	0.083
			2.332

Since $2.332 < 16.812$, H_0 is not rejected. The unpaid balances are uniformly distributed by size.

18. H_0: Income and scholastic achievement not related.
H_1: They are related.
6 df. Reject H_0 if $\chi^2 > 12.592$. $\chi^2 = 8.391$. H_0 not rejected.

19. The null and alternate hypotheses are:
H_0: Quarter and group are not related.
H_1: Quarter and group are related.
Using MINITAB the following cell frequencies were developed:

Group Rank	I	II	III	IV	Total
Low	21	28	35	38	122
Medium	34	22	29	37	122
High	36	41	28	17	122
Total	91	91	92	92	366

There are 6 degrees of freedom, so H_0 is rejected if $\chi^2 > 12.592$. The computed value of χ^2 is 20.680, so H_0 is rejected. Quarter and group are related. It is concluded that the draft order is not random.

20. H_0: Years of service is normally distributed.
H_1: Years of service are not normally distributed.
df $= 6$, Critical value $= 12.592$ (Since we are dealing with a population, no additional df are lost).

Years	z Areas	f_0	f_e
<5	.1314	12	11.169
5–10	.1462	18	12.427
10–15	.1945	12	16.532
15–20	.2015	16	17.128
20–25	.1604	11	13.634
25–30	.0992	7	8.432
30 or more	.0668	9	5.678
Total	1.000	85	6.574

Computed $\chi^2 = 6.574$. H_0 is not rejected. Length of service normally distributed.

21. *a.* H_0: No relationship between pool and township.
H_1: There is a relationship.

	Township				
Pool	1	2	3	4	5
0	7	6	6	8	2
1	5	9	13	10	9

df $= 4$. 9.488 is critical value. Computed $\chi^2 = 4.571$. Do not reject H_0. No relationship shown between pool and township.

b. H_0: No relationship between garage and township.
H_1: There is a relationship.

	Township				
Garage	1	2	3	4	5
0	4	4	7	7	2
1	8	11	12	11	9

df $= 4$. Reject if $\chi^2 > 9.488$. Computed $\chi^2 = 1.768$. Do not reject H_0. No relationship shown between garage and township.

c.

Beds	f_0	z probability	f_e
2	18	.3156	23.67
3	21	.2597	19.48
4	16	.2798	17.24
5	8	.1319	9.89
6	9	.0491	8.68
7	3	.0139	1.04
	75	1.0000	75.00

$\chi^2 = 13.282$. H_0 is rejected because computed $\chi^2(13.282) >$ critical value of 11.345. df $= 6 - 1 - 2 = 3$. Not normally distributed.

22.

Attendance	Winning Season	Losing Season	Total
less than 20	5	5	10
2.0 or more	13	3	16
Total	18	8	26

H_0: There is no relationship between attendance and winning.
H_a: There is a relationship between attendance and winning.
H_0 is rejected if $\chi^2 > 3.841$. The computed χ^2 is 2.821, so H_0 is not rejected. No relationship between winning and attendance is established.

CHAPTER 17:   NONPARAMETRIC METHODS: ANALYSIS OF RANKED DATA

1. *a.* If the number of pluses (successes) in the sample is 9 or more, reject H_0.
   b. Reject H_0 because the cumulative probability associated with nine successes (.073) does not exceed the significance level (.10).

2. *a.* Reject H_0 if number of + signs is either ≤ 1 or ≥ 8.
   b. Do not reject H_0.

3. *a.* H_0:$p = .50$, H_1:$p < 50$; $n = 10$.
   b. H_0 is rejected if there are nine or more plus signs.
      A " + " represents a loss.
   c. Reject H_0. It is an effective program, because there was only one person who gained weight.

4. *a.* H_0:$p = .50$, H_1 $p > .50$, $n = 13$.
   b. Reject H_0 if number of + signs ≥ 10.
   c. Reject H_0. 12 persons improved their self confidence.

5. *a.* H_0:$p = .50$ (There is no change in weight.)
      H_1:$p > .50$ (There is a loss of weight. The program was effective.)
   b. Do not reject H_0 if the computed value of z is between 0 and 1.645. Otherwise, reject H_0. (A weight loss is considered a " + ".)
   c.
   $$z = \frac{(32 - .50) - .50(45)}{.50\sqrt{45}}$$
   $$= \frac{1.5 - 22.5}{3.335}$$
   $$= 2.69$$
   d. Reject H_0 because 2.69 falls to the right of 1.645. The weight loss program is effective.

6. *a.* H_0:$p = .50$, H_1:$p > 50$.
   b. Reject H_0 if $z > 1.645$. $z = 2.97$, found by $(42 - .50 - 30)/3.87$.
   c. Reject H_0. Program effective.

7. *a.* H_0:$p = .50$, H_1:$p > .50$.
      H_0 is rejected if $z > 2.05$.
   $$\mu = 81(.50) = 40.5$$
   $$\sigma = \sqrt{81(.50)(.50)} = 4.5$$
   $$z = \frac{42.5 - 40.5}{4.5} = .44$$

Since $.44 < 2.05$ do not reject H_0. No preference.

8. H_0:$p = .50$, H_1:$p > .50$. Critical value is 1.645. Computed $z = 2.80$, found by $(20 - .50 - 12.5)/2.5$.
   Reject H_0. Workers prefer to assemble entire computer.

9. *a.* H_0:Median = \$40,000, H_1:Median > \$40,000.
   b. H_0 is rejected if $z > 1.645$.
   c.
   $$\mu = 200(.50) = 100$$
   $$\sigma = \sqrt{200(.50)(.50)} = 7.07$$
   $$z = \frac{170 - .5 - 100}{7.07} = 9.83$$

   H_0 is rejected. The median income is greater than \$40,000.

10. H_0:Median = \$503.
    H_1:Median < \$503.
    Reject if $z < -1.645$
    $z = -3.95$, found by
    $(160 + .5 - 200)/10$.
    Reject H_0. Median is less than \$503.

11. *a.* H_0: The two samples distributions come from the same population.
       H_1: The two sample distributions do not come from the same population.
    b. $n_1 = 6$, $n_2 = 5$. Using Appendix J, the critical value is 3. Reject H_0 if computed U is 3 or less.
    c.
    $$U = (6)(5) + \frac{6(6 + 1)}{2} - 48$$
    $$= 30 + 21 - 48$$
    $$= 3$$
    $$U' = (6)(5) + \frac{5(5) + 1}{2} - 18$$
    $$= 30 + 15 - 18$$
    $$= 27$$

    The smaller of 3 and 27 is 3 (observations ranked from low to high).

d. The computed value of U is equal to or less than 3. Reject H_0 at the .05 significance level. There is a difference between the two groups. The distributions are not the same.

12. a. H_0: Populations are the same. H_1: Populations are different.
    b. Reject H_0 if smaller of U or U^1 is $\le$ 10.
    c. $U^1 = 22$.
    d. Do not reject H_0. No difference.

13. H_0: The distributions of ages of the two groups are the same.
    H_1: The country-western musicians are older.
    $n_1 = 10$, $n_2 = 12$. H_0 is rejected if the smaller of U or $U' \le 34$.

Rock		Country	
Age	Rank	Age	Rank
28	8.0	26	6.0
16	1.0	42	16.5
42	16.5	65	22.0
29	9.5	38	13.0
31	11.0	29	9.5
22	3.0	32	12.0
50	20.0	59	21.0
42	16.5	42	16.5
23	4.0	27	7.0
25	5.0	41	14.0
	94.5	46	19.0
		18	2.0
			158.5

$$U = 10(12) + \frac{10(11)}{2} - 94.5 = 80.5$$

$$U' = 10(12) + \frac{12(13)}{2} - 158.5 = 39.5$$

H_0 is not rejected (since 39.5 is greater than 34). There is no difference in the two age distributions.

14. H_0: The times are the same.
    H_1: Experimental times are less.
    Reject H_0 if smaller U or $U^1 \le 12$. $U = 3.5$. Reject H_0. Experimental times are less.

15. ANOVA requires that we have three or more populations, the data are interval or ratio-level, the populations are normally distributed, and the population standard deviations are equal. Kruskal-Wallis requires only ordinal-level data, and no assumptions are made regarding the shape of the populations.

16. When there are more than two populations the Mann-Whiting test is used.

17. a. H_0: The three population distributions are equal.
    b. If the computed value of H is greater than 5.991, reject H_0. If it is 5.991 or less, do not reject H_0. (Use Appendix I; the chi-square distribution.)
    c. $H = 8.98$, found by:

Rank	Rank	Rank
8	5	1
11	6.5	2
14.5	6.5	3
14.5	10	4
16	12	9
64	13	19
	53	

$$H = \frac{12}{16(16 + 1)} \left[\frac{(64)^2}{5} + \frac{(58)^2}{6} + \frac{(19)^2}{5} \right] - 3(16 + 1)$$

$$= .0441176[1,359.6] - 51$$

$$= 59.98 - 51 = 8.98$$

   d. Reject H_0 because $8.98 > 5.991$. The three distributions are not equal.

18. a. H_0: Distributions are not the same.
    b. Reject if $\chi^2 > 9.210$.
    c. $H = 7.324$
    d. H_0 not rejected.

19. H_0: The distributions of the lengths of life are the same.
    H_1: The distributions of the lengths of life are not the same.
    H_0 is rejected if $H > 9.210$. (Refer to the χ^2 table, Appendix I, for the critical value.)

Salt		Fresh		Others	
Hours	Rank	Hours	Rank	Hours	Rank
167.3	3	160.6	1	182.7	13
189.6	15	177.6	11	165.4	2
177.2	10	185.3	14	172.9	7
169.4	6	168.6	4	169.2	5
180.3	12	176.6	9	174.7	8
	46		39		35

$H = .62$, found by:

$$\frac{12}{15(16)} \left[\frac{(46)^2}{5} + \frac{(39)^2}{5} + \frac{(35)^2}{5} \right] - 3(16)$$

H_0 is not rejected. There is no difference in the three distributions.

20. H_0: The distributions are the same.
    H_1: They are not the same.
    Reject H_0 if $\chi^2 > 5.991$. Computed H = .312.
    Do not reject.

21.

Absolute difference	Rank	Correctly signed
70	1	−1
90	2	2
120	3	−3
130	4	4
190	5	5
250	6	6
550	7	7

Sums: −4, +24. So T = 4 (the smaller of the two sums). From Appendix K, .05 level, one-tailed test, N = 7, the critical value is 3. Since the T of 4 > 3, do not reject H_0 (one-tailed test). There is no difference in square footage. Yuppies do not live in larger homes.

22. H_0: Mileage is the same. H_1: mileage not the same. H_0 rejected if T ≤ 5. Computed T = 11. Do not reject H_0.

23. a. H_0: The production is the same for the two systems.
    H_1: Production using the Mump method is greater.
    b. H_0 is rejected if T ≤ 21, N = 13.
    c. The calculations for the first three employees are:

Employee	Old	Mump	d	Rank	R^+	R^-
A	60	64	4	6	6	
B	40	52	12	12.5	12.5	
C	59	58	−1	2		2

The sum of the negative ranks is 6.5, which is smaller than the sum of the positive ranks. Since 6.5 is less than 21, H_0 is rejected. Production using the Mump method is greater. Note: Answers will vary, .05 level used in this solution.

24. a. H_0: Production has not changed.
    b. H_1: Production has increased (one tail).
    c. .05
    d. Reject H_0 if T ≤ 21.
    e. Computed T = 34, do not reject H_0.

25. a. Two-tailed.
    b. N = 19. H_0 is rejected if there are either 5 or fewer "+" signs, or 14 or more. The total of 12 "+" signs falls in the acceptance region. H_0 is not rejected. There is no preference between the two shows.

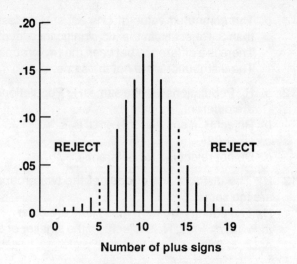

c. The two westerns would be equally popular.

26. a. One-tailed because it states that Bic is preferred over Pilot.
    b. 17, found by 20 − 3.
    c. Reject H_0 if there are 13 or more pluses.

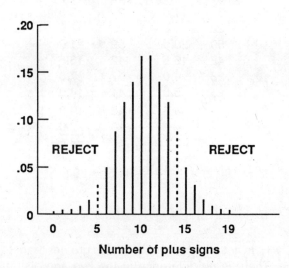

d. Do not reject H_0.

27. H_0: Community responsibility is the same before and after marriage.
    H_1: Community responsibility is not the same.
    H_0 is rejected if T ≤ 3, N = 8.
    The calculations for the first four women are:

Name	Before	After	d	Rank	R^+	R^-
Beth	110	114	4	3	3	
Jean	157	159	2	2	2	
Sue	121	120	−1	1		1
Cathy	96	103	7	4.5	4.5	

The smaller sum of ranks is 13.5, which is the computed T. It lies in the acceptance region beyond 3.
Do not reject H_0.

28. H_0: Rates are the same. H_1: The rates are not the same.
   H_0 is rejected if $\chi^2 > 5.991$. H $= .082$. Do not reject H_0.

29. H_0: Idle minutes are same.
   H_1: Idle minutes are not the same.
   $n_1 = 5, n_2 = 6$. H_0 is rejected if U or U' is less than or equal to 3.

Day		Night	
Minutes	Rank	Minutes	Rank
92	7	96	8
103	9	114	10
116	11	80	1
81	2	82	3
89	5	88	4
	34	91	6
			32

   $$U = 5 \times 6 + \frac{5 \times 6}{2} - 34 = 11$$

   $$U' = 5 \times 6 + \frac{6 \times 7}{2} - 32 = 19$$

   H_0 is not rejected. There is no difference in the idle minutes.

30. H_0: The populations are the same.
   H_1: The populations differ.
   Reject H_0 if $\chi^2 > 7.815$. H $= 14.30$
   Reject H_0, accept H_1.

31. H_0: Median $= \$1,200$
   H_1: Median $> \$1,200$
   H_0 is rejected if $z > 1.645$.

   $$\mu = 144.(50) = 72$$

   $$\sigma = .50\sqrt{144} = 6$$

   $$z = \frac{74.5 - 72}{6} = 0.42$$

   H_0 is not rejected. The median is not greater than $\$1,200$.

32. H_0: p $= .50$, H_1: p $\neq .50$. $\mu = 100$, s $= 7.071$.
   Reject if $z > 1.96$ or $z < -1.96$.
   Computed z $= 8.42$, found by $(160 - .5 - 100)/7.071$.
   Reject H_0. There is a difference in the preference for the two types of orange juice.

33. H_0:p $= .50$
   H_1:p $\neq .50$
   H_0 is rejected if there are 12 or more or 3 or less plus signs. Since there are only 8 plus signs, H_0 is not rejected. There is no preference with respect to the two brands of components.

34. H_0: The distribution of the ranks is the same for all months.
   H_1: The distribution of the ranks is not the same for all months.
   H_0 is rejected if $\chi^2 > 19.675$.
   The data from exercise 19 in chapter 16 is in 12 columns, so using MINITAB the H value is computed to be 25.95. H_0 is rejected. The draft dates were not random.

```
MTB    > stack c1–c12 into c20;
SUBC   > subscripts c21.
MTB    > kruskal c20 c21
```

LEVEL	NOBS	MEDIAN	AVE. RANK	Z VALUE
1	31	211.0	201.2	0.97
2	29	210.0	203.0	1.03
3	31	256.0	225.8	2.33
4	30	225.0	203.7	1.09
5	31	226.0	208.0	1.35
6	30	207.5	195.7	0.66
7	31	188.0	181.5	−0.11
8	31	145.0	173.5	−0.55
9	30	168.0	157.3	−1.42
10	31	201.0	182.5	−0.06
11	30	131.5	148.7	−1.88
12	31	100.0	121.5	−3.41
OVERALL	366		183.5	

$H = 25.95$ d.f. = 11 $p = 0.007$

Reject H_0 if $\chi^2 > 19.675$.
$H = 25.95$. Reject H_0 Lottery numbers not random.

35. H_0: Incomes are the same.
H_1: Incomes are different.
Critical value of χ^2 is 7.815.
:MTB > krusk c10 c21
:

LEVEL	NOBS	MEDIAN	AVE. RANK	Z VALUE
1	10	13.20	16.5	−0.98
2	13	13.70	18.3	−0.46
3	9	14.90	20.1	0.19
4	6	17.00	26.0	1.56
OVERALL	38		19.5	

$H = 2.92$ d.f. = 3 $p = 0.404$
$H = 2.93$ d.f. = 3 $p = 0.403$ (adj. for ties)

H_0 is not rejected. No differences in salaries.

36. *a.* H_0: The distributions of prices are the same in the six townships.
H_1: The distributions of prices are not the same in the six townships.
H_0 is rejected if $\chi^2 > 9.488$.
MTB > kruskal c1 c6

LEVEL	NOBS	MEDIAN	AVE. RANK	Z VALUE
1	12	153.8	28.3	−1.68
2	15	160.0	43.0	0.99
3	19	173.3	40.0	0.47
4	18	154.3	36.4	−0.35
5	11	164.5	40.8	0.46
OVERALL	75		38.0	

$H = 3.58$ d.f. = 4 $p = 0.466$
$H = 3.58$ d.f. = 4 $p = 0.466$ (adj. for ties)

H_0 is not rejected. No difference in price.

b. H_0: Prices are the same with respect to bedroom.

H_1: Prices are not the same with respect to bedroom.

Reject H_0 if $\chi^2 > 9.488$.

MTB > code (2)2 (3)3 (4)4 (5)5 (6:10)6 c2 c20

MTB > kruskal c1 c20

LEVEL	NOBS	MEDIAN	AVE. RANK	Z VALUE
2	18	148.7	29.1	-1.98
3	21	160.6	34.3	-0.93
4	16	151.1	34.4	-0.74
5	8	179.3	48.2	1.40
6	12	216.4	55.9	3.10
OVERALL	75		38.0	

$H = 13.87$ d.f. $= 4$ $p = 0.008$

$H = 13.87$ d.f. $= 4$ $p = 0.008$ (adj. for ties)

H_0 is rejected. The distribution of prices is different depending on the number of bedrooms.

c. H_0: Distances are the same with respect to having a pool.

H_1: Distances are not the same with respect to having a pool.

H_0 is rejected if $\chi^2 > 3.841$.

MTB > kruskal c5 c4

LEVEL	NOBS	MEDIAN	AVE. RANK	Z VALUE
0	29	16.00	42.1	1.31
1	46	14.00	35.4	-1.31
OVERALL	75		38.0	

$H = 1.70$ d.f. $= 1$ $p = 0.192$.

$H = 1.71$ d.f. $= 1$ $p = 0.191$ (adj. for ties).

H_0 is not rejected.

CHAPTER 18: INDEX NUMBERS

1. *a.* 127.8, found by ($115,500/$90,400)(100). Price increased by 27.8 percent from 1981 to 1991.

    b. 129.1, found by ($87,200/$67,550)(100). The loan amount increased 29.1 percent between 1981–82 and 1991.

2. *a.* Lumber 146.5, found by (9.14/6.24)100. Furniture 165.4, found by (8.70/5.26)(100). Stone 158.2, found by (11.25/7.11)100. Instruments 180.5, found by (11.73/6.50)100.

    b. Hourly earnings in lumber increased 46.5% from December 1979 to March 1991, etc.

3. *a.* 121.0, found by ($97.71/$80.75)(100).

	Price 1983,	Amount consumed,		Price 1992,	
Fruit	p_0	q_0	$p_0 q_0$	p_t	$p_0 p_t$
Bananas	$0.23	100	$23.00	$0.35	$35.00
Grapefruit	0.29	50	14.50	0.27	13.50
Apples	0.35	85	29.75	0.35	29.75
Strawberries	1.02	8	8.16	1.69	13.52
Oranges	0.89	6	5.34	0.99	5.94
			$80.75		$97.71

   b. Prices of fruits in 1992 were 21.0 percent more than they were in 1983.

4. *a.*

	1985 Price	Production		1992 Price	
Item	p_0	q_0	$p_0 q_0$	p_t	$p_t q_t$
Washer	$0.07	17,000	$ 1,190	$0.10	$ 1,700
Pin	0.04	125,000	5,000	0.03	3,750
Bolt	0.15	40,000	6,000	0.15	6,000
Nut	0.08	62,000	4,960	0.05	3,100
			$17,150		$14,550

$$P = \frac{\$14,550}{\$17,150}(100) = 84.8$$

   b. Prices declined 15.2 percent from 1985 to 1992, found by 100.0 − 84.8.

5. *a.* $Q = 90.4$, found by ($1,975.92/$2,186.53)(100).
    $V = 93.8$, found by ($2,051.81/$2,186.53)(100).

	p_0	q_0	$p_0 q_0$	pt	q_t	$p_0 q_t$	$p_t q_t$
Oats	$1.52	200	$ 304.00	$1.87	214	$ 325.28	$ 400.18
Wheat	2.10	565	1,186.50	2.05	489	1,026.90	1,002.45
Corn	1.48	291	430.68	1.48	203	300.44	300.44
Barley	3.05	87	265.35	3.29	106	323.30	348.74
			$2,186.53			$1,975.92	$2,051.81

Quantity declined 9.6% between 1977 and 1992.

b. Value declined 6.2% between 1977 and 1992.

6.

Item	p_0q_0	p_0q_t	p_tq_t
Motor	$ 41,536	$100,512.40	$122,659.20
Compound	255,892	186,329.04	193,882.92
Nails	3,784	8,948.00	10,737.60
	$301,212	$295,789.44	$327,279.72

a. $Q = (\$295,789.44/\$301,212.00)(100) = 98.2$ indicating a decline of 1.8 percent.

b. $V = (\$327,279.72/\$301,212.00)(100) = 108.7$, indicating an increase of 8.7 percent in value.

7. *a.* $\dfrac{6.8}{5.3}(100)(.20) = 25.66$

$\dfrac{362.26}{265.88}(100)(.40) = 54.50$

$\dfrac{115.2}{109.6}(100)(.25) = 26.28$

$\dfrac{\$622,864}{\$529,917}(100)(.15) = \dfrac{17.63}{124.07}$

b. Business activity increased 24.07 percent from 1989 to 1991.

8. Answers will vary depending on weights selected.

	Chasen weight	
New businesses	.15	16.02*
Business failures	.10	8.29
Income tax	.40	33.93
Enrollment	.10	12.01
Sales tax	.25	23.98
	100.00	94.23

*(1162/1088)(100)(.15) = 16.02

Economic activity has declined 5.77% between 1987 and 1992, found by 100.0 − 94.23.

9.

Period	Money income	CPI	Real income
1982–84	$19,800	100	$19,800
1991	$32,000	135	$23,704

A nurse's purchasing power has increased since 1982–84. The amount of the increase is about $3,904.

10. *a.* $2.13M, found by $[(0.4 + 1.1 + 4.9)/3] \times 100$.
Real income for 1990 = $(4.6/130.7)\,100 = \$3.52M$.

b. For 1985, $11.4M.
For 1990, first $(130.7/107.6)\,100 = 121.5$
Then $(4.6/121.5)\,100 = \$3.79M$.
Thus his real income declined from $11.4M in 1985 to $3.79M in 1990.

c. Prices in 1980 were 17.6% below the 1982–84 level, found by 100.0 − 82.4.

11. *a.* Real incomes

	Mining	Apparel	Printing/ Publishing	Retail Trade
1989	$459.48	$188.98	$332.54	$152.19
1990	459.53	183.53	326.23	149.40
1991	460.21	178.32	316.96	144.45

b. Except for mining, real weekly wages declined meaning that the weekly wages of employees in apparel, printing and publishing, and retail trade did not keep up with inflation.

12. *a.* 280.0, found by (1.40/.50) 100. Cash dividends increased 180.0% from 1980 to 1990.

b. 311.1, found by (1.40/.45) 100.

13. 82.1, found by (55,000/67,000) 100. Employment decreased 17.9% from 1979 to 1990.

14. 68.5, found by (236,000,000/344,568,000) 100. Long-term debt down 31.5% from 1979 to 1990.

15. 198.7 found by (6,285,000,000/3,162,505,000) 100. Revenue increased 98.7% between 1979–80 and 1990.

16.

	Index
Construction	149.4
Finance	193.9
Trade	168.9
Utilities	154.6

Construction had the smallest increase (49.4%), finance the largest (93.9%).

17. Wholesale trade up 68.9%, transportation and public utilities increased 54.6%.

18.

	Real hourly wage	Change from base period
Service	$7.56*	$0.29
Retail trade	5.14	−0.55
Manufacturing	8.21	−0.63

* ($10.20/135.0)100

19. 1982–84 = 100. Purchasing power of a dollar is $1.00. For March 1991 = $ .74, found by ($1/135.0) 100.
    Purchasing power of a dollar declined $ .26 between those two periods.

20. Real income in 1986 was $1,861.31, found by ($2,040/109.6) 100. In 1991 it was $1548.15 found by ($2,090/135.0) 100. Thus, it declined $313.16 a month.

21. a. For 1992:

Retail Sales	34.01*
Bank deposits	10.46
Industrial production	41.48
Employment	37.09
	123.04

    * (1971.0/1,159)(100)(.20)
    b. Economy up 23.04% from 1983 to 1992.

22. Using 1950 = 100; for 1980 the indexes are:
    a. Letting 1950 be 100.0 (the base period):

Year	CPI	Labor Force	Productivity	GNP
1950	100.0	100.0	100.0	100.0
1967	138.7	126.6	154.1	275.9
1971	168.2	135.9	170.0	371.6
1975	223.6	148.4	177.0	529.8
1980	342.3	167.2	225.9	917.5

    b. From 1950 to 1980 consumer prices increased 242.3 percent, the labor force 67.2 percent, productivity 125.9 percent, and the GNP 817.5 percent.

23.

Item	p_0q_0	p_tq_t	p_tq_0	p_0q_t
Cabbage	$120	$ 75	$100	$ 90
Carrots	20	24	24	20
Peas	80	90	72	100
Endive	15	30	15	30
	$235	$219	$211	$240

a. P = ($211/$235)100 = 89.8. Prices down 10.2 percent from 1977 to 1992.
b. P = ($219/$240)100 = 91.3. Prices down 8.7 percent.
c. Laspeyres uses 1977 quantities for the base, Paasche uses 1992 quantities for the base.
d. Q = ($240/$235)100 = 102.1. Production increased 2.1 percent from 1977 to 1992.
e. V = ($219/$235)100 = 93.2. Value down 6.8 percent from 1977 to 1992.

24. a. Prices rose 603.6 percent, found by

    P = ($1,818,260/$258,437)(100) = 703.6.

    subtracting 100.0 gives 603.6.
    b. Quantity produced increased by 5.1 percent, found by ($271,624.40/$258,437)(100) = 105.1.

Item	p_0q_0	p_0q_t	p_tq_0
Aluminum	$ 287	$ 344.40	$ 760
Gas	850	680	12,500
Petroleum	190,800	190,800	1,560,000
Platinum	66,500	79,800	245,000
	$258,437	$271,624.40	$1,818,260

25. a. 686.6, found by (1,864,912/271,624.40)100.
    b. 721.6, found by (1,864,912/258,437)100.

26. There are two CPI's. One measures the change in prices of a fixed market basket of goods and services for urban wage earners and clerical workers. The other is for all consumers. The base period is 1982–84.

27. Basically, if the CPI increases from 140.5 to 141.0 wages go up 5 cents an hour—or a certain percent.

28. Contracts vary.

SOLUTIONS CHAPTER 19: TIME SERIES AND FORECASTING

1.

Year	failures	t	tY	t^2
1987	79	0	0	0
1988	120	1	120	1
1989	138	2	276	4
1990	184	3	552	9
1991	200	4	800	16
	721	10	1,748	30

$$b = \frac{1,748 - 721(10)/5}{30 - (10)^2/5} = 30.6$$

$$a = \frac{721}{5} - 30.6\left(\frac{10}{5}\right) = 83$$

$Y' = 83 + 30.6t$
For 1994, $Y' = 83 + 30.6(7)$
$Y' = 297.2$

2. $Y' = 37.6 + 1.75t$

Year	phone	t	tY	t^2
1986	37.9	0	0	0
1987	39.8	1	39.8	1
1988	40.4	2	80.8	4
1989	42.7	3	128.1	9
1990	44.1	4	176.4	16
1991	47.1	5	235.5	25
	252	15	660.6	55

$$b = \frac{660.6 - 252(15)/6}{55 - (15)^2/6} = 1.749$$

$$a = \frac{252}{6} - 1.749\left(\frac{15}{6}\right) = 37.628$$

$Y' = 37.628 + 1.749t$
For 1994, $Y' = 37.628 + 1.749(8)$
$Y' = 51.62$

3.

Year	Scrap	Code	Yt	t^2
1988	2.0	0	0	0
1989	4.0	1	4.0	1
1990	3.0	2	6.0	4
1991	5.0	3	15.0	9
1992	6.0	4	24.0	16
	20.0	10	49.0	30

$$b = \frac{49 - (20)(10)/5}{30 - (10)^2 5} = 0.90 \quad a = \frac{20}{5} - 0.90\left(\frac{10}{5}\right) = 2.2$$

$Y' = 2.2 + 0.90t$
$2.2 + 0.90(6) = 7.60$ (tons)

4.

Year	Vending	Code	Yt	t^2
1988	$17.5	0	0	0
1989	19.0	1	19.0	1
1990	21.0	2	42.0	4
1991	22.7	3	68.1	9
1992	24.5	4	98.0	16
	104.7	10	227.1	30

$$b = \frac{227.1 - (104.7)(10)/5}{30 - (10)^2/5} = 1.77$$

$$a = \frac{104.7}{5} - 1.77\left(\frac{10}{5}\right) = 17.4$$

$Y' = 17.4 + 1.77t$
$\quad 17.4 + 1.77(6) = 28.02$

5. a. $Y' = 0.0572 + 0.110(t)$, found by MINITAB with 1987 code 0.
   b. 28.82%, found by antilog of 0.110, which is 1.2882. Then 1.2882 − 1 = .2882. This is percent by which sales increased on average during the period.
   c. Estimated sales for 1994 = 6.717, found by:
   $Y' = 0.0572 + 0.110(7)$
   $Y' = .8272$
   Then the antilog of 0.8272 is 6.717.

6. a. 1.96 + 0.0415(t), found by MINITAB with 1984 coded 0.
   b. 10.03%, found by antilog of 0.0415, which is 1.1003.
   Then 1.1003 − 1 = .1003. This is the percent by which sales increased during the period.
   c. Estimated sales for 1994 = 237.14, found by:
   $Y' = 1.96 + 0.0415(10)$
   $Y' = 2.375$
   Then the antilog of 2.375 is 237.14

7. The output from the CBS System is as follows.

Classical Seasonal Indices

Period	Quarter	Value	Trend	S-I
1	1	4	—	—
	2	10	—	—
	3	7	6.1250	1.1429
	4	3	6.5000	0.4615
2	1	5	7	0.7143
	2	12	7.3750	1.6271
	3	9	7.6250	1.1803
	4	4	8.2500	0.4848
3	1	6	9.1250	0.6575
	2	16	9.5000	1.6842
	3	12	—	—
	4	4	—	—

Seasonal Index by Quarter

Quarter	Average SI Component	Seasonal Index
1	0.6859	0.6911
2	1.6557	1.6682
3	1.1616	1.1704
4	0.4732	0.4768

8. The results from the CBS package are as follows.

Period	Quarter	Value	Trend	S-I
1	1	5.3000	—	—
	2	4.1000	—	—
	3	6.8000	5.6625	1.2009
	4	6.7000	5.5625	1.2045
2	1	4.8000	5.3750	0.8930
	2	3.8000	5.2375	0.7255
	3	5.6000	5.1875	1.0795
	4	6.8000	5.1250	1.3268
3	1	4.3000	5.1375	0.8370
	2	3.8000	5.0500	0.7525
	3	5.7000	5.1125	1.1149
	4	6	5.3750	1.1163
4	1	5.6000	5.5625	1.0067
	2	4.6000	5.6375	0.8160
	3	6.4000	—	—
	4	5.9000	—	—

Seasonal Index by Quarter

Quarter	Average SI Component	Seasonal Index
1	0.9122	0.9077
2	0.7647	0.7609
3	1.1318	1.1261
4	1.2159	1.2098

9.

t	estimated pairs (millions)	Seasonal index	Quarterly forecast (millions)
21	40.05	110.0	44.055
22	41.80	120.0	50.160
23	43.55	80.0	34.840
24	45.30	90.0	40.770

10. Sales for each quarter are 500, found by 2000/4. The estimated sales for the second quarter are 725, found by 500(1.45).
Note: The first quarter of 1990 is coded 1.

11.

ROW	Qtrs	Index	Absent	Deseason	Time
1	1	0.6911	4	5.7879	1
2	2	1.6682	10	5.9945	2
3	3	1.1704	7	5.9809	3
4	4	0.4768	3	6.2919	4
5	1	0.6911	5	7.2348	5
6	2	1.6682	12	7.1934	6
7	3	1.1704	9	7.6897	7
8	4	0.4768	4	8.3893	8
9	1	0.6911	6	8.6818	9
10	2	1.6682	16	9.5912	10
11	3	1.1704	12	10.2529	11
12	4	0.4768	4	8.3893	12

Using MINITAB the results are as follows.
MTB > regr c4 1 c5;
The regression equation is
Deseason = 5.17 + 0.378 Time

Predictor	Coef	Stdev	t-ratio	P
Constant	5.1658	0.3628	14.24	0.000
Time	0.37805	0.04930	7.67	0.000

Using the regression equation $Y' = 5.1658 + .37805t$, the following estimates were obtained.

Estimate	Index	Seasonally adjusted
10.080	0.6911	6.966
10.458	1.6682	17.446
10.837	1.1704	12.836
11.215	0.4768	5.347

12.

ROW	Qtr	Index	Sales	Deseason	Time
1	1	0.9077	5.3	5.83893	1
2	2	0.7609	4.1	5.38836	2
3	3	1.1261	6.8	6.03854	3
4	4	1.2098	6.7	5.53811	4
5	1	0.9077	4.8	5.28809	5
6	2	0.7609	3.8	4.99409	6
7	3	1.1261	5.6	4.97292	7
8	4	1.2098	6.8	5.62076	8
9	1	0.9077	4.3	4.73725	9
10	2	0.7609	3.8	4.99409	10
11	3	1.1261	5.7	5.06172	11
12	4	1.2098	6.0	4.95950	12
13	1	0.9077	5.6	6.16944	13
14	2	0.7609	4.6	6.04547	14
15	3	1.1261	6.4	5.68333	15
16	4	1.2098	5.9	4.87684	16

The regression equation is
Deseason = 5.48 − 0.0112 Time

Predictor	Coef	Stdev	t-ratio	P
Constant	5.4832	0.2530	21.67	0.000
Time	−0.01121	0.02616	−0.43	0.675

Fitted	Index	Forcecast
5.293	0.9077	4.8045
5.282	0.7609	4.0191
5.270	1.1261	5.9345
5.259	1.2089	6.3576

13. a. Y' = 18,000 − 400t, assuming the straight line starts at 18,000 in 1970 and goes down to 10,000 in 1990.
 b. 400
 c. 8,000, found by 18,000 − 400(25).

14. a. Y' = 4,000 + 933t assuming a straight line goes from 4,000 to 18,000.
 b. $933

15. a. MTB > plot c3 vs c1

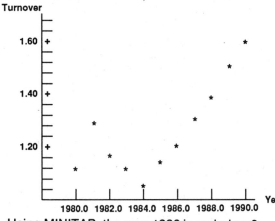

 b. Using MINITAB, the year 1980 is coded as 0, 1981 as 1 and so on.
 MTB > regr c3 1 c2
The regression equation is
Turnover = 1.05 + 0.0441 Code

Predictor	Coef	Stdev	t-ratio	P
Constant	1.04864	0.06665	15.73	0.000
Code	0.04409	0.01127	3.91	0.004

 Y' = 1.05 + 0.0441t
 c. 1983: Y' = 1.05 + 0.0441(3) = 1.1823
  1989: Y' = 1.05 + 0.0441(9) = 1.4469
 d. 1995: Y' = 1.05 + 0.0441(15) = 1.7115
 e. .0441 per year.

16. a.

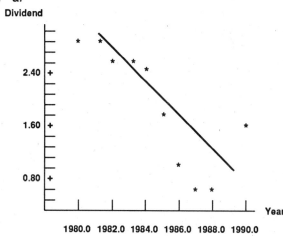

 b. The year 1980 is coded as 0, 1981 as 1 and so on.
The regression equation is
Dividend = 3.06 − 0.263 Code

Predictor	Coef	Stdev	t-ratio	P
Constant	3.0636	0.2518	12.17	0.000
Code	−0.26303	0.04717	−5.58	0.000

 c. 1982: Y' = 3.06 − 0.263(2) = 2.534
  1989: Y' = 3.06 − 0.263(9) = .693
 d. 1994: Y' = 3.06 − 0.263(14) = −0.622
 e. The dividends decreased about 0.263 per year over the period.

 Note: The year 1982 is coded 0.

17. a.

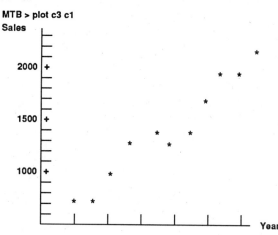

MTB > regr c3 1 c2
The regression equation is
Sales = 786 + 127 Code

Predictor	Coef	Stdev	t-ratio	P
Constant	786.45	53.66	14.66	0.000
Code	127.109	9.070	14.01	0.000

b. $Y' = 786 + 127(t)$, found by MINITAB with 1982 coded as 0, 1983 as 1, and so on.
c. 1984: $Y' = 786 + 127(2) = \$1,040$.
   1990: $Y' = 786 + 127(8) = \$1,802$.
d. \$127 million.
e. \$2,691 million.

18. a.

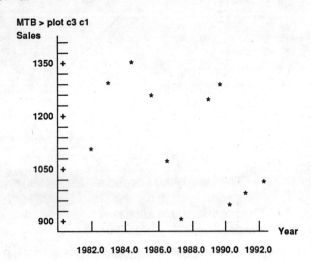

MTB > regr c3 1 c2
The regression equation is
Sales = 1258 − 23.6 Code

Predictor	Coef	Stdev	t-ratio	P
Constant	1257.68	79.24	15.87	0.000
Code	− 23.61	13.39	− 1.76	0.112

   log $Y' = 1,258 − 23.6(t)$, found by MINITAB, with 1982 as 0.
c. 1983: $1,258 − 23.6(1) = \$1,234.40$
   1989: $1,258 − 23.6(7) = \$1,092.80$
d. 1997: $1,258 − 23.6(16) = \$880.4$
e. A \$23.6 million decrease per year.

19. Using the MINITAB system the output is as follows. The year 1983 is coded as 0.
    a. log Y′ = .903900 + 0.113669t is the regression equation.

Predictor	Coef	Stdev	t-ratio	P
Constant	0.903900	0.002316	390.35	0.000
Code	0.113669	0.000391	290.41	0.000

    b. For 1983 the code is 3.
    log Y′ = 0.903900 + 0.113669(3) = 1.244907. Antilog is 17.575.
    For 1990 the code is 8.
    log Y′ = 0.903900 + 0.113669(8) = 1.813252. Antilog is 65.051.
    c. The yearly rate of increase is 29.9%, found by taking the antilog of 0.113669 and subtracting 1.
    d. log Y′ = 0.903900 + 0.113669(11) = 2.154259. Antilog is 142.646 ($millions).

20. a. The regression equation is as follows. The year 1984 is coded as 0.
    Log Y′ = 1.94769 + 0.0300431t

Predictor	Coef	Stdev	t-ratio	P
Constant	1.94769	0.00252	773.81	0.000
Code	0.0300431	0.0006981	43.04	0.000

    b. Y′ = 1.94769 + 0.0300431(9) = 2.2180779. The antilog is 165.226.
    c. The antilog of .0300431 is 1.0716, so the rate of increase is about 7.16% per year.

21. a. The regression equation is (1980 is coded as 0).
    log Y′ = 0.00909 + .21978t

Predictor	Coef	Stdev	t-ratio	P
Constant	0.00909	0.07390	0.12	0.905
Code	0.21978	0.01384	15.88	0.000

    b. Y′ = 0.00909 + .21978(13) = 2.86623. The antilog is 734.903.
    c. The antilog of .21978 is 1.659, so the households increased about 65.9% per year.

22. *a.* July 44.2, August 72.3, September 197.5

b.

Month	Total	Mean	Seasonal
Jan.	345.3	86.325	86.5
Feb.	424.1	106.075	106.3
March	697.8	174.45	174.8
April	483.9	120.975	121.2
May	239.2	59.800	59.9
June	190.3	47.575	47.7
July	180.6	45.15	45.2
August	295.6	73.905	74.0
Sept.	798.5	199.625	200.0
Oct.	351.9	87.975	88.1
Nov.	424.6	106.15	106.4
Dec.	358.6	89.65	89.8
		1197.65	

Correction = 1200/1197.65 = 1.001962

c. Sales for September and March are considerably above average and below average for May, June, and July.

23. *a.* July 87.5; August 92.9; September 99.3; October 109.1.

b.

Month	Total	Mean	Corrected
July	348.9	87.225	86.777
Aug.	368.1	92.025	91.552
Sept.	395.0	98.750	98.242
Oct.	420.4	105.100	104.560
Nov.	496.2	124.050	123.412
Dec.	572.3	143.075	142.340
Jan.	333.5	83.375	82.946
Feb.	297.5	74.375	73.993
March	347.3	86.825	86.379
April	481.3	120.325	119.707
May	396.1	99.025	98.516
June	368.1	92.025	91.552
		1206.200	

Correction = 1200/1206.2 = 0.99486

c. April, November, and December are periods of high sales, while February is low.

24. *a.* The seasonal indexes are computed using the CBS software.
Model: Seasonal Indices
Number of Periods: 20

Classical Seasonal Indices

Period	Quarter	Value	Trend	S-I
1	1	7.8000	—	—
	2	10.2000	—	—
	3	14.7000	10.3875	1.4152
	4	9.3000	10.4500	0.8900
2	1	6.9000	10.9750	0.6287
	2	11.6000	11.3250	1.0243
	3	17.5000	11.5750	1.5119
	4	9.3000	11.5875	0.8026
3	1	8.9000	11.0750	0.8036
	2	9.7000	10.9000	0.8899
	3	15.3000	11.2250	1.3630
	4	10.1000	11.7875	0.8568
4	1	10.7000	12.3125	0.8690
	2	12.4000	12.5750	0.9861
	3	16.8000	12.4625	1.3480
	4	10.7000	12.4250	0.8612
5	1	9.2000	12.6125	0.7294
	2	13.6000	12.6000	1.0794
	3	17.1000	—	—
	4	10.3000	—	—

Seasonal Index by Quarter

Quarter	Average SI Component	Seasonal Index
1	0.7577	0.7558
2	0.9949	0.9924
3	1.4095	1.4060
4	0.8526	0.8505

b. The third quarter is more than 40% above a typical quarter. The production activity is below average in the first and fourth quarters.

c. The trend equation, as determined by MINITAB is as follows, using the first quarter of 1986 as code 1.
The regression equation is
Adj = 10.1 + 0.142 year

Predictor	Coef	Stdev	t-ratio	P
Constant	10.0989	0.4473	22.58	0.000
Year	0.14213	0.03734	3.81	0.001

d. The projections for 1991 are as follows

Period	Production	Index	Forecast
21	13.084	.7558	9.889
22	13.226	.9924	13.125
23	13.368	1.4060	18.795
24	13.510	.8505	11.490

25. *a.* The output from the CBS software is as follows.
Model: Seasonal Indices
Number of Periods: 24

Classical Seasonal Indices

Period	Quarter	Value	Trend	S-I
1	1	142	—	—
	2	312	—	—
	3	488	288	1.6944
	4	208	289.2500	0.7191
2	1	146	293	0.4983
	2	318	296.5000	1.0725
	3	512	298.7500	1.7138
	4	212	302	0.7020
3	1	160	314.7500	0.5083
	2	330	322.8750	1.0221
	3	602	319.5000	1.8842
	4	187	320.2500	0.5839
4	1	158	317.5000	0.4976
	2	338	312.3750	1.0820
	3	572	311.5000	1.8363
	4	176	317.2500	0.5548
5	1	162	321.3750	0.5041
	2	380	323.2500	1.1756
	3	563	326.2500	1.7257
	4	200	324	0.6173
6	1	162	324.7500	0.4988
	2	362	328.3750	1.1024
	3	587	—	—
	4	205	—	—

Seasonal Index by Quarter

Quarter	Average SI Component	Seasonal Index
1	0.5014	0.5027
2	1.0909	1.0936
3	1.7709	1.7753
4	0.6354	0.6370

b. The production is the largest in the third quarter. It is 77.5% above the average quarter. The second quarter is also above average. The first and fourth quarters are well below average, with the first quarter at about 50% of a typical quarter.

26. *a.* The results from the CBS system are as follows.

Model: Seasonal Indices

Number of Periods: 28

Classical Seasonal Indices

Period	Quarter	Value	Trend	S-I
1	1	210	—	—
	2	180	—	—
	3	60	174.5000	0.3438
	4	246	179.5000	1.3705
2	1	214	186.7500	1.1459
	2	216	187.5000	1.1520
	3	82	189.5000	0.4327
	4	230	195	1.1795
3	1	246	197.6250	1.2448
	2	228	205	1.1122
	3	91	212.7500	0.4277
	4	280	217	1.2903
4	1	258	222.5000	1.1596
	2	250	227.5000	1.0989
	3	113	232.3750	0.4863
	4	298	237.1250	1.2567
5	1	279	239.6250	1.1643
	2	267	240.7500	1.1090
	3	116	244.3750	0.4747
	4	304	250.1250	1.2154
6	1	302	252.7500	1.1949
	2	290	253.2500	1.1451
	3	114	256.3750	0.4447
	4	310	258.8750	1.1975
7	1	321	259.7500	1.2358
	2	291	261.7500	1.1117
	3	120	—	—
	4	320	—	—

Seasonal Index by Quarter

Quarter	Average SI Component	Seasonal Index
1	1.1909	1.1939
2	1.1215	1.1243
3	0.4350	0.4361
4	1.2516	1.2548

b. From the MINITAB system the output is as follows, using the first quarter as a code 1.
The regression equation is
Deseason = 163 + 4.13 Code

Predictor	Coef	Stdev	t-ratio	P
Constant	163.208	5.431	32.05	0.000
Code	4.1253	0.3272	12.61	0.000

Period	Sales	Index	Forecast
29	282.8417	1.1939	337.6847
30	286.967	1.1243	322.6370
31	291.0923	.4361	126.9454
32	295.2176	1.2548	370.4390

27. The CBS system was used to determine the seasonal indexes.
    Model: Seasonal Indices
    Number of Periods: 20

Classical Seasonal Indices

Period	Quarter	Value	Trend	S-I
1	1	4.4000	—	—
	2	6.1000	—	—
	3	11.7000	7.3125	1.6000
	4	7.2000	7.3375	0.9813
2	1	4.1000	7.3250	0.5597
	2	6.6000	7.4250	0.8889
	3	11.1000	7.5750	1.4653
	4	8.6000	7.5750	1.1353
3	1	3.9000	7.7125	0.5057
	2	6.8000	7.9625	0.8540
	3	12	8.2375	1.4568
	4	9.7000	8.4125	1.1530
4	1	5	8.5375	0.5857
	2	7.1000	8.5375	0.8316
	3	12.7000	8.3625	1.5187
	4	9	8.0375	1.1198
5	1	4.3000	7.5625	0.5686
	2	5.2000	7.1500	0.7273
	3	10.8000	—	—
	4	7.6000	—	—

Seasonal Index by Quarter

Quarter	Average SI Component	Seasonal Index
1	0.5549	0.5577
2	0.8254	0.8296
3	1.5102	1.5178
4	1.0973	1.1029

b. The MINITAB system was used to determine the trend equation.
The regression equation is
Deseason = 7.67 + 0.0023 Code

Predictor	Coef	Stdev	t-ratio	P
Constant	7.6696	0.3196	24.00	0.000
Code	0.00227	0.02876	0.08	0.938

c.

Period	Production	Index	Forecast
21	7.7150	0.5577	4.3026
22	7.717	0.8296	6.4020
23	7.7200	1.5178	11.7174
24	7.7218	1.1029	8.5163

28. The MINITAB output for the two models are as follows with the first period as $t = 0$.
Linear:
MTB > regr c2 1 c4
The regression equation is
Students = 12823 + 494 Code

Predictor	Coef	Stdev	t-ratio	P
Constant	12823.0	296.2	43.30	0.000
Code	494.42	21.15	23.37	0.000

= 762.7   R-sq = 96.0%   R-sq(adj) = 95.8%

LOG
MTB > regr c3 1 c4
The regression equation is
Log-stu = 4/12 + 0.0117 Code

Predictor	Coef	Stdev	t-ratio	P
Constant	4.12461	0.00733	562.90	0.000
Code	0.0116772	0.0005234	22.31	0.000

= 0.01887   R-sq = 95.6%   R-sq(adj) = 95.4%

The year 1967 is coded 0, so 1993 is coded 26.
   Linear Y' = 12,823 + 494.42(26) = 25,678
   Log Y' = 4.12461 + .0116772(26) = 4.4282172
   The antilog is 26,805.
The linear estimate is probably better, because the fitted values are about the same and the linear estimates are easier to understand.

29. Using the CBS system the index for each quarter was:

Seasonal Index by Quarter

Quarter	Average SI Component	Seasonal Index
1	1.1962	1.2053
2	1.0135	1.0212
3	0.6253	0.6301
4	1.1371	1.1457

The MINITAB output is:
The regression equation is
Y' = 43.6 + 7.22 C1

Predictor	Coef	Stdev	t-ratio	P
Constant	43.611	7.600	5.74	0.000
Year	7.2153	0.4579	15.76	0.000

Period	Visitors	Index	Forecast
29	252.86	1.2053	304.77
30	260.07	1.0212	265.58
31	267.29	0.6301	168.42
32	274.50	1.1457	314.50

In 1992 there were a total of 928 visitors. A ten percent increase in 1993 means there will be 1021 visitors. The quarterly estimates are 1021/4 = 255.25 visitors per quarter.

Period	Visitors	Index	Forecast
Winter	255.25	1.2053	307.65
Spring	255.25	1.0212	260.66
Summer	255.25	0.6301	160.83
Fall	255.25	1.1457	292.44

The regression approach is probably superior because the trend is considered.

30. *a.* Using the CBS system the seasonal indexes are:

Seasonal Index by Quarter

Quarter	Average SI Component	Seasonal Index
1	0.8925	1.0438
2	0.8283	0.9688
3	0.4449	0.5203
4	1.2621	1.4761

So the indexes are 104.38, 96.88, 52.03, and 147.61.

b. Fall quarter enrollment is the largest, 47% above average and the summer quarter is the lowest, almost 48% below average.

Using MINITAB, the regression equation is
The regression equation is
$Y' = 1589 + 50.4 C1$

Predictor	Coef	Stdev	t-ratio	P
Constant	1589.2	149.7	10.62	0.000
Year	50.43	13.83	3.65	0.002

The estimates for the next four quarters are:
s = 304.4 R-sq = 45.4% R-sq (adj) = 42.0%

Period	Students	Index	Forecast
19	2547.3	1.0438	2658.9
20	2597.7	.9688	2516.7
21	2648.2	.5203	1377.9
22	2698.6	1.4761	3983.4

CHAPTER 20:   AN INTRODUCTION TO DECISION MAKING UNDER UNCERTAINTY

1. $EMV(A_1) = .30(\$50) + .50(\$70) + .20(\$100) = \$70$

   $EMV(A_2) = .30(\$90) + .50(\$40) + .20(\$80) = 63$

   $EMV(A_3) = .30(\$70) + .50(\$60) + .20(\$90) = 69$

   Decision: Choose alternative 1.

2. Choose returnables because EMV (returnables) is higher.

   EMV (returnables) $= \$80(.70) + \$40(.30)$

   $= \$68$ thousand

   EMV (nonreturnables) $= \$25(.70) + \$60(.30)$

   $= \$35.5$ thousand

   Use returnable bottles

3.
	Opportunity loss		
	S_1	S_2	S_3
A_1	\$40	\$ 0	\$ 0
A_2	0	30	20
A_3	20	10	10

4.
	Opportunity loss (\$000)	
Type of bottle	Passed	Not passed
Returnable	0	\$20
Nonreturnable	\$55	0

5. (Answers in \$000)

   $EOL(A_1) = .30(\$40) + .50(\$0) + .20(\$0) = \$12$

   $EOL(A_2) = .30(\$0) + .50(\$30) + .20(\$20) = 19$

   $EOL(A_3) = .30(\$20) + .50(\$10) + .20(\$10) = 13$

6. (Answers in \$000)

   EOL (Returnables) $= \$0(.70) + \$20(.30)$

   $= \$6$ thousand

   EOL (Nonreturnables) $= \$55(.70) + 0(.30)$

   $= \$38.5$ thousand

7. Expected value under conditions of certainty is \$82, found by $.30(\$90) + .50(\$70) + .20(\$100) = \$82$

   $EVPI = \$82 - \$70 = \$12$

8. Condition of Certainty $= \$80(.70) + \$60(.3)$

   $= \$74$ thousand

   Then $EVPI = \$74 - \$68 = \$6$ thousand

9. Yes, it changes the decision. Choose alternative 2. (Answers in \$000).

   $EMV(A_1) = .50(\$50) + .20(\$70) + .30(\$100) = \$69$

   $EMV(A_2) = .50(\$90) + .20(\$40) + .30(\$80) = \$77$

   $EMV(A_3) = .50(\$70) + .20(\$60) + .30(\$90) = \$74$

10. Choose returnables. Does not alter decision.

   EMV (Returnable)   = $80(.30) + $40(.70)
                           = $52 thousand
   EMV (Nonreturnables) = $25(.30) + $60(.70)
                           = $49.5 thousand

11. *a.* (Answers in $000)

   EMV(neither) = .30($0) + .50($0) + .20($0)
                           = $0
   EMV(1) = .30($125) + .50($65) +
                  .20($30) = $76.00
   EMV(2) = .30($105) + .50($60) +
                  .20($30) = $67.50
   EMV(both) = .30($220) + .50($110) +
                  .20($40) = $129.00

   b. Choose both.

   c.

	Opportunity loss		
	S_1	S_2	S_3
Neither	$220	$110	$40
1	95	45	10
2	115	50	10
Both	0	0	0

   d.

   EOL(neither) = .30($220) + .50($110) + .20($40) = $129.00
   EOL(1) = .30($95) + .50($45) + .20($10) = $53.00
   EOL(2) = .30($115) + .50($50) + .20($10) = $61.50
   EOL(both) = .30($0) + .50($0) + .20($0) = $ 0

   e. EVPI = $0, found by $129 − $129.
   Certainty = .30($220) + .50($110) + .20($40)
                  = $129

12.

	Weather	
Transportation	*Good*	*Bad*
Plane	$115	$122.50
Train	80	110
Car	110	140

   EMV (plane)
    $115(.40) + $122.50(.60) = $119.50
   EMV (train)
    $80(.40) + $110(.60) = $98.00
   EMV (car)
    $110(.40) + $140(.60) = $128.00
   Choose the train because $98 is the least cost.
    Certainty = $80(.40) + $110(.60) = $98
       EVPI = $98 − $98 = $0

13. The payoff table is as follows in $000.

	Recession S_1	No Recession S_2
Production	$ – 10.0	$15.0
Stock	$ –5.0	$12.0
CD	$ 6.0	$ 6.0

a. Purchase a CD
b. Increase production.
c. (Answers in $000)

EMV(Prod.) = .2(– 10) + .8(15.0) = 10.0
EMV(Stock) = .2(– 5) + .8(12.0) = 8.6
EMV(CD) = .2(6) + .8(6) = 6.0
Expand production
d. EVPI = [.2(6) + .8(15)] – [10.0] = 13.2 – 10.0 = 3.2

14. Payoff Table

a.

	S_1	S_2	S_3
No Inspection	$ 7.2	$14.4	$21.60
Inspect	10.0	10.0	10.00

b. EMV (Inspect) = .7(7.2) + .2(14.4) + .1(21.60) = $10.08
Inspect = $10.0
The decision is to inspect.
c. EVPI = [.7(7.2) + .2(10) + .1(10)] – 10.0 = – 1.96

15. a.

	Event				
Act	10	11	12	13	14
10	$500	$500	$500	$500	$500
11	200	550	550	550	550
12	– 100	250	600	600	600
13	– 400	– 50	300	650	650
14	– 700	– 350	0	350	700

b.

Act	Expected profit
10	$500.00
11	504.50
12	421.50
13	233.50
14	– 31.50

Order 11 mobile homes because expected profit of $504.50 is the highest.

c.

	Opportunity loss				
Supply	10	11	12	13	14
10	$ 0	$ 50	$100	$150	$200
11	300	0	50	100	150
12	600	300	0	50	100
13	900	600	300	0	50
14	1,200	900	600	300	0

d.

	Act				
	10	11	12	13	14
Expected opportunity loss	$95.50	$91	$174	$362	$627

Decision: Order 11 homes because the opportunity loss of $91 is the smallest.

e. $91, found by:

$595.50	profit under certainty
– 504.50	profit under uncertainty
$ 91.00	value of perfect information

16. a.

	Event			
Act	7	8	9	10
7	$35	$35	$35	$35
8	15	40	40	40
9	–5	20	45	45
10	– 25	0	25	50

b. Expected profits are:

Demand	Expected Payoff
7	$35.00
8	37.50
9	33.75
10	18.75

The computations for 9 snowmobiles are:

Event X	Probability P(X)	Payoff Y	Expected Profit P(X)Y
7	0.10	$ – 5	$ – 0.50
8	.25	20	5.00
9	.45	45	20.25
10	.20	45	9.00
Total			$33.75

c. Lease 8 snowmobiles because the expected profit of $37.50 is the highest.
d. Opportunity loss table is:

Act Number Available	Opportunity loss			
	7	8	9	10
7	0	5	10	15
8	20	0	5	10
9	40	20	0	5
10	60	40	20	0

e. Computations for 8 snowmobiles:

Demand X	Probability P(X)	Opportunity Loss OL	Expected Loss P(X)OL
7	0.10	$20	$2.00
8	.25	0	0.00
9	.45	5	2.25
10	.20	10	2.00
Total			$6.25

The expected opportunity losses are:

	Number Available			
	7	8	9	10
Expected Opportunity Loss	$8.75	$6.25	$10.00	$25.00

f. Lease 8 snowmobiles.

g. Value of perfect information is $6.25. Profit under certainty is $43.75, found by:

Event	Profit	Total Profit	Probability	Expected Profit
7	$5	$35	0.10	$ 3.50
8	5	40	.25	10.00
9	5	45	.45	20.25
10	5	50	.20	10.00
Total				$43.75

Then, $43.75 − $37.50 = $6.25

h. All evidence indicates that leasing 8 snowmobiles would be the most profitable.

17. a.

	Event					
Act	41	42	43	44	45	46
41	$410	$410	$410	$410	$410	$410
42	405	420	420	420	420	420
43	400	415	430	430	430	430
44	395	410	425	440	440	440
45	390	405	420	435	450	450
46	385	400	415	430	445	460

b.

Act	Expected profit
41	$410.00
42	419.10
43	426.70
44	432.20
45	431.70
46	427.45

c. Order 44 because $432.20 is the largest expected profit.

d. Expected opportunity loss:

41	42	43	44	45	46
$28.30	$19.20	$11.60	$6.10	$6.60	$10.85

e. Order 44 because the opportunity loss of $6.10 is the smallest. Yes, it agrees.

f. $6.10, found by:

$438.30	profit under certainty
− 432.20	profit under uncertainty
$ 6.10	value of perfect information

The maximum we should pay for perfect information is $6.10.

18. The cost per car is $4,000, found by $6000 − $2000. If Kevin purchased 20 cars and he can rent 20 cars the payoff is $12,500. It is computed as follows:

(20 cars)(5 days)(50 weeks)($20 − $1.50) − (20 cars)($4,000) = $92,500 − $80,000 = $12,500
The other payoffs are computed in a similar fashion.

		Payoff (in $000) States of Nature				
		20	21	22	23	EMV(A_i)
	A_1 20	12.5	12.5	12.5	12.5	12.5
	A_2 21	8.5	13.125	13.125	13.125	12.6625
Choices	A_3 22	4.5	9.125	13.75	13.750	11.90
	A_4 23	.5	5.125	9.75	14.375	8.825

EMV(A_2 = .10(8.5) + .20(13.125) = 12.6625
EMV(A_3 = .10(4.5) + .20(9.125) + .70(13.75) = 11.90
EMV(A_4 = .10(0.5) + .20(5.125) + .50(9.75) + .20(14.375) = 8.825
EVCP = .1(12.5) + .2(13.125) + .5(13.75) + .2(14.375) = 13.625
EVPI = 13.625 − 12.6625 = 0.9625
$962.50

CHAPTER 21:   STATISTICAL QUALITY CONTROL

1. Chance variations are usually large in number and random in nature and usually cannot be eliminated. Assignable variation is usually non-random and can be eliminated.

2. Variable charts are concerned with actual measurements (weight, diameter, etc.). Attribute charts are based on a classification of acceptable or not acceptable (door lock either works or it does not).

3. *a.* The A_2 factor is 0.729.
   b. The value for D_3 is 0, and for D_4 it is 2.282.

4. .1075, found by

   $$[(.577)(.25)(\sqrt{5})]/3$$

5. *a.*

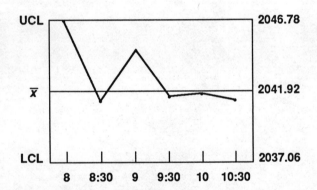

	$\bar{X}$	
Time	*Arithmetic means*	*R range*
8:00 A.M.	46	16
8:30 A.M.	40.5	6
9:00 A.M.	44	6
9:30 A.M.	40	2
10:00 A.M.	41.5	9
10:30 A.M.	39.5	1
	251.5	40

UCL $= \bar{\bar{X}} + A_2\bar{R}$

$= 41.92 + 0.729(6.67)$

$= 46.78$

LCL $= \bar{\bar{X}} - A_2\bar{R}$

$= 41.92 - 0.729(6.67)$

$= 37.06$

b. Interpreting, the mean reading was 2,041.92 degrees Fahrenheit. If the oven continues operating as evidenced by the first six hourly readings, about 99.7 percent of the mean readings will lie between 2,037.06 degrees and 2,046.78 degrees.

6. *a.* UCL $= D_4\bar{R} = 2.282 (6.67) = 15.22$.
      LCL $= D_3\bar{R} = 0$.
   b. Oven is operating within bounds. The first range (8 A.M.) is outside the control limits.

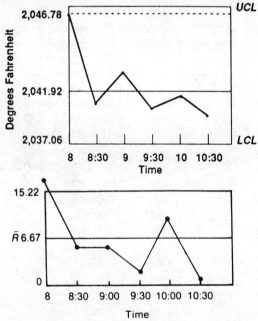

7a. $\bar{p} = \dfrac{.48}{10} = .048$

$$.048 \pm 3 \sqrt{\frac{.048(1-.048)}{50}} = .048 \pm .091$$

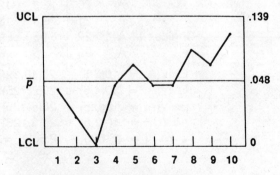

The limits are from 0 to .139.

b. 10/50 = .20, so this reading is out of control. The process should be adjusted.

8. *a.* $\bar{p}$ = 1.88/20 = .094.

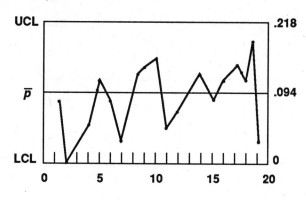

b. 9.4% of bolts are defective. 99.7% of the checks will reveal a percent defective between 0 and 21.8%.

9. *a.* $\bar{c} = \dfrac{24}{10} = 2.40$ $2.40 \pm 3\sqrt{2.40} = 2.40 \pm 4.65$

The limits are from 0 to 7.05.

b. The unit that had 6 defects is not out of control because 6 < 7.05; that is, 6 falls below the UCL of 7.05.

10. *a.* $\bar{c}$ = 72/12 = 6
LCL and UCL = $\bar{c} \pm 3\sqrt{\bar{c}} = 6 \pm 3\sqrt{6} = 0$ and 13.348.

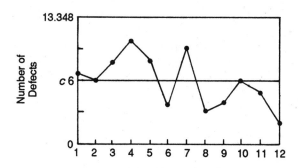

b. Mean number of defects is 6. About 99.7% of means will be between 0 and 13.348.

11.

Percent defective	Probability of accepting lot
10	.889
20	.558
30	.253
40	.083

12.

Percent defective	Probability of accepting lot
10	.956
20	.698
30	.355
40	.124

13. $P(X \leq 1 \mid n = 10, p = .10) = .736$
$P(X \leq 1 \mid n = 10, p = .20) = .376$
$P(X \leq 1 \mid n = 10, p = .30) = .149$
$P(X \leq 1 \mid n = 10, p = .40) = .046$

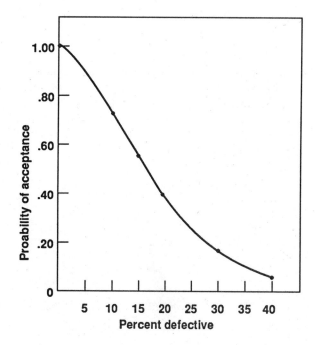

14. $P(x \leq 3/n = 25, p = .10) = .764$
$P(x \leq 3/n = 25, p = .20) = .234$
$P(x \leq 3/n = 25, p = .30) = .033$
$P(x \leq 3/n = 25, p = .40) = .002$

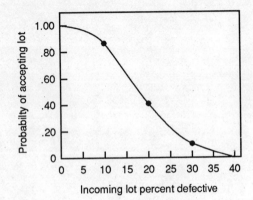

15. *a.* $\bar{\bar{X}} = 10.0, \bar{R} = .25$. For mean chart UCL = $10.0 + .577 (.25) = 10.14$
   LCL = 9.86. For range chart UCL = 2.115 (.25) = .53, LCL = 0.
   b. Process is out of control for means, but in control for variation.

16. *a.* $\bar{c} = 4.0$, UCL = 10, LCL = 0.
   b. Yes. 11.3 is beyond the upper limit.

17. *a.* $\bar{p} = 93/15 = 6.2$. Then 6.2/200 = .031.
   b. UCL = .068, LCL = 0.
   c. No. 10 packages = .05 which does not exceed UCL of .068.

18. $\bar{c} = 137/10 = 13.7$.
   UCL = $\bar{c} + 3 \sqrt{\bar{c}} = 13.7 + 3 \sqrt{13.7} = 24.8$
   LCL = 2.6

19. *a.* and *b.* For the mean chart: central line = 45.2; UCL = 54.3; LCL = 36.1. Control limits computed by $\bar{\bar{X}} \pm A_2\bar{R} = 45.2 \pm .729(12.5)$. The factor A_2 is from Appendix L. For the range chart: central line = 12.5; UCL = 28.5; LCL = 0. Control limits computed by:
$$D_4\bar{R} = 2.282(12.5)$$
$$D_3\bar{R} = (0)(12.5)$$

20. *a.* and *b.*

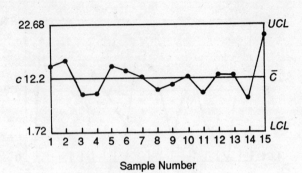

Sample Number

$\bar{c} = 183/15 = 12.2$
UCL and LCL found by:
$\bar{c} \pm 3 \sqrt{\bar{c}}$
$12.2 \pm 3 \sqrt{12.2}$
$12.2 \pm (3)(3.49285)$
12.2 ± 10.48
UCL 22.68
LCL 1.72

   c. Based on the initial check of 15 bowls, the probability is 0.997 that a bowl will have between 1.72 stones and 22.68 stones in it. The average number is 12.2.

21. *a.*

$$\bar{p} = \frac{.80}{10} = .08$$

To find UCL and LCL:

$$.08 \pm 3 \sqrt{\frac{(.80)(92)}{50}}$$

$$.08 \pm 3(.038)$$

UCL = .1951

LCL = 0

   b.

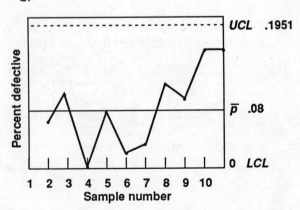

Sample number

c. The upper and lower control limits indicate that 99.73 percent of the percent defectives will be between 0 and 19.51, with an average of 8 percent.

22. *a.* $\bar{\bar{X}}$ = 87.36, UCL = 88.11, LCL = 86.61
$\bar{R}$ = 1.3, UCL = 2.75, LCL = 0

b.

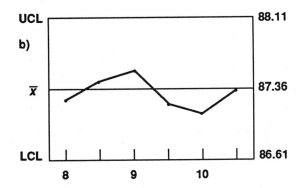

c.

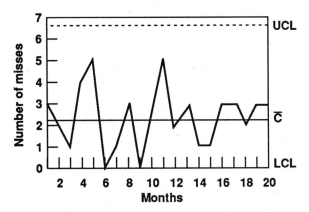

d. Mean is 87.36 outside diameter. Mean range is 1.3. 99.7% sample means between 86.61 and 88.11; range between 0 and 2.75.

23. $\bar{c}$ = 47/20 = 2.35.
UCL and LCL = $2.35 \pm 3\sqrt{2.35}$ = 0 and 6.95.

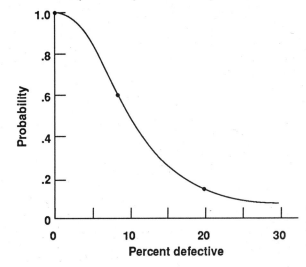

There is no upward trend.

24. *a.* $P(X \le 2 | n = 25, p = .10)$ = .537
$P(X \le 2 | n = 25, p = .20)$ = .098
$P(X \le 2 | n = 25, p = .30)$ = .009
b. $P(X \le 2 | n = 25, p = .15)$ = .0172 + .0759
+ .1607
= .2538
c. $P(X \le 2 | n = 25, p = .05)$ = .2774 + .3650
+ .2305
= .8729

The probability (.8729) is somewhat less than desired (.90). (*Note:* A more extensive table, or some computer system such as MINITAB, is required for parts b and c.)

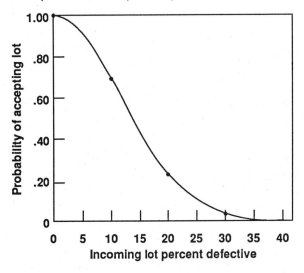

25. $P(x \le 3/n = 20, p = .10)$ = .867
$P(x \le 3/n = 20, p = .20)$ = .411
$P(x \le 3/n = 20, p = .30)$ = .107

PART III

Solutions to Review Section Exercises

ANSWERS TO SECTION ONE EXERCISES
A Review of Chapter 1–4

1. *a.* Sample.
   b. Ratio.
   c. $11.60, found by $58/5. Or, see MINITAB below.
   d. $11.70. Half of the employees earn below $11.70 an hour and the other half earn above $11.70 an hour.
   e. 5.845, found by 23.38/4. Or using MINITAB, $s_2 = (2.42)^2 = 2.845$.
   MTB > descb c1

	N	MEAN	MEDIAN	TRMEAN	STDEV	SEMEAN
C1	5	11.60	11.70	11.60	2.42	1.08

	MIN	MAX	Q1	Q3
C1	9.00	14.80	9.25	13.90

   f. -1.241, found 3 ($11.60 - $11.70)/$\sqrt{5.845}$
   Negative skewness.

2. *a.* population.
   b. 5 hours, found by 30/6.
   c. 4.5. Half of the hours are above 4.5, half below it.
   d. No mode.
   e. 2.67 hours, found by 16/6.
   f. 3.56 hours, found by $\sqrt{12.6667}$.
   g. 71 percent, found by (3.56/5)(100).

3. *a.*

Number of Rolls	f
3–5	2
6–8	6
9–11	8
12–14	3
15–17	1
Total	20

   b.

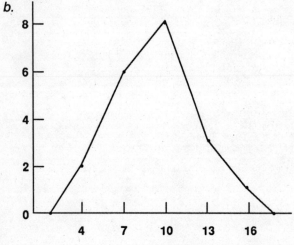

LABEL?

c. 9.25, found by 185/20

d. 9.25, found by

$$8.5 + \frac{10-8}{8}(3)$$

e. 10, using the frequency distribution and the midpoint of the 9 to 11 class.

f. 14 using the frequency distribution, found by 17 − 3, or 13 using the ungrouped data.

g. 9.355, found by

$$\frac{1,889 - \dfrac{(185)^2}{20}}{20-1}$$

	N	MEAN	MEDIAN	TRMEAN	STDEV	SEMEAN
C1	20	9.300	9.000	9.278	3.045	0.681

	MIN	MAX	Q1	Q3
C1	3.000	16.000	8.000	11.000

h. 3.059, found by $\sqrt{9.355}$ ·

i. 3.132 to 15.368, found by 9.25 ± 2(3.059).

4. a. ratio.

b.

Amount Spent ($ millions)	Frequency	Cumulative Frequency	Midpoint
$ 6–$10	3	3	$ 8
11– 15	5	8	13
16– 20	8	16	18
21– 25	8	24	23
26– 30	4	28	28
31– 35	2	30	33
Total	30		

c.

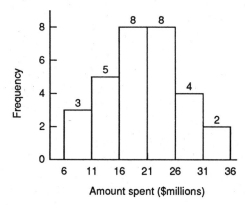

d.

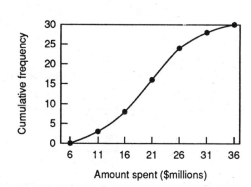

e. About $19 or $20 million

f. $19.83 using the grouped data, found by $595/30.

g. Answers will vary slightly. Interquartile range = $9 million found by $24 − $15. Quartile deviation = $4.5 million, found by ($24 − $15)/2.

5. a. 8.82%, found by 44.1/5.

b. 7.479%.

c. Geometric mean since it is not highly influenced by the 19.5%.

6. 20.24% found by $\sqrt[5]{\dfrac{284}{113}} - 1$

7.

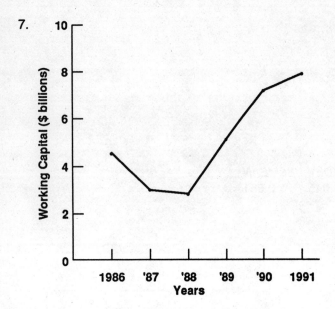

8.

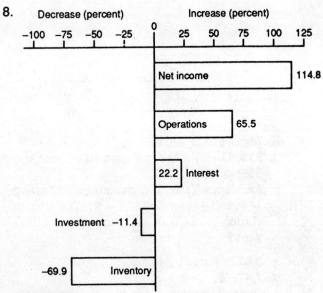

9. Ordinal.

10. Statistic.

11. Less-than-cumulative frequency polygon. About 45; about 35; 10, 5 found by 10/2; 35, found by 55 − 20.

12. Frequency polygon. Positive skewness. Mean would be larger than the median.

13. 9.375%.

14. 1.5

15. Coefficient of variation.

16. 24. To explain, the range is about 6 times the standard deviation for a symmetrical distribution.

17. 92 and 108, found by 100 ± 2(4).

18. Geometric mean.

19.
and
20. *a.* The following histogram is from MINITAB.

Histogram of C1   N = 50

Midpoint	Count	
0	1	*
40	7	*******
80	3	***
120	8	********
160	15	***************
200	10	**********
240	3	***
280	3	***

N	MEAN	MEDIAN	TRMEAN	STDEV	SEMEAN
50	147.90	148.50	146.11	69.24	9.79

MIN	MAX	Q1	Q3
14.00	299.00	106.00	186.25

The distribution is fairly symmetrical because the mean ($147.90) and the median ($148.50) are quite close. The mean ± 2s indicates that the middle 95% of the deposits are between $147.90 ± 2 ($69.24) = $9.42 and $286.38. Range = $299.00 − $14.00 = $285.00. There is a very slight negative skewness (because the mean is less than the median.

21. *a.* From MINITAB:
MTB > descb c1

	N	MEAN	MEDIAN	TRMEAN	STDEV	SEMEAN
C1	85	15.06	15.00	14.79	9.63	1.04

	MIN	MAX	Q1	Q3
C1	0.00	36.00	6.00	22.50

Typical length of service is about 15 years (mean or median).

b. Range is 36 years, found by 36 (MAX) − 0 (MIN).

c. Only slight positive skewness because the mean of 15.06 is slightly larger than the median (15.00).

d. Stem-and-leaf of *C*1   *N* = 85
   Leaf Unit = 1.0
   12   0   011222333444
   30   0   5555555566677788999
   42   1   000133334444
   (16) 1   5555566666788899
   27   2   00001233333
   16   2   6667889
    9   3   00123344
    1   3   6

22. *a.*

Per capita income ($000)	Number of states
$8–$ 9.9	1
10– 11.9	12
12– 13.9	17
14– 15.9	13
16– 17.9	5
18– 19.9	3
Total	51

b. From MINITAB, either $13,767 (mean) or $13,600 (median).

	N	MEAN	MEDIAN	TRMEAN	STDEV	SEMEAN
C10	51	13.767	13.600	13.667	2.305	0.323

	MIN	MAX	Q1	Q3
C10	9.500	19.200	11.900	15.100

c. Range = $9,700, found by $19,200 – $9,500.
   CV = 16.72%, found by $2.305/$13.767.
   AD = $1.827

d. Positively skewed. Sk = 0.243, found by 3 ($13.787 – $13.600)/2.305.

e. State per capita incomes range from $9,500 to $19,200. The mean income is $13,767 and half of the states have per capital incomes above $13,600 and half below it. The distribution is somewhat symmetrical with the mean ($13,767) and median ($13,600) quite close. A stem and leaf chart verifies the approximate symmetrical shape.
   Steam-and-leaf   *N* = 51
   LEAF UNIT = 0.10
    1   9   5
    4   10   577
   13   11   111124899
   20   12   2234789
   (10) 13   2222567889
   21   14   1345777
   14   15   111449
    8   16   68
    6   17   157
    3   18   39
    1   19   2

23.   Median: Women $15,762, men $24,345.
         Mode: Women $12,500, men $37,500.
     Lowest 25%: Women $11,053, men $15,732.
      Upper 25%: Women $22,231, men $39,858.
     The distribution of the annual earnings of men
     significantly higher than the women. Note: mean
     cannot be computed because of open-ended
     class.

24. Typical age at inauguration is 55. Range is 27
    years, found by 69 (oldest) − 42 (youngest).

	N	MEAN	MEDIAN	TRMEAN	STDEV	SEMEAN
Years	41	55.073	55.000	55.027	6.267	0.979

	MIN	MAX	Q1	Q3
Years	42.000	69.000	51.000	59.000

Stem-and-leaf chart reveals that the distribu-
tion of ages is somewhat symmetrical.
MTB>   stem c1;
SUBC> increment 5.
Stem-and-leaf of years   N = 41
Leaf Unit = 1.0
```
  2    4  23
  7    4  67899
 19    5  001111224444
(12)   5  555566677778
 10    6  011124
  4    6  5589
```

ANSWERS TO SECTION TWO EXERCISES
A Review of Chapters 5–7

1. Subjective.

2. An experiment.

3. An event.

4. Mutually exclusive.

5. Complement rule. $1 - P(x) = .999$.

6. 1.00

7. Discrete.

8. *1.* An outcome of an experiment is classified
      into mutually exclusive categories of a "suc-
      cess" or a "failure."
   2. The resulting data result from counts.
   3. The probability of a success and the probabil-
      ity of a failure stay the same from trial to trial.
   4. The trials are independent.

9. Discrete.

10. Only Mu.

11. Bellshaped, symmetrical, asymptotic.

12. Standard normal distribution.

13. *a.* .10, found by 20/200.
    b. .725, found by 145/200.
    c. .925, found by 1 – 15/200.

14. *a.* .035 from Appendix A where p = .8 and n = 15.
    b. .018, found by .001 + .003 + .014.
    c. .648, found by .250 + .231 + .132 + .035.

15. *a.* 1353, found from Appendix C, where μ = 2.0.
    b. 346, found by 400(.1353) = 54. Then 400 – 54 = 346.
    c. .3233, found by 1 – (.1353 + .2707 + .2707).

16. *a.* .0401, found by (13,500 – 10,000)/2,000 = 1.75. The area is .4599. Then .5000 – .4599 = .0401.
    b. .6147, found by (8,000 – 10,000)/2,000 = – 1.00. Area is .3413.
    (11,500 – 10,000)/2,000 = .75. Area is .2734.
    Then .3413 + .2734 = .6147.
    c. 7,440, found by – 1.28 = (X – 10,000)/2,000.

17. *a.* .417, found by 223/535.
    b. .407, found by 177/435.
    c. .914, found by (435/535) + (312/535) – 258/535.

18. .345 for a p of .20.
    .579 for a p of .30.
    Use the binomial as an approximation. Let n = 6, p = .20, P(r ≥ 2) = 1 – P(r ≤ 1) = 1 – (.262 + .393) = .345. If p = .30, then P(r ≥ 2) = 1 – P(r ≤ 1) = 1 – (.118 + .303) = .579.

19. *a.* $1.84 million, found by 0 + .64 + 1.2.
    b. .98.
    c. .20, found by .004/.02.
    d. Yes. The $2 million premium is greater than the expected loss of $1.84 million. Thus the expected profit is $.16 million.

20. *a.* The mean number of children is 1.10 and the standard deviation is 1.18 children, found by

0	P(X)	XP(X)	$(X-\mu)^2$ P(X)
0	.40	.00	0.4840
1	.30	.30	0.0030
2	.15	.30	0.1215
3	.10	.30	0.3610
4	.05	.20	0.4205
	1.00	1.10	1.3900

$\sigma = \sqrt{1.39} = 1.18$

b. 550, found by 500(1.1) rounded up.

c. The probability distribution for those families with children is computed below.

Number of Children X	Prob	Prob given children P(X)	XP(X)
1	.30	.500	.500
2	.15	.250	.500
3	.10	.167	.501
4	.05	.083	.332
	.60	1.000	1.833

Among those families with children, the mean number of children is 1.833.

ANSWERS TO SECTION THREE EXERCISES
Review of Chapters 8–10

1. b   6. e
2. d   7. e
3. c   8. b
4. a   9. a
5. d 10. b

11. $H_0: \mu = 36$, $H_1: \mu < 36$ Reject H_0 if z < −1.645.

Computed z = −3.60, found by $\dfrac{35.5 - 36}{.9/\sqrt{42}}$

Reject H_0.

12. *a.* $H_0: p = .08$, $H_1: p > .08$.

b. Alpha = .01

c. $\dfrac{\bar{p} - p}{\sqrt{\dfrac{p(1-p)}{n}}}$

d. Reject H_0 if z > 2.33

e. Computed z = .7372, computed by

$$z = \dfrac{.10 - .08}{\sqrt{\dfrac{.08(92)}{100}}}$$

f. Do not reject H_0. The difference can be attributed to sampling error.

13. *a.* 457, found by $n = .05(1 - .05)\left(\dfrac{1.96}{.02}\right)^2$

b. Raise the level of confidence to say .05, or raise the allowable error.

14. 42, found by $n = \left(\dfrac{(2.58)\,(.50)}{.20}\right)^2$

15. a. $H_0: \mu_c \neq \mu_k$; $H_1: \mu_c \neq \mu_k$
    b. two-tailed. No direction given.
    c.
    $$z = \dfrac{\bar{X}_c - \bar{X}_k}{\sqrt{\dfrac{s_c^2}{n_c} + \dfrac{s_k^2}{n_k}}}$$

    d. -1.96, $+1.96$.
    e. Computed $z = -2.0203$, found by
    $$\dfrac{10.92 - 11.05}{\sqrt{\dfrac{(.78)^2}{180} + \dfrac{(.39)^2}{200}}}$$

    Reject H_0 and accept H_1. The means are not equal.

16. a. $H_0: p_c = p_d$. $H_1: p_c \neq p$ where p_c is Chicago and p_d is Dallas.
    b. Two tailed. No direction given.
    c.
    $$z = \dfrac{p_1 - p_2}{\sqrt{\dfrac{\bar{p}_c\,(1 - \bar{p}_c)}{n_1} + \dfrac{\bar{p}_c\,(1 - \bar{p}_c)}{n_2}}}$$

    d. Reject H_0 if computed z is > 1.96 or < -1.96.
    e. $p_c = 180/200 = .89$; $p_1 = 180/200 = .90$; $p_2 = 87/100 = .87$; $\dfrac{180 + 87}{300} = .89$

    Computed $z = .7829$. Do not reject H_0. There is no significant difference in the two proportions.

SOLUTIONS TO REVIEW
of Chapters 11 and 12

1. b   7. d
2. b   8. d
3. a   9. b
4. b   10. d
5. d   11. e
6. c   12. a

Part II   Problems

13. $H_0: \mu = 20$, $H_1: \mu > 20$, reject H_0 if $t > 1.860$.

    H_0 is not rejected. The mean amount of break time is not more than 20 minutes.

14. $H_0: \mu_1 = \mu_2$, $H_1: \mu_1 \neq \mu_2$, reject H_0 if $t < 2.845$ or $t > 2.845$.

    $$S_p^2 = \dfrac{(12 - 1)(5)^2 + (10 - 1)(8)^2}{12 + 10 - 2} = 42.55$$

    $$t = \dfrac{250 - 252}{\sqrt{42.55\left(\dfrac{1}{12} + \dfrac{1}{10}\right)}} = -0.716$$

    H_0 is not rejected. There is no difference in the mean strength of the two glues.

15. $H_0: \mu_d = 0$ $H_1: \mu_d > 0$ Reject H_0 if $t > 1.833$
    $\bar{d} = 0.4$ $s_d = 6.11$ $t = \dfrac{.4}{6.11/\sqrt{10}} = 0.21$

    H_0 is not rejected. There is no difference in the paints.

16. $H_0: \mu_1 = \mu_2 = \mu_3 = \mu_4$, H_1: The means are not the same. H_0 rejected if $F > 3.29$.

Source	SS	df	MS	F
Treatments	20.736	3	6.91	1.04
Error	100.00	15	6.67	
Total	120.736	18		

    H_0 is not rejected. There is no difference in the mean sales.

17. $H_0: \mu_1 = \mu_1 = \mu_2 = \mu_3 = \mu_4 = \mu_5$ H_1: Means not equal $F = 3.84$
    $H_0: \mu_1 = \mu_2 = \mu_3$ H_1: Means not equal $F = 4.46$

Source	SS	df	MS	F
Treatments	165.73	4	41.43	11.098
Blacks	22.8	2	11.40	3.054
Error	29.87	8	3.73	
Total	218.40	14		

    There is a difference in fertilizer types, but not soil conditions.

18. $H_0\ \sigma_N^2 = \sigma_E^2$ $H_1: \sigma_N^2 = \sigma_E^2$ H_0 is rejected if $F > 1.95$.
    $F = (3.9)^2/(2.85)^2 = 1.87$.
    H_0 is not rejected. There is no difference in the variation of the two groups.

ANSWERS TO
A Review of Chapters 13–15

1. Coefficient of correlation, coefficient of determination.

2. Strong negative association.

3. $H_0: \rho = 0$, $H_1: \rho > 0$. Critical value of t is 1.671 computed $t = 3.324$. H_0 rejected. There is positive correlation.

4. Only 4% of the variation in Y is not explained by X.

5. The independent variables are entered into the equation in the order in which they increase R^2 the fastest.

6. Net profit.

7. $Y' = \alpha + \beta_1 X_1 + \beta_2 X_2 + \beta_3 X_3 + \beta_4 X_4$.

8. $163,200.

9. $(86)^2 = .7396$. About 74% of the variation in net profit is explained by the four variables.

10. About 68 percent of the net profits would be within 1($3,000) of the estimates, about 95 percent would be within 2($3,000), or $6,000, of the estimates. And, 99.7 percent would be within 3($3,000) of the estimates.

11. *a.*

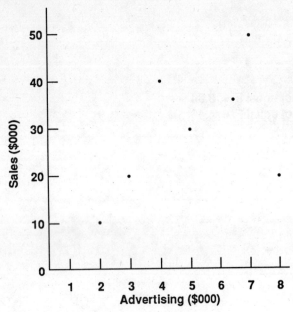

b. R = .9042
c. $R^2 = .8176$, $1 - R^2 = .1824$
d. $Y' = -1.12622 + 7.4324 X$
e. $32.23 in thousands.
f. Strong positive correlation.

12. *a.*

Bowler	X	Y	Rank X	Rank Y	d	d^2
1	81	76	2.5	3	−0.5	0.25
2	18	36	10	9	+1	1.00
3	41	46	8	6	+2	4.00
4	91	88	1	1	0	0
5	50	42	7	7	0	0
6	29	36	9	9	0	0
7	62	60	5	5	0	0
8	77	36	4	9	−5	25
9	81	87	2.5	2	+0.5	0.25
10	56	72	6	4	+2	4.00
					0.0	34.5

b. $r_s = 1 - \dfrac{6\Sigma d^2}{n(n^2-1)} = 1 - \dfrac{6(34.5)}{10(99)}$

$= 1 - \dfrac{207}{990} = 1 - 0.209 = .791$

	$\alpha = .05$	$\alpha = .01$
	$n = 10$	$n = 10$
critical values =	.564	= .746
	.791 > .564	.791 > .746

There is a strong relationship between the two rankings and the relationship is statistically significant at both the .05 and .01 levels.

13. *a.* .9261, found by 1050.4/1134.6.
b. 2.0469, found by $\sqrt{83.8/20}$
c. $H_0: \beta_1 = \beta_2 = \beta_3 = \beta_4 = 0$, H_1: not all coefficients are zero. Reject if F > 2.87. F = 62.697, found by 262.70/4.19.
d. Could delete X_2 because t-ratio (1.29) is less than critical t value of 2.086. Otherwise reject H_0 for X_1, X_3 and X_4 because all of those t-ratios are greater than 2.086.

Solutions to Review of Chapters 16 and 17

1. frequency observed and frequency expected.

2. Contingency table.

3. Chi-square distribution.

4. 6, found by $(4-1)(3-1)$

5. Not rejected because 11.248 is less than 12.592.

6. H_0 is rejected.

7. There is no difference between the observed and the expected set of frequencies.

8. At least interval.

9. Nominal level

10. Ordinal

11. To determine if two populations are the same.

12. No assumptions are necessary.

13. To determine if three or more populations are the same.

14. To determine if the distribution of difference in paired observations has a median of 0.

15. Kruskal-Wallis

16. Sign test and the Wilcoxon test.

17. Yes

18. One-tailed

19. No. It is positively skewed.

20. The number of categories minus one.

21. H_0: Median = \$27,000, H_1: Median $\neq$ \$27,000. Use .05 significance level and the sign test. The critical values are $z < -1.96$ and $z > 1.96$. Count the number of values above the median, compute z, assuming a large sample, and make a decision.

PART IV

All Answers to the
Chapter Assignments in the Study Guide

Answers to Study Guide Chapter Assignments
Chapter 1

There is no assignment for Chapter 1

Chapter 2
Part I

1. b   3. a   5. c   7. a   9. a
2. a   4. d   6. c   8. a   10. a

Part II

11. horizontal

12. Shows how components of the total have changed relative to each other.

13. Shows an increase or decrease in two or more components over time.

14. The difference between the upper and lower class limit.

15. A frequency distribution reports the actual frequency, a relative frequency converts each frequency to a fraction or percent of the total number of observations.

16. *a.* and *b.*

Miles	Frequency	Cumulative Frequency
0– 2	2	2
3– 5	3	5
6– 8	10	15
9–11	10	25
12–14	5	30
	30	

16. *c.*

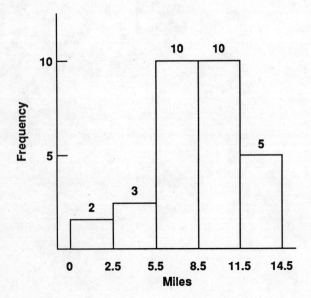

17.

Status	Millions	Cumulative	Percent
Married	107.0	107.0	64%
Single	36.0	143.0	85
Widowed	12.8	155.8	93
Divorced	12.0	167.8	100
	167.8		

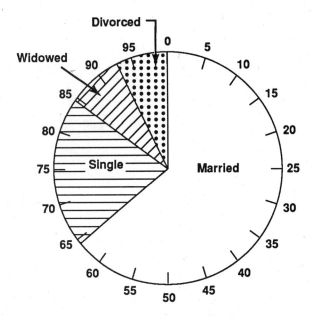

18. *a.* 30
    b. 51, 99
    c. 8
    d. 15
    e. 51, 54, 57

Chapter 3
Part I

1. b
2. a
3. c
4. a
5. d
6. a
7. a
8. b
9. b
10. a

Part II

11. median.

12. zero.

13. There is no class midpoint.

14. The midpoint of the class with the most frequencies.

15. Half the distance between the middle two observations.

Part III

16. *a.* $\bar{X} = 104/8 = 13.0$.
    b. The mode is 12, found by $(11 + 13)/2$.
    c. No mode. No value appears more than once.

17. unemployed = .067(7,480) + .072(12,890) + .089(120,650) + .052(15,980)
    = 13,022.17
    weighted mean is $\bar{X}_w$ = 13,022.17/157,360 = .083

18.
$$GM = \sqrt[6]{\frac{50}{28}} - 1 = \frac{\log 1.785714}{6} = 0.0419687 - 1.0$$

antilog 0.0419687 − 1.0 = 1.10146 − 1.0 = .10146
The rate of increase in 10.146% per year.

19.

Hour	f	X	fX	CF
0– 9	3	4.5	13.5	3
10–19	7	14.5	101.5	10
20–29	15	24.5	367.5	25
30–39	10	34.5	345.0	35
40–49	5	44.5	222.5	40
			1050.0	

a. Frequency distribution

b. $\bar{X} = \dfrac{1050}{40} = 26.25$

c. Median $= 19.5 + \dfrac{20-10}{15}(10) = 26.17$

d. The mode is 24.5 hours.

Chapter 4

Multiple choice

1. c   3. d   5. b   7. d   9. a
2. a   4. b   6. d   8. a   10. b

Fill in the blanks

11. 0.56

12. median

13. two

14. 4

15. 17

Problems

16. a. range = 150 − 120 = 30
    b. AD = 60/7 = 8.5714
    c.
$$s = \sqrt{\frac{130,280 - \dfrac{(952)^2}{7}}{7-1}} = 11.6046$$

17.

Passengers	f	X	fX	fX²	CF
15–19	4	17	68	1,156	4
20–24	9	22	198	4,356	13
25–29	11	27	297	8,019	24
30–34	8	32	256	8,192	32
35–39	6	37	222	8,214	38
40–44	2	42	84	3,528	40
	40		1125	33,465	

a. range = 44 − 15 = 29

b.
$$s = \sqrt{\frac{33{,}465 - \frac{(1125)^2}{40}}{40 - 1}} = 6.8395$$

c.
$$Q_1 = 19.5 + \frac{10 - 4}{9}(5) = 22.83$$

$$Q_3 = 29.5 + \frac{30 - 24}{8}(5) = 33.25$$

$$QD = \frac{33.25 - 22.83}{2} = 5.21$$

18. a. $1 - \dfrac{1}{(1.6)^2} = 0.61$

b. about 95%

c.
$$CV = \frac{0.75}{9.5} = 0.079$$

$$CV = \frac{2.0}{6.5} = 0.308$$

There is more relative dispersion in the time spent.

d.
$$sk = \frac{3(9.5 - 10.0)}{0.75} = -2.00$$

Moderate amount of negative skewness.

Chapter 5
Part I

1. d	3. c	5. a	7. c	9. d
2. d	4. a	6. b	8. b	10. b

Part II

11. A new permutation occurs each time a new arrangement of the objects occurs. Combinations are not dependent on order.

12. classical, realtive frequency, subjective

13. An event is a particular result of an experiment. An outcome is a collection of events.

Part III

14. a. .30, found by 30/100
     b. .40, found by 40/100
     c. .10, found by 10/100
     d. .80, found by 1 − (20/100)

15. a. .216, found by $(.60)^3$
     b. .936, found by $1 - ((1 - .6)^3)$

16. a. .45, found by

$$\frac{140}{400} + \frac{90}{400} - \frac{50}{400}$$

   b. .556, found by 50/90
   c. .846, found by 220/260

17. .682 found by $P(\text{Bus/Late}) = \dfrac{.30(.25)}{.70(.05) + .30(.25)}$

Chapter 6
Part I

1. c	3. c	5. d	7. c	9. d
2. a	4. a	6. b	8. b	10. b

Part II

11. A random variable list the outcomes but not the probability. A probability distribution includes the probability of the outcomes.

12. Only two outcomes, p is constant, independent trials, fixed number of trials.

13. For the hypergeometric distribution the trials are not independent.

14. When n is large and p is small.

15. A discrete random variable can assume only certain values, but a continuous random variable can assume an infinite number of values within a certain range.

Part III

16. a. $\mu = 0(.1) + 1(.3) + 2(.3) + 3(.2) + 4(.1) = 1.90$
     b. $\sigma^2 = (0 - 1.9)^2.1 + (1 - 1.9)^2.3 + (2 - 1.9)^2.3 + (3 - 1.9)^2.2 + (4 - 1.9)^2.1 = 1.29$

17. a. $\mu = 8(.3) = 2.4$
         $\sigma^2 = 8(.3)(.7) = 1.68$
         $\sigma = 1.30$
     b. $P(X = 4/n = 8, p = .30) = .136$
     c. $P(X \geq 4/n = 8, P = .30) = .136 + .047 + .010 + .001 = .194$

18. a. $P(X = 5/\mu = 5) = .1755$
     b. $P(X < 5) = .0067 + .0337 + .0842 + .1404 + .1755 = .4405$
     c. $P(X \geq 5) = 1 - P(X < 5) = 1 - .4405 = .5595$

19.

$$\frac{_8C_2\,_4C_2}{_{12}C_4} = \frac{\left[\dfrac{8 \cdot 7}{2}\right]\left[\dfrac{4 \cdot 3}{2}\right]}{\left[\dfrac{12 \cdot 11 \cdot 10 \cdot 9}{4 \cdot 3 \cdot 2 \cdot 1}\right]} = \frac{[28][6]}{495} = .339$$

Chapter 7
Part I

1. a	3. c	5. b	7. d	9. a
2. a	4. d	6. b	8. c	10. d

Part II

11. continuous; described by μ and σ; mean, median, and mode equal; there is a family of normal distributions

12. np and n(1 – p) should be 5 or more.

13. When a continuous distribution is used to estimate a discrete distribution.

14. The standard normal distribution is one of many normal distributions. It has a mean of 0 and a standard deviation of 1.

15. $= 50(.40) = 20$, $\sigma^2 = 50(.4)(.6) = 12.0$

Part III

16. *a.* $z = (350 - 320)/25 = 1.20$
      $.5000 - .3849 = .1151$
   b. $z = (275 - 320)/25 = -1.80$
      $.4641 + .3849 = .8490$
   c. $z = (300 - 320)/25 = -0.80$
      $.4641 - .2881 = .1760$
   d. $.52 = \dfrac{x - \$320}{\$25}$

      $x = 333$

17. *a.* p = .20, n = 200, independent samples, only 2 outcomes. Also 200(.20) = 40, and 200(.8) = 160, both larger than 5.
   b. $\mu = 200(.20) = 40$, $\sigma^2 = 200(.2)(.8) = 32$
      $\sigma = \sqrt{32} = 5.6569$
   c. $z = (30.5 - 40)/5.6569 = -1.68$
      $.4535 + .5000 = .9535$
   d. $z = (29.5 - 40)/5.6569 = -1.86$
      $.4686 - .4535 = .0151$
   e. $z = (44.5 - 40.0)/5.6569 = 0.80$
      $z = (50.5 - 40.0)/5.6569 = 1.86$
      $.4686 - .2881 = .1805$

Chapter 8
Part I

1. c	3. b	5. d	7. a	9. b
2. a	4. b	6. c	8. b	10. c

Part II

11. The test is destructive, impossible to check all items, costly to study all items, sample results are adequate, contact all items in the population is time consuming.

12. A population parameter is a value determined from the entire population, a sample statistic is a value calculated from the sample information.

13. When the sample is more than 5 percent of the population.

14. The sampling error is the difference between the sample statistic and the population parameter.

15. The level of confidence, the size of the sample, variability in the population.

Part III

16. *a.* $_6C_2 = \dfrac{6!}{2!4!} = 15$

b.

Samples	Mean	Samples	Mean
8,10	9	10,12	11
8,10	9	10,12	11
8,12	10	10,12	11
8,12	10	10,12	11
8,12	10	12,12	12
10,10	10	12,12	12
10,12	11	12,12	12
10,12	11		

c.

X	f	fX
9	2	18
10	4	40
11	6	66
12	3	36
	15	160

d. The population mean is 10.67, found by 64/6. The mean of the sampling distribution is also 10.67, found by 160/15.

17. *a.* $5.67 \pm 1.645\,(1.56/\sqrt{40})$
  5.67 ± 0.406

  b. $5.67 \pm 1.645 \left(\dfrac{1.56}{\sqrt{40}}\right)\left(\sqrt{\dfrac{300-40}{300-1}}\right)$

  5.67 ± 0.378

18. *a.* $0.40 \pm 1.96 \sqrt{\dfrac{(.40)(.60)}{200}}$

  0.40 ± 0.068

  b. $0.40 \pm 1.96 \sqrt{\dfrac{(.40)(.60)}{200}}\left(\sqrt{\dfrac{1000-200}{1000-1}}\right)$

  0.40 ± 0.061

19. $n = (.5)(.5)\left[\dfrac{1.96}{.04}\right]^2 = 601$

20. $n = [(2.05)(15,000)/3000]^2 = 106$

Chapter 9
Part I

1. d	3. a	5. a	7. d	9. c
2. b	4. b	6. b	8. b	10. a

Part II

11. decision rule

12. state H_0 and H_1, determine the level of significance, determine the test statistic, state the decision rule, conduct the test and make the decision on H_0.

13. A Type I error is rejecting a true H_0 and Type II error is accepting a false H_0.

14. The p-value is the probability of finding a value of the test statistic as extreme or more extreme than that calculated, when H_0 is true.

Part III

15. $H_0{:}\mu = 50$, $H_1{:}\mu < 50$. Reject H_0 if $z < -2.33$.

$$z = \frac{48.2 - 50}{4.2/\sqrt{36}} = -2.571$$

H_0 is rejected. The mean number of minutes of music is less than 50.

16. $H_0{:} \mu_y = \mu_0$, $H_1{:} \mu_y > \mu_0$. Reject H_0 if $z > 1.645$.

$$z = \frac{590 - 545}{\sqrt{\dfrac{75^2}{35} + \dfrac{56^2}{40}}} = 2.910$$

H_0 is rejected. The mean amount owed is larger for the younger customers. p-value is .0018, found by .5000 − .4982.

17. $H_0{:} \mu = 13.0$
    $H_1{:} \mu > 13.0$
    b.

$$1.645 = \frac{\bar{X}_c - 13.00}{\dfrac{7}{\sqrt{40}}}$$

$$\bar{X}_c = 13.00 + 1.82 = 14.82$$

c.
$$z = \frac{14.82 - 14.00}{\dfrac{7}{\sqrt{40}}} = .74$$

Then .5000 + .2704 = .7704

Chapter 10
Part I

1. a   3. b   5. b   7. a
2. c   4. c   6. a   8. d

Part II

9. constant probability of success, independent trials, only two outcomes, fixed sample size.

10. proportion

Part III

11. $H_0: p = .30$, $H_1: p > .30$. Reject H_0 if $z > 1.645$.

$$z = \frac{.35 - .30}{\sqrt{\frac{.30(.70)}{200}}} = 1.54$$

H_0 is not rejected. The proportion watching TV-13 has not increased.
The p-value is .0618, found by $.5000 - .4382$

12. $H_0: p_a = p_d$, $H_1: p_a > p_d$. Reject H_0 if $z > 2.33$.

$$\bar{p}_c = \frac{15 + 18}{120 + 80} = 0.165$$

$$z = \frac{0.225 - 0.125}{\sqrt{\frac{.165(1 - .165)}{80} + \frac{.165(1 - .165)}{120}}} = 1.866$$

H_0 is not rejected. There is no difference in the proportion absent on the day and the afternoon shift.
The p-value is .0307, found by $.5000 - .4693$

Chapter 11
Part I

1. a   3. a   5. d   7. c   9. b
2. d   4. a   6. a   8. d   10. b

Part II

11. independent sample, normal populations, equal variances, interval scale.

12. $n - 1$

13. known

Part III

14. $H_0 : \mu = 50$, $H_1 : \mu > 50$. Reject H_0 if $t > 1.895$.

$$\bar{X} = \frac{438}{8} = 54.75 \qquad s = \sqrt{\frac{24330 - 438^2/8}{8-1}} = 7.066$$

$$t = \frac{54.75 - 50.00}{7.066/\sqrt{8}} = 1.901$$

H_0 is rejected. The mean weight of the luggage is greater than 50 pounds. The p-value is between .05 and .025.

15. $H_0 : \mu_g = \mu_k$, $H_1 : \mu_g > \mu_k$. Reject H_0 if $t > 2.508$.

$$s_p^2 = \frac{(10-1)(35)^2 + (14-1)(41)^2}{10 + 14 - 2} = 1494.45$$

$$t = \frac{435 - 380}{\sqrt{1494.45\left(\frac{1}{14} + \frac{1}{10}\right)}} = \frac{55.00}{16.00} = 3.436$$

H_0 is rejected. The commissioner can conclude that the mean insurance premium is more in Georgia.

16.

Worker	After	Before	Difference	d^2
1	30	28	2	4
2	28	29	−1	1
3	27	26	1	1
4	28	32	−4	16
5	33	33	0	0
6	27	33	−6	36
7	30	36	−6	36
8	31	29	2	4
9	29	34	−5	25
10	32	25	7	49
11	33	25	8	64
12	30	25	5	25
			3	261

$H_0 : \mu_d = 0$, $H_1 : \mu_d \neq 0$. Reject H_0 if $t < -2.201$ or $t > 2.201$.

$$\bar{X}_d = \frac{3}{12} = 0.25 \qquad s_d \sqrt{\frac{261 - (3)^2/12}{12-1}} = 4.864$$

$$t = \frac{0.25}{4.864/\sqrt{12}} = 0.178$$

H_0 is not rejected. The p-value is greater than .20.

Chapter 12
Part I

1. b	3. c	5. c	7. b	9. d
2. a	4. a	6. c	8. d	10. d

Part II

11. independent sample, normal populations, equal variances, interval scale.

12. positively skewed, continuous distribution, based on two sets of degrees of freedom, never negative.

Part III

13. $H_0: \sigma_1^2 = \sigma_2^2$ $H_1: \sigma_1^2 \neq \sigma_2^2$. Reject H_0 if $F > 2.03$.
    $F = 7.35^2/5.75^2 = 1.63$
    H_0 is not rejected. The no difference in the variation when carrying the bag and walking.

14. $H_0: \mu_1 = \mu_2 = \mu_3$, H_1:Not all means are equal. Reject H_0 if $F > 3.89$.

    SS total $= 283 - (61)^2/15 = 34.93$

    $$\text{SST} = \frac{(20)^2}{5} + \frac{(14)^2}{5} + \frac{(27)^2}{5} - \frac{(61)^2}{15} = 16.93$$

    SSE $= 34.93 - 16.93 = 18$

Source	SS	df	MS	F
Treatment	16.93	2	8.467	5.64
Error	18.00	12	1.5	
Total	34.93	14		

    H_0 is rejected. There is a difference in the mean time.

15. *a.* Treatments   Blocks
    $$H_0: \mu_d = \mu_e = \mu_n$$ $$[H_0: \mu_s = \mu_m = \mu_t = \mu_w = \mu_t = \mu_t = \mu_s]$$
        H_1:Not all treatment means equal H_1:Not all Blocks means equal
    b. H_0 for treatment means is rejected if $F > 3.89$ and for blocks if $F > 3.00$.
    c.
Source	SS	df	MS	F
Treatment	1154.7	2	577.3	16.59
Blocks	499.8	6	83.3	2.42
Error	417.3	12	34.8	
Total	2071.8	20		

    d. See part c.
    e. Reject H_0 for treatment means. There is a difference in the mean number of cases by shift.
        Accept H_0 for block means. There is no difference in the mean number of cases by day of the week.

Chapter 13
Part I

1. b	3. b	5. c	7. a	9. a
2. d	4. b	6. c	8. b	10. c

Part II

11. A value of 0 indicates no correlation, 1.00 and − 1.00 indicate perfect correlation, sign indicates the direction of the correlation, interval scale required.

12. Spearman is used on ranked data, Pearson on interval or higher data.

13. The direction of the relationship. Some indication of the strength.

Part III

    a.

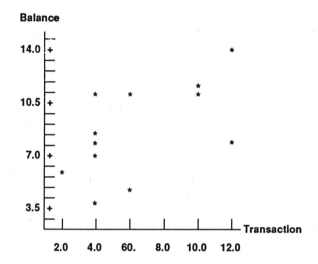

Balance Y	Transactions X	XY	Y^2	X^2
9	4	36	81	16
8	4	32	64	16
14	12	168	196	144
11	6	66	121	36
6	2	12	36	4
11	4	44	121	16
12	10	120	144	100
7	4	28	49	16
11	10	110	121	100
9	12	108	81	144
5	6	30	25	36
4	4	16	16	16
107	78	770	1055	644

$$r = \frac{770 - (107)(78)/12}{\sqrt{[1055 - (107)^2/12][644 - (78)^2/12]}} = \frac{74.5}{\sqrt{(100.91)(137)}} = 0.634$$

$H_0: \rho = 0$, $H_1: \rho > 0$. Reject H_0 if t > 1.812.

$$t = \frac{0.634\sqrt{12-2}}{\sqrt{1-(0.634)^2}} = 2.591$$

H_0 is rejected. There is positive correlation.
15. H_0: There is no correlation among the ranks.
H^1: There is postitive correlation among the ranks.
Reject H_0 if t > 2.552.

$$t = \frac{0.45\sqrt{20-2}}{\sqrt{1-(0.45)^2}} = 2.138$$

H_0 is not rejected. The correlation among the ranks in the population could be 0.

Chapter 14
Part I

1. b	3. a	5. c	7. b	9. b
2. c	4. a	6. a	8. d	10. c

Part II

11. standard error of estimate

12. *a.* The independent and the dependent variable are linearly related.
b. For each X, the values are normally distributed around Y′.
c. The variation is the same for each X.
d. The Y–Y′ values are independent.

13. coefficient of determination

14. Y and Y′

Part III

a. $b = \dfrac{770-(107)(78)/12}{644-(78)^2/12} = \dfrac{74.5}{137.0} = 0.544$

$a = \dfrac{107}{12} - 0.544\left(\dfrac{78}{12}\right) = 5.381$

$Y' = 5.381 + 0.544X$

b.
$S_{y \cdot x} = \sqrt{\dfrac{1055 - 5.381(107) - 0.544(770)}{12-2}} = \sqrt{\dfrac{60.353}{10}} = 2.457$

c. $Y' = 5.381 + 0.544(5) = 8.101$

d.
$8.101 \pm 2.228(2.457)\sqrt{\dfrac{1}{12} + \dfrac{(5-6.5)^2}{137.0}}$

8.101 ± 1.729

$[6.372, 9.830]$

e.

$$8.101 \pm 2.228(2.457)\sqrt{1 + \frac{1}{12} + \frac{(5-6.5)^2}{137}}$$

8.101 ± 5.741

$[2.360, 13.842]$

Chapter 15
Part I

1. c	3. c	5. a	7. b	9. a
2. a	4. c	6. c	8. b	10. d

Part II

11. autocorrelation

12. There is a linear relationship between the dependent variable and the independent variables, the dependent variable is continuous and of interval scale, the residual term is the same for all Y', no autocorrelation, and the independent variables are not correlated.

13. the coefficient of determination

14. dependent variable, independent variables

Part III

15. *a.* There is no problem with correlation among the independent variables. The strongest correlation is between salary and years.
   b. $H_0: \beta_1 = \beta_2 = \beta_3 = 0$, H_1: at least one β_i is not equal to zero. H_0 is rejected if $F > 3.59$. Since the computed F is 13.91, H_0 is rejected. At least one of the regression coefficients does not equal 0.
   $R^2 = 641.10/810.04 = 0.791$. Nearly 80 percent of the variation in salary is explained by the three independent variables.
   c. $H_0: \beta_1 = 0$ $H_0: \beta_2 = 0$ $H_0: \beta_3 = 0$
   $H_1: \beta_1 \neq 0$ $H_1: \beta_2 \neq 0$ $H_1: \beta_3 \neq 0$
   Reject H_0 if $t < -2.201$ or $t > 2.201$.
   The H_0 is rejected for years and performance, and not rejected for absences.

Answers to Chapter 16
Part 1

1. d	6. d
2. b	7. d
3. b	8. a
4. a	9. a
5. a	10. c

Part II

11. Based on degrees of freedom, positively skewed, continuous, approaches normal as the degrees of freedom increase.

12. Independent, or not related.

13. Accidents are not evenly distributed through the week.

Part III

14. H_0: Positions are equally likely
H_0: Positions are not equally likely
H_0 is rejected if $x^2 > 7.815$

Position	f_0	f_e	$\frac{(f_0 - f_e)^2}{f_e}$
1	35	27	2.37
2	30	27	0.33
3	26	27	0.04
4	17	27	3.70
	108		6.44

H_0 is not rejected. Political candidates are equally likely to win in any of the positions.

15. H_0: There is no relationship between smoking and heart attack.
H_1: There is a relationship between smoking and heart attack.
H_0: is rejected if $\chi^2 > 9.210$.

$$x^{22} = \frac{(50-73.33)^2}{73.33} + \dots + \frac{(10-15.83)^2}{15.83} = 35.167$$

H_0 is rejected. There is a relationship between smoking and heart attack.

16. H_0: The distribution is normal.
H_1: The distribution is not normal.
H_0 is rejected if $\chi^2 > 9.488$.

Wage	Area	f_e	f_0	$\frac{(f_0-f_e^2)}{f_e}$
< $8.00	.0918	36.72	25	3.7407
8.00 to 10.00	.1596	63.84	70	.5944
10.00 to 12.00	.2486	99.44	110	1.1214
12.00 to 14.00	.2486	99.44	101	.0245
14.00 to 16.00	.1596	63.84	57	.7329
16 or more	.0918	36.72	37	.0021
		400	400	6.2160

Answers to Chapter 17
Part I

1. d	6. c
2. c	7. a
3. a	8. b
4. b	9. d
5. a	10. a

Part II

11. *a.* Kruskal-Wallis
b. Mann-Whitney

12. When np and n(p − 1) both are greater than 5.

13. The mean of the ranks involved.

Part III

14. H_0: There is no difference in the tax to be paid.

H_1: There is a difference in the tax to be paid.

H_0 is rejected if there are 1 or less or 7 or more + signs. There are 2 + signs, so H_0 is not rejected. There is no difference in the amount paid.

15. *a.* H_0: There is no difference in the tax to be paid.

H_1: There is a difference in the tax to be paid.

b. H_0 is rejected if R^+ or R^- is 5 or absolute less.

Rooney	Swanson	difference	difference	Rank	R –	R +
1600	1910	– 310	310	5.0	5.0	
1970	1920	50	50	2.5		2.5
2120	2080	40	40	1.0		1.0
2140	2340	– 200	200	4.0	4.0	
2340	2390	– 50	50	2.5	2.5	
2510	2850	– 340	340	6.0	6.0	
2560	2980	– 420	420	7.0	7.0	
2710	3340	– 630	630	8.0	8.0	
						3.5

Because 3.5 is less than 5.0, H_0 is rejected. There is a difference in the amount to be paid.

16. H_0: The distributions are the same.

H_a: The distributions of the males is to the right of the females.

Reject H_0 if U or U' is less than or equal to 17.

Male	Rank	Female	Ranks
$9.90	4	$9.10	1
10.10	5	9.50	2
11.30	10	9.60	3
11.70	11	10.30	6
12.10	12	10.40	7
12.80	13	10.50	8
14.60	14	10.70	9
14.80	15		36
15.40	16		
17.10	17		
	117		

$$U = (10)(7) + \frac{10(11)}{2} - 117 = 8$$

$$U' = (10)(7) + \frac{7(8)}{2} - 36 = 62$$

Because 8 is less than 17 H_0 is rejected. The males spend more money.

17. H_0: The distribution of sales are the same.
H_1: The distribution of sales are not the same.
H_0 is rejected if $\chi^2 > 5.991$.

Red	Rank	Blue	Rank	Green	Rank
437	2	448	3	402	1
450	4	455	6	452	5
460	7	469	10	553	16
464	8.5	513	12	560	17
464	8.5	519	13	567	18
477	11	539	15	580	19
530	14	607	20		
	55		79		76

$$H = \frac{12}{20(21)}\left[\frac{(55)^2}{7} + \frac{(79)^2}{7} + \frac{(76)^2}{6}\right] - 3(21) = 2.33$$

H_0 is not rejected. No difference in the distributions.

Chapter 18 Answers

Part I

1. a 6. b
2. a 7. d
3. a 8. c
4. c 9. a
5. d 10. c

Part II

11. 668

12. 2142.86

13. The base changes each year

14. Units

Part III

15.

Year	Sales	Index
87	$521,123	100.0
88	609,205	116.9
89	643,566	123.5
90	750,931	144.1
91	711,555	136.5

16. a. $P = (7.10/5.70)(100) = 124.50$

b. $P = \dfrac{\$1.80(500) + \$1.10(200) + \$1.20(100) + \$3.00(50)}{\$1.30(500) + \$.90(200) + \$1.00(100) + \$2.50(50)} = \dfrac{\$1390}{\$1055}(100) = 131.70$

c. $P = \dfrac{\$1.80(700) + \$1.10(250) + \$1.20(200) + \$3.00(40)}{\$1.30(700) + \$.90(250) + \$1.00(200) + \$2.50(40)} = \dfrac{\$1895}{\$1435}(100) = 132.06$

d. The Paasche Price Index use current period quantities as weights, whereas, the Laspeyres Price Index uses base period quantities as weights.

17. *a.* Purchasing power is $\dfrac{1}{150.7}(100) = .663$

b. 1980 Real Income $= \dfrac{\$45,380}{82.4}(100) = \$55,073$

1992 Real Income $= \dfrac{\$63,750}{150.7}(100) = \$42,303$

c. Mr. Jerdoneck's earnings did not keep up with inflation. In fact, he lost $12,770 in base period dollars.

Answers to Chapter 19

Part I

1. a	6. b
2. d	7. a
3. b	8. b
4. d	9. b
5. a	10. c

Part II

11. time series

12. episodic, random

13. specific seasonal

14. seasonal index

Part III

15. *a.*

Year	Y Earning	t Code	Yt	t^2
1987	$.94	1	.94	1
1988	1.81	2	3.62	4
1989	4.05	3	12.15	9
1990	3.92	4	15.68	16
1991	4.18	5	20.90	25
1992	5.20	6	31.20	36
	20.10	21	84.49	91

$$b = \frac{84.49 - (20.10)(21)/6}{91 - (21)^2/6} = \frac{14.14}{17.50} = 0.808$$

$$a = \frac{20.10}{6} - 0.808\left(\frac{21}{6}\right) = 0.522$$

b. $Y' = 0.522 + 0.808(9) = 7.794$

Year	Qtr.	Passengers	4-Qtr. Moving Total	4-Qtr. Moving Avg.	Centered Moving Avg.	Specific Seasonal
1989	I	5				
	II	9				
			30	7.50		
	III	8			7.625	1.04918
			31	7.75		
	IV	8			7.750	1.03226
			31	7.75		
1990	I	6			7.875	0.76190
			32	8.00		
	II	9			8.000	1.12500
			32	8.00		
	III	9			8.000	1.12500
			32	8.00		
	IV	8			8.125	0.98462
			33	8.25		
1991	I	6			8.375	0.71642
			34	8.50		
	II	10			8.375	1.19403
			33	8.25		
	III	10			8.250	1.21212
			33	8.25		
	IV	7			8.250	0.84848
			33	8.25		
1992	I	6			8.125	0.73846
			32	8.00		
	II	10			8.125	1.23077
			33	8.25		
	III	9				
	IV	8				

Quarter

Year	I	II	III	IV	
1989			1.04918	1.03226	
1990	.76190	1.12500	1.12500	0.98462	
1991	.71642	1.19403	1.21212	0.84848	
1992	.73846	1.23077			
Total	2.21678	3.54980	3.38630	2.8653	Total
Mean	0.7389	1.1833	1.1288	0.9551	4.0061
Typical Index	73.78	118.15	112.71	95.36	400.00

Answers to Chapter 20

1. c   6. c
2. b   7. a
3. a   8. a
4. a   9. a
5. a   10. b

Part II

11. unknown future event

12. The cost of uncertainty.

13. Expected value of perfect information.

14. (1) find the optimum payoff for each state of nature, (2) subtract the payoff for each act from the optimum value.

Part III

Payoff Table

	Improves	*Recession*
a. Build new	$100,000	− $40,000
Expand	30,000	− 4,000
Do nothing	0	0

b. $E(A_1) = .30(\$100,000) + .70(-\$40,000) = \$2,000$
$E(A_2) = .30(\$30,000) + .70(-\$4,000) = \$6,200$
$E(A_3) = .30(0) + .70(0) = 0$

c. $EMV = 3(\$100,000) + .7(0) = \$30,000$
$EVPI = \$30,000 - \$6,200 = \$23,800$

d.

Loss Table

	Improves	*Recession*
Build	0	$40,000
Expand	$70,000	$4,000
Do nothing	$100,000	0

$EOL(A_1) = .3(0) + .7(\$40,000) = \$28,000$
$EOL(A_2) = .3(\$70,000) + .7(\$4000) = \$23,800$
$EOL(A_3) = .3(\$100,000) + .7(0) = \$30,000$

e. Expand, because the expected payoff is the largest and the opportunity cost the smallest.

Answers Chapter 21
Part I

1. b   6. a
2. b   7. c
3. c   8. a
4. d   9. a
5. d   10. a

Part II

11.　OC Curve

12.　Consumer's risk

13.　binomial

14.　$\bar{c}$, percent defective

15.　Poisson

16.　99.7

Part III

Month	Total	Mean	Range
January	6.0	1.20	0.6
February	5.7	1.14	0.9
March	3.5	0.70	0.7
April	6.6	1.32	1.0
May	3.9	0.78	0.9
		5.14	4.1

$\bar{\bar{X}} = 5.14/5 = 1.028$　$\bar{R} = 4.0/5 = 0.82$

$\bar{\bar{X}} \pm A_2\bar{R} = 1.028 \pm .577(0.82) = 1.028 \pm 0.473$

　　UCL = 1.501　　　LCL = .555

　　UCL = $D_4\bar{R}$ = 2.115(.82) = 1.734

18.　　$\bar{p} = \dfrac{51}{300} = .17$

$.17 \pm 3\sqrt{\dfrac{.17(83)}{30}}$

$.17 \pm 0.206$

　(0, .376)

19.　$\bar{c} = 65/15 = 4.333$

　　$\bar{c} \pm \sqrt{\bar{c}} = 4.333 \pm 3\sqrt{4.333}$

　　　　　4.333 ± 6.25

　　　　　0, 10.583

20.　$P(x \le 2/p = .10, n = 20) = .667$

　　　　　$P(x \le 2/\rho = .20, n = 20) = .206$